The Billion-Dollar Bet

How Shayne Coplan Built Polymarket and Changed Prediction Markets Forever

J.F. Sachs

Copyright and Legal Disclaimer

Copyright Notice

Legal Disclaimer and Important Notice

Accuracy and Attribution

This book is a work of narrative nonfiction. The events, individuals, companies, and circumstances described herein are based on extensive research, including publicly available documents, court filings, regulatory records, media reports, and other sources as detailed in the Research and Source Notes section. Where possible, facts have been verified through multiple independent sources.

Dialogue and internal thoughts have been reconstructed based on interviews, contemporaneous notes, public statements, and reasonable inference. Some scenes have been dramatized for narrative purposes while maintaining factual accuracy to the best of the author's ability.

No Official Affiliation

This book is an independent work of journalism and analysis. The author is not affiliated with, endorsed by, or sponsored by Polymarket, Shayne Coplan, or any companies, individuals, or organizations discussed in this book. The views and opinions expressed are those of the author based on research and do not necessarily reflect the views of any person or entity mentioned herein.

Financial and Investment Disclaimer

This book is not financial, investment, or legal advice. Nothing in this book should be construed as:

- A recommendation to buy, sell, or trade any securities, cryptocurrencies, or prediction market contracts
- Investment advice of any kind
- Legal guidance regarding regulatory compliance
- Tax advice or planning recommendations
- An endorsement of any platform, technology, or business model discussed

Prediction markets, cryptocurrency trading, and related activities involve substantial risk and may not be legal in all jurisdictions. Readers should consult qualified financial, legal, and tax advisors before engaging in any activities discussed in this book.

Past performance is not indicative of future results. The success or failure of Polymarket or any platform discussed does not predict outcomes for other ventures or investments.

Regulatory and Legal Status Disclaimer

Regulatory and legal matters discussed in this book were accurate as of the time of writing. Laws, regulations, and enforcement priorities change rapidly, particularly in emerging technology sectors. The regulatory status of prediction markets, cryptocurrency, and related activities varies by jurisdiction and evolves constantly.

This book describes legal proceedings, investigations, and regulatory actions that may be ongoing or unresolved at the time of publication. References to investigations, allegations, or legal matters should not be construed as determinations of guilt, wrongdoing, or liability. All parties are presumed innocent until proven guilty in a court of law.

Cryptocurrency and Blockchain Technology Disclaimer

This book discusses blockchain technology, cryptocurrencies, and decentralized systems. These technologies are:

- Highly volatile and risky
- Subject to regulatory uncertainty
- Potentially subject to hacking, fraud, or technical failures
- Not suitable for all investors
- Not insured or guaranteed by any government agency

Readers should conduct independent research and risk assessment before engaging with any cryptocurrency or blockchain-based platform.

Forward-Looking Statements

This book contains analysis, predictions, and speculation about future developments in prediction markets, technology, regulation, and related fields. These forward-looking statements are based on information available at the time of writing and involve substantial uncertainty. Actual outcomes may differ materially from any scenarios, predictions, or possibilities discussed.

Privacy and Confidentiality

Where individuals are quoted or described, the author has made reasonable efforts to obtain consent or verify public availability of information. Some names, identifying details, or circumstances may have been changed to protect privacy where appropriate. Any such changes are noted in the text or source notes.

Third-Party Trademarks

All trademarks, service marks, trade names, product names, and logos mentioned in this book are the property of their respective owners. Use of these marks does not imply endorsement by or affiliation with their owners.

Polymarket®, Kalshi®, and other marks are trademarks of their respective companies. This book's use of these marks is for identification and commentary purposes only under fair use doctrine.

Fair Use Statement

This book makes use of copyrighted material including quotes, data, and analysis for purposes of criticism, commentary, news reporting, teaching, scholarship, and research, which the author believes constitutes fair use under Section 107 of the U.S. Copyright Act.

If you believe any material has been used inappropriately, please contact the publisher.

Limitation of Liability

To the fullest extent permitted by law, the author and publisher disclaim all liability for any loss, damage, or injury arising from the use of information in this book, including but not limited to:

- Financial losses from trading or investment decisions
- Legal consequences from activities undertaken based on information herein
- Technical failures or security breaches of any platforms discussed

- Reliance on analysis, predictions, or forward-looking statements

Readers use information in this book at their own risk.

Table of Contents

PART I: THE FOUNDER

Chapter 1

The Youngest Billionaire

The knock came at 6:00 AM.

Shayne Coplan was still in bed in his SoHo apartment when FBI agents demanded entry on the morning of November 13, 2024. Outside his door, numerous federal law enforcement officers had assembled for what would become one of the most controversial raids in recent tech history. The 26-year-old founder and CEO of Polymarket, the crypto-fueled prediction market that had just correctly called the presidential election was about to have his world turned upside down.

The agents seized his phone and electronic devices, methodically collecting evidence for an investigation whose full scope wouldn't become clear for months. Coplan complied, handing over his computers, his smartphones, the digital infrastructure of his entire life. No arrest was made. No charges were filed. But the message was unmistakable, someone, somewhere in the machinery of federal law enforcement, had taken notice of what Polymarket had accomplished and they weren't happy about it.

Within hours, the raid would make headlines around the world. "FBI raids home of Polymarket CEO," the news alerts blared, each story adding its own spin to a narrative that seemed almost too perfect in its timing. The raid came just one week after the presidential election, during which Polymarket had gained mainstream attention for its eerily accurate prediction markets. While traditional polls had shown a dead heat between Donald Trump and Kamala Harris right up until election day, Polymarket's traders had consistently given Trump the edge and they had been right.

A Polymarket spokesperson would later call the raid "obvious political retribution by the outgoing administration against Polymarket for providing a market that correctly called the 2024 presidential election." Whether that assessment was accurate or paranoid would become the subject of intense debate. What was undeniable was the symbolism, a young entrepreneur who had built something genuinely new, something that had challenged the conventional wisdom of America's polling establishment, was now under federal investigation.

That afternoon, with characteristic millennial defiance, Coplan posted to X: "new phone, who dis?"

The joke landed with his followers, but it couldn't mask the gravity of the situation. Sources close to the matter described the raid as "grand political theater," suggesting the FBI could have simply asked Coplan's lawyer for the materials instead of staging a dawn raid designed to generate headlines.

It would have been easy, in that moment, to write Shayne Coplan off as just another crypto bro who had flown too close to the sun. Another twenty-something hustler who had built something controversial, skirted regulations, and was now facing the consequences. The tech industry had seen this movie before, and it usually ended badly.

But Coplan's story was about to take a very different turn.

From Bathroom Office to Billionaire

Fast forward eleven months to October 2025. Intercontinental Exchange, the owner of the New York Stock Exchange, announced it would invest up to $2 billion in Polymarket at an $8 billion pre-money valuation. The deal transformed Polymarket from a regulatory pariah into a Wall Street-backed financial institution. And it made Shayne Coplan, at 27 years old, the world's youngest self-made billionaire.

The number was almost incomprehensible. Coplan owns approximately 11% of Polymarket, a stake now worth more than a billion dollars. He had achieved what most entrepreneurs only dream about, building something from nothing, surviving regulatory attacks, and emerging not just vindicated but triumphant.

The journey from that November morning, confused, his devices seized and his company under federal scrutiny to October's validation by one of Wall Street's most prestigious institutions represented one of the most dramatic turnarounds in recent tech history. In between came months of legal limbo, strategic maneuvering, and ultimately, total vindication. In July 2025, both the Justice Department and the CFTC dropped their investigations without filing charges. That same month, Polymarket acquired QCEX, a CFTC-licensed exchange and clearinghouse for $112 million, giving it legal grounds to operate in the United States.

The kid who had started his company from a makeshift bathroom office while broke and desperate had not just survived, he had won.

The Paradox of Success

But how do you make sense of someone like Shayne Coplan? How does a 27-year-old dropout become a billionaire by creating a platform where people bet on literally everything, from presidential elections to celebrity deaths to whether aliens will be confirmed by a certain date?

The answer is more complex than either Coplan's boosters or critics typically acknowledge. This is not a simple story of a visionary genius, nor is it a cautionary tale about crypto excess and regulatory evasion. It's something more nuanced: the story of a young man who genuinely believed that markets could reveal truth in ways that experts and institutions couldn't, who built a platform that tested that theory at massive scale, and who found himself at the center of debates about democracy, gambling, free speech, and the future of information itself.

Coplan's ascent illuminates something fundamental about our current moment. We live in an age of radical epistemic uncertainty where traditional sources of truth (newspapers, polls, experts, institutions) have lost credibility with large swaths of the population, where misinformation spreads at light speed, where conspiracy theories compete with fact on equal footing. In this environment, Polymarket offered something seductive: a mechanism for aggregating collective wisdom, weighted by actual money at stake.

The platform's supporters saw it as a revolutionary tool for discovering truth. Its critics saw it as online gambling dressed up in libertarian philosophy. Both were partially right.

What makes Coplan's story particularly fascinating is the timing. He built Polymarket during the pandemic, grew it during America's most contentious political period in modern history, survived a regulatory crackdown that would have killed most companies, and emerged as a billionaire just as prediction markets moved from fringe curiosity to mainstream financial instrument. His biography is inseparable from this tumultuous period in American life.

A Study in Contradictions

Shayne Coplan embodies a series of contradictions that make him both compelling and enigmatic.

He's a college dropout who disrupted the polling industry with sophisticated market mechanics. He's a crypto native who just partnered with the 233-year-old New York Stock Exchange. He's a self-described non-partisan who has photos with Donald Trump Jr. and attended events for Democrats. He's a believer in decentralization who built a centralized platform. He's an advocate for transparent prediction markets who operate in regulatory gray zones.

In 2020, Coplan was so broke he was taking inventory of belongings in his Lower East Side apartment to figure out what he could sell to make rent. He was running Polymarket as a solo founder from what he called his "makeshift bathroom office", a MacBook propped up on a washing basket, literally building a company from his bathroom. Five years later, he would be courted by the most powerful financial institutions in America and named the youngest self-made billionaire on earth.

This trajectory from bathroom office to billionaire is the stuff of tech industry legend. But it also raises questions. How did he do it? What decisions did he make along the way? What principles did he hold onto, and which ones did he compromise? What does his success say about our economy, our culture, our politics?

The Raid in Context

To understand the full arc of Coplan's story, you have to understand what that November morning represented. The FBI raid wasn't just about Polymarket's compliance with a 2022 settlement with the Commodity Futures Trading Commission, which had required the platform to block U.S. users. It was about power, specifically about who gets to define truth in America.

On election morning 2024, Polymarket showed Trump with a 58.6% chance of winning while Vice President Kamala Harris sat at 41.4%. Traditional polls showed a dead heat. Nearly every major news organization was calling the race "too close to call." The entire apparatus of American political journalism, built on decades of polling methodology and expert analysis, was telling America one story. Polymarket was telling a different story.

And Polymarket was right.

The platform had processed over $3.6 billion in bets on the presidential election, creating what was effectively the largest prediction market in history. Tens of thousands of traders, many of them international, were putting real money behind their beliefs about American politics. The result was a forecast that outperformed virtually every professional pollster.

On election night, sources say Donald Trump's campaign team watched Polymarket graphs, with the president-elect himself using the platform to gauge the election. When Trump won, Polymarket became the story. How had a crypto betting site outsmarted the entire polling industry?

This is why the raid, coming just one week later, felt so loaded with meaning. To Polymarket's supporters, it looked like the establishment was striking back, punishing success, attacking innovation and trying to shut down a platform that had exposed the failures of legacy institutions. To skeptics, it looked like overdue accountability for a company that had been flouting regulations and potentially manipulating markets.

The truth, as usual, was more complicated.

What This Book Will Explore

This book is the story of how Shayne Coplan built Polymarket and became the world's youngest billionaire. But it's also about much more than one person's success.

It's about the collision between crypto libertarianism and government regulation. About the wisdom of crowds versus expert forecasting. About the thin line between prediction markets and gambling. About whether betting on elections strengthens democracy or corrupts it. About the future of truth in a post-institutional age.

It's about risk and reward, about surviving federal investigations, about the price of success at 27. It's about bathroom offices and billion-dollar valuations, about FBI raids and Wall Street partnerships, about political controversy and technological innovation.

Most of all, it's about a simple but profound idea: that markets can reveal truth. That if you give people a financial incentive to be right, they will collectively produce better forecasts than any expert, any poll, any model. And that in an age of information chaos, this might matter more than ever.

Shayne Coplan didn't invent prediction markets, the idea goes back centuries. But he built the first platform to bring them into the mainstream, to test their potential at massive scale, to prove that they could actually work. In doing so, he became a billionaire, survived an FBI raid, and changed how millions of people think about the future.

Whether that change is for better or worse remains hotly debated. What's undeniable is that the change is real, and it's accelerating.

The Morning After

Eight months after the FBI raid, Coplan posted on X: "On election night, we were on top of the world after Polymarket called the election. 8 days later, the FBI broke down my door at 6am and took all my computers and phones, looking for anything that could imply foul play. While traumatic, it etched the story..."

The post came after the government dropped its investigations. "After cooperating and engaging, we've been cleared of any wrongdoing. Justice prevailed," Coplan wrote. "God Bless America."

It was a moment of triumph, but also a reminder of how precarious his position had been. For months, Coplan had lived in legal limbo, not knowing whether he would be charged, whether his company would survive, whether everything he had built would be dismantled by federal prosecutors.

He kept building anyway.

That decision to keep pushing forward despite the uncertainty, despite the risk, despite the very real possibility of criminal charges tells you something essential about Shayne Coplan. He's a true believer. Whether that belief is rooted in naivety or genius, whether it's visionary or reckless, is precisely what makes his story so compelling.

The billion-dollar valuation would suggest genius. But the FBI raid suggests recklessness. The truth is probably both.

A Generation's Voice

Coplan represents something larger than just his own success. He's emblematic of a generation that came of age during the financial crisis, that saw institutions fail, that lost faith in traditional authorities, and that turned to technology, especially cryptocurrency as a solution.

This generation doesn't trust the Federal Reserve, so they created Bitcoin. They don't trust banks, so they built DeFi. They don't trust polling, so they created prediction markets. They don't trust traditional media, so they get their news from podcasts and Twitter threads.

Whether this represents progress or chaos depends largely on your perspective. But it's undeniably reshaping how information, money, and power work in America.

Coplan is a product of this moment. He participated in Ethereum's initial coin offering in 2014 when it was priced significantly lower, getting in early on what would become one of the most important blockchain platforms. He dropped out of NYU to pursue crypto ventures. He was, in many ways, a typical crypto entrepreneur.

What set him apart was his focus. While many in crypto chased get-rich-quick schemes, Coplan became interested in something more substantive: the epistemic value of prediction markets, the idea that you could use financial incentives to aggregate human knowledge and produce accurate forecasts. He read the academic literature on prediction markets.

He studied economist Robin Hanson's work. He thought deeply about information aggregation and collective intelligence.

And then he built something.

The Structure Ahead

This book traces Coplan's journey from college dropout to billionaire, from bathroom office to Wall Street partnership, from regulatory outlaw to government-approved operator. But it also examines the broader phenomenon of Polymarket itself, how it works, why it matters, who uses it, and what it reveals about our society.

We'll explore the technical architecture that makes the platform possible, the regulatory battles that nearly destroyed it, the 2024 election that made it famous, and the FBI investigation that tested Coplan's resolve. We'll meet the traders who've won and lost fortunes on the platform, the investors who bet on Coplan's vision, and the regulators who tried to shut him down.

We'll examine the criticisms: that Polymarket is just gambling, that it enables manipulation, that it could influence elections rather than just predict them. And we'll explore the defenses, that markets are truth-seeking mechanisms, that prediction markets improve democracy, that Polymarket represents the future of forecasting.

Most importantly, we'll try to answer the central question at the heart of Coplan's story: Did he build something genuinely valuable, or did he just get lucky betting on chaos?

The answer to that question will determine not just Coplan's legacy, but the future of prediction markets themselves. If Polymarket succeeds in becoming a permanent part of how we understand and predict the future, it will be because Shayne Coplan was right about something fundamental.

If it fails or if it succeeds in ways that corrupt rather than enlighten then this story will serve as a cautionary tale about the limits of market-based truth.

Either way, at 27 years old with a billion-dollar net worth and the backing of the New York Stock Exchange, Shayne Coplan has already secured his place in the history of technology, finance, and politics. What comes next will determine whether that place is celebrated or condemned.

The journey from that November morning, when FBI agents took his phones, to October, when ICE wrote a two-billion-dollar check, is one of the most remarkable stories in recent business history. It's a story about belief and risk, about innovation and regulation, about truth and money.

It's a story worth telling in full.

This is that story.

Chapter 2

Before Polymarket

A Manhattan Childhood

Shayne Coplan was born in 1998 and grew up on the Upper West Side of New York City, raised by his mother. He attended public school in Hell's Kitchen, the bustling neighborhood near the theater district. This was a New York that was simultaneously gritty and glamorous. Hell's Kitchen had shed much of its rougher reputation from decades past, but it still retained an edge, a sense of possibility mixed with unpredictability.

The Upper West Side and Hell's Kitchen provided an interesting duality for a young mind. The Upper West Side represented old money, cultural institutions, tree-lined streets, and the kind of stability that money can buy. Hell's Kitchen, meanwhile, was evolving rapidly, caught between its working-class roots and an influx of development and gentrification. It was the perfect environment for someone who would later build a platform that existed in the gray zones between established systems and disruptive innovation.

Coplan attended The Beacon School, a highly selective public high school in Hell's Kitchen. Beacon was known for its progressive approach to education, emphasizing collaborative learning and inquiry-based methods. It wasn't the kind of pressure-cooker environment of elite private schools, but it attracted smart, creative kids who thought differently. Students at Beacon were encouraged to question conventional wisdom, to think critically about systems and structures. These formative years would prove crucial in shaping Coplan's approach to building Polymarket.

From an early age, Coplan learned to code as a teenager. This wasn't unusual for his generation, millennials and Gen Z grew up with the internet as a given, technology as air they breathed but Coplan took to it with particular intensity. He wasn't just using technology; he was interested in how it worked, how it could be rebuilt, how systems could be reimagined from first principles.

The Ethereum Epiphany

The moment that would define Coplan's trajectory came when he was just sixteen years old. In 2014, at age fourteen, Coplan first became interested in cryptocurrency, drawn to the multi-trillion dollar industry while it was still in its infancy. At sixteen, he participated in Ethereum's initial coin offering, purchasing the cryptocurrency for around thirty cents per token. According to crypto lore, he became one of the youngest participants in the Ethereum ICO.

To understand the significance of this decision, you have to understand what Ethereum represented in 2014. Bitcoin had proven that decentralized digital currency was possible, but Ethereum promised something more ambitious: a world computer, a platform for decentralized applications, smart contracts that could execute automatically without intermediaries. Vitalik Buterin, Ethereum's founder, was selling a vision of a new internet, one where code, not corporations, determined the rules.

For a sixteen-year-old to grasp this vision and commit money to it (however little) required a particular kind of mind. It required someone who could see potential in abstraction, who could imagine systems that didn't yet exist, who was willing to bet on ideas that most people dismissed as crazy. The fact that Ethereum tokens were trading for thirty cents while, by 2024, they would be worth around twenty-four hundred dollars, represented a roughly eight-thousand-fold return. But more important than the financial windfall was what the investment represented: a young person aligning himself with a movement that believed in radical decentralization, in code as law, in technology as a solution to institutional failure.

This early exposure to cryptocurrency fundamentally shaped how Coplan would think about markets, information, and trust. The crypto ethos, don't trust, verify; code is law; decentralization is resilience would become the philosophical foundation of Polymarket.

The Education of a Dropout

Coplan pursued a computer science degree at New York University, one of the premier programs in the country. NYU's computer science department was rigorous, filled with brilliant students and faculty pushing the boundaries of what was possible with code. For someone who had already dipped his toes into the world of blockchain, NYU provided the theoretical foundations and technical skills to turn ideas into reality.

But Coplan left before completing his degree to pursue his interests in cryptocurrencies and prediction markets. This decision to drop out of a prestigious program, to abandon the traditional path to success would later be romanticized as visionary boldness. But at the time, it must have felt terrifying. What did he have? Some technical skills, a belief in crypto, and an obsession with an obscure concept called prediction markets.

Before founding Polymarket, Coplan had work experience that gave him insight into both technology and information systems. He interned at Chronicled from June to August 2016, and at Genius from April to July 2015. Genius, the lyric annotation site that had expanded into annotating the internet itself, was particularly influential. It was a company built on the idea that collective intelligence could add context and meaning to information, a concept that would later manifest in a different form with Polymarket.

The decision to leave NYU wasn't made lightly. Rob Hadick, a partner at venture capital firm Dragonfly and one of Polymarket's investors, would later describe Coplan as someone who "wants to be able to talk about it forever. This is his life. He lives it". At an initial meeting, Coplan eschewed a formal pitch in a conference room and instead proposed a walk, which turned into a two-hour stroll around New York, during which Coplan talked Hadick's ear off about prediction markets.

This intensity, this all-consuming focus, is what distinguishes people who actually build things from people who just have ideas. Coplan wasn't dabbling in prediction markets as an interesting side project. He was consumed by them.

The Intellectual Foundations

What exactly had captured Coplan's imagination? The answer lies in the academic literature on prediction markets, particularly the work of economist Robin Hanson.

Coplan was inspired by economist Friedrich Hayek's theories on decentralized information systems and George Mason University professor Robin Hanson's work on futarchy. This intellectual lineage is crucial to understanding what Polymarket would become.

Friedrich Hayek, the Austrian economist and philosopher, had argued in his seminal 1945 paper "The Use of Knowledge in Society" that the central problem of economic organization was not just how to allocate resources, but how to aggregate dispersed knowledge. Price signals in free markets, Hayek argued, served as a mechanism for transmitting information that no central planner could possibly possess. This idea that markets are fundamentally information processing systems would become the philosophical core of prediction markets.

Robin Hanson took this insight further. Hanson is an associate professor of economics at George Mason University, known for his work on prediction markets since 1988. He proposed "futarchy," a form of governance based on the slogan "vote values, but bet beliefs". In Hanson's vision, elected officials would define measures of national wellbeing, and prediction markets would be used to determine which policies would have the most positive effect.

The idea was radical: instead of relying on experts, pundits, or politicians to predict the consequences of policy decisions, you would create markets where people could bet on outcomes. Speculative markets, stock markets, commodity markets and betting markets had this remarkable property of aggregating information very well from diverse people. The idea was to harness that mechanism purposefully to get better information about particular topics.

Coplan was always interested in seeing the world through the lens of probabilities. He described an interest in data-driven websites such as FiveThirtyEight as foundational in building that worldview. FiveThirtyEight, Nate Silver's statistical analysis website, had gained fame by correctly predicting electoral outcomes using sophisticated polling aggregation. But Coplan saw limitations in this approach. Polls asked people what they thought would happen, but didn't require them to put anything on the line. What if you could create a system where people had skin in the game?

The theoretical case for prediction markets was compelling. Prediction markets claim to produce uniquely accurate estimates and provide more accurate data than can be acquired from anywhere else. When people bet their own money on outcomes, they have every incentive to be right. The collective wisdom of many participants, each with different information and perspectives, weighted by their confidence (as measured by how much they're willing to bet), should theoretically produce superior forecasts.

The Failure of Existing Platforms

But if prediction markets were such a good idea, why didn't they already exist at scale? The answer: they did, sort of and they had mostly failed.

During the 2020 lockdown, Coplan explored prediction platforms like Augur, an Ethereum-based market that launched in 2015 but failed to gain much traction. Understanding why Augur failed is essential to understanding what Coplan would do differently with Polymarket.

Augur raised funds through a crowdfunding campaign in August 2015 and launched in July 2018. The project was ambitious, technically sophisticated, and backed by credible people in the crypto space. Ethereum founder Vitalik Buterin served as an adviser to the project. On paper, everything looked promising.

But reality was harsh. Soon after the platform launched, users had created death pools or assassination markets on famous people. This wasn't just a PR nightmare; it represented a fundamental challenge for decentralized prediction markets. If you build a truly permissionless system where anyone can create any market, some people will create deeply problematic markets. Augur's founder Joey Krug hinted that someone might try to create illegal wagers, requiring extensive moderation somewhat antithetical to the permissionless ideals of crypto.

Augur's user numbers dropped off sharply after launch: from two hundred sixty-five daily users in early July 2018 to just thirty-seven on August eighth. Three years after its August 2015 launch, it disclosed just thirty-seven daily average users as of August 2018. For a project that had raised significant funds and generated enormous hype, this was a disaster.

What went wrong? Several factors contributed to Augur's failure:

User Experience: Augur was built by developers for developers. The interface was clunky, confusing for normal users. The platform required users to download a desktop application rather than accessing it through a web browser. In an era when people expected seamless web experiences, this was a significant barrier.

Complexity: The underlying mechanism, dispute resolution, reputation tokens, multiple rounds of verification was technically elegant but cognitively overwhelming. Users didn't want to understand Byzantine consensus mechanisms; they wanted to place bets and collect winnings.

Liquidity: Without sufficient users, markets lacked depth. Spreads were wide, making it expensive to trade. This created a vicious cycle: low liquidity deterred users, which further decreased liquidity.

Regulatory Uncertainty: In July 2018, the Commodity Futures Trading Commission noted the resemblance of Augur contracts to binary options, which would fall under its jurisdiction. The specter of regulatory action hung over the project. Founder Joey Krug later admitted that Augur might be unwelcome in the State of California and quietly abandoned the project.

Ethical Problems: Beyond assassination markets, Augur faced questions about market manipulation, wash trading, and whether betting on tragic events was morally acceptable. These weren't just theoretical concerns; they actively damaged the platform's reputation.

Augur's REP token declined ninety-nine point eight percent from its all-time high. The project wasn't entirely dead, but it had clearly failed to achieve its ambitions.

Other platforms faced similar fates. InTrade, another major prediction market, succumbed to regulatory pressure and ceased trading in 2013. PredictIt, an academic research project allowed to operate with CFTC approval, remained small and limited by restrictions on bet sizes and market types.

The Inefficiency of Traditional Forecasting

While prediction market platforms were struggling, traditional forecasting methods were also showing their limitations. This gap between the promise of prediction markets and the failure of existing platforms on one side, and the inadequacy of polls and expert predictions on the other was the opportunity that Coplan identified.

Traditional polling had become increasingly unreliable. Response rates were plummeting. People were harder to reach via landlines. Younger voters were especially difficult to poll accurately. Methodology disputes raged about how to weight different demographic groups. And most fundamentally, polls measured stated preferences at a moment in time, not actual behavior or aggregate wisdom.

The 2016 presidential election had exposed these weaknesses dramatically. Nearly every poll and expert forecast gave Hillary Clinton a comfortable lead. The consensus was overwhelming. And the consensus was wrong. This wasn't just an embarrassment for pollsters; it represented an epistemological crisis. If the entire apparatus of professional forecasting could be so wrong, what good was it?

Expert predictions fared no better. Pundits confidently asserted outcomes that never materialized. Political scientists built elaborate models that failed to predict reality. The problem wasn't that individual experts were stupid, many were brilliant but that the incentive structure was broken. Being wrong carried no cost. You could make wildly inaccurate predictions and face no consequences beyond momentary embarrassment. There was no skin in the game.

Robin Hanson had pointed out this problem years earlier: prediction markets can provide information that is detrimental to the status quo, telling people and organizations things they don't want to hear. This was threatening to established institutions. Hanson described dramatic cases where management and officials forecast one outcome while prediction market data revealed a different reality particularly around project deadlines. Organizations didn't necessarily want more accurate information if that information undermined their preferred narratives.

But by 2020, the moment was ripe for something new. The pandemic had disrupted everything. Misinformation was rampant. Trust in institutions was at historic lows. People were desperate for better ways to understand an uncertain world.

Why Prediction Markets? Why Blockchain?

Coplan's insight was that the failure of previous prediction market platforms wasn't a fundamental flaw in the concept, it was a failure of execution. The idea was sound. The implementations were flawed.

Blockchain technology had matured significantly since Augur's early days. Coplan founded Polymarket in 2020, operating as a prediction market using smart contracts on the Polygon blockchain. The choice of Polygon, a Layer 2 scaling solution for Ethereum was crucial. It offered the security and decentralization of Ethereum with dramatically lower transaction costs and faster settlement times. This solved one of Augur's core problems: gas fees that made small trades prohibitively expensive.

But technology alone wasn't enough. Coplan understood that building a successful prediction market required solving several problems simultaneously:

User Experience: It had to be as easy as any mainstream website. No downloading software, no managing private keys directly, no technical jargon that scared away normal users.

Market Design: The platform needed mechanisms to ensure liquid markets, fair pricing, and protection against manipulation. Automated market makers could provide constant liquidity even when natural market makers weren't present.

Content Moderation: Unlike Augur's pure decentralization, Polymarket would need some centralized control over which markets could be created. This was pragmatic rather than ideological. Assassination markets and other obviously illegal content would be prohibited.

Regulatory Strategy: Rather than pretending regulations didn't exist, Polymarket would need a coherent legal strategy for operating globally while managing U.S. regulatory risk.

Community Building: Success would require cultivating a community of sophisticated traders who could provide liquidity and signal quality to other users.

These insights didn't come from nowhere. They came from Coplan's years of studying both the theory and practice of prediction markets, from his understanding of crypto infrastructure, from his obsessive focus on the problem.

The Vision Crystallizes

By early 2020, Coplan had clarity about what needed to be built. Four years before Polymarket would become a household name during the 2024 election, Coplan was just another entrepreneur, hacking away in a makeshift bathroom office at his passion project, a prediction market that would blend gambling with real world events.

Coplan started the project from his bathroom with very limited resources, working solo and setting up a makeshift office where he ran the initial operations. He often spent long nights coding and refining his ideas. This wasn't glamorous. There were no venture capital rounds yet, no press coverage, no validation from the outside world. Just one person in a bathroom, writing code, driven by a vision that markets could reveal truth in ways that polls and experts couldn't.

The pandemic created an unusual moment. With the world in lockdown, uncertainty was everywhere. People were desperate for information about when things would return to normal, whether vaccines would work, what would happen to the economy. Traditional institutions seemed paralyzed. The moment demanded something new.

Coplan later posted on social media: "2020, running out of money, solo founder, HQ in my makeshift bathroom office. little did I know Polymarket was going to change the world".

At the time, this probably seemed like delusional optimism. A kid in his early twenties, working alone in a bathroom, claiming his project would change the world? It fit every stereotype of tech hubris.

But sometimes the delusional optimists are right.

The Moment Before

Understanding Coplan before Polymarket is essential to understanding what Polymarket would become. This wasn't a project conceived by a committee or designed by consultants. It emerged from one person's obsessive conviction that markets could solve information problems that democracy and expertise couldn't.

Coplan brought together several threads: the crypto ethos learned from early involvement in Ethereum, the theoretical foundations from Hayek and Hanson, the lessons from Augur's failure, the technical skills from NYU and his internships, and the urgency created by the pandemic and the breakdown of trusted information sources.

He also brought youth. At twenty-two, Coplan had no baggage from traditional finance, no investment in existing systems, no fear of institutional consequences. He could be audacious in ways that someone with more experience might not dare. He could drop out of college, work from a bathroom, and genuinely believe he was building something world-changing.

Whether that belief was justified would depend entirely on what came next. The intellectual foundations were solid. The timing seemed right. The previous failures had taught valuable lessons. But none of that guaranteed success.

What happened next would determine whether Shayne Coplan was a visionary or just another crypto dreamer with a bathroom office.

The answer would come sooner than anyone expected.

Chapter 3

The Vision Takes Shape (2019-2020)

From Theory to Reality

By late 2019, Shayne Coplan had reached a crossroads. He had dropped out of NYU. He had spent years studying prediction markets, reading academic papers, exploring failed platforms like Augur. He had earned money from his early Ethereum investment, giving him a financial cushion and practical experience with blockchain technology. He understood the theory. He saw the opportunity. But theory and opportunity are cheap. Execution is everything.

What separated Coplan from the thousands of other crypto enthusiasts with grand ideas was that he actually started building. While others debated in Discord channels and wrote whitepapers that would never become products, Coplan began the unglamorous work of turning his vision into reality.

The timeline is revealing. Coplan founded Polymarket in 2020, but the intellectual and practical work began earlier. Throughout 2019, he was exploring existing prediction platforms, talking to developers, sketching out architecture, and most importantly, thinking deeply about what had gone wrong with previous attempts. This wasn't impulsive. It was methodical.

"This is too good of an idea to just exist in whitepapers," Coplan would later recall thinking. The sentiment captures something essential about his approach. The academic literature on prediction markets was extensive and compelling. Robin Hanson had been writing about futarchy for decades. Researchers had demonstrated the accuracy of prediction markets in controlled settings. But these ideas remained largely theoretical, confined to academic journals and small-scale experiments. Someone needed to bring them into the real world at scale.

The Pandemic as Catalyst

And then COVID-19 arrived.

In March 2020, the world locked down. Suddenly, everyone was stuck at home, glued to screens, desperate for information about a rapidly evolving crisis. Would there be a vaccine? When would things reopen? How deadly was this virus really? Traditional authorities, government health agencies, media outlets, and expert epidemiologists were giving contradictory information. Predictions changed weekly. The fog of uncertainty was overwhelming.

For Coplan, this was the perfect moment. People needed better ways to aggregate information and forecast outcomes. They needed skin-in-the-game predictions, not expert pronouncements that carried no cost if wrong. And crucially, millions of people were stuck at home with time to explore new platforms.

Coplan began building Polymarket from his bathroom during this period. The image would later become iconic, the young founder hunched over a laptop balanced on a washing basket, writing code in the cramped space of a bathroom-turned-office. It wasn't a metaphor. It was literally where he worked.

The bathroom office was in his Lower East Side apartment. He was running out of money, taking inventory of possessions to figure out what he could sell to make rent. This was not the glamorous world of venture-backed startups with ping-pong tables and catered lunches. This was one person, nearly broke, betting everything on an idea that most people would dismiss as crazy.

But the pandemic gave him focus and urgency. As COVID questions dominated public discourse, Coplan saw immediate applications for prediction markets. Would masks become mandatory? Would schools reopen in the fall? Would there be a second wave? These were questions that mattered to everyone, and no one knew the answers with certainty.

The Technical Architecture: Why Blockchain?

Before Polymarket could predict anything, Coplan had to solve a fundamental technical challenge: How do you build a prediction market that actually works?

The choice to build on blockchain wasn't ideological or rather, it wasn't only ideological. It was practical. Blockchain technology offered several crucial advantages for a prediction market:

Transparency: Every transaction would be recorded on an immutable public ledger. This meant users could verify that markets were being resolved fairly, that their bets were recorded accurately, and that no one was manipulating the system behind the scenes.

Smart Contracts: Automated execution meant that when a market resolved, payouts happened automatically. No central entity deciding who gets paid. No delays. No disputes about whether someone had actually won. The code would execute impartially.

Censorship Resistance: By building on blockchain, Polymarket would be harder for any single entity to shut down. This mattered enormously for a platform that would inevitably create controversial markets.

Global Access: Cryptocurrency made it possible for anyone, anywhere to participate, without needing a traditional bank account or payment processor. This was crucial for building international liquidity.

But which blockchain? This decision would prove pivotal.

Ethereum was the obvious choice in many ways, it had the most developers, the strongest ecosystem, the best smart contract infrastructure. But Ethereum in 2020 had a fatal flaw, gas fees. During periods of high network activity, transaction costs on Ethereum could spike to $50 or more. For a prediction market where people might want to place small bets of $10, $20 and $50 this was prohibitive. You couldn't build a mainstream platform where the cost of making a bet exceeded the bet itself.

Coplan chose Polygon (formerly Matic Network), a Layer 2 scaling solution for Ethereum. Polygon was elegant: it offered the security and decentralization of Ethereum but processed transactions on a separate, faster, cheaper sidechain. Transaction fees on Polygon were measured in fractions of a cent rather than tens of dollars. Settlement was nearly instant rather than minutes or hours.

This choice demonstrated Coplan's pragmatism. Pure blockchain maximalists might have insisted on using only Ethereum mainnet, accepting slow, expensive transactions as the price of true decentralization. Coplan understood that users didn't care about ideological purity, they cared about user experience. Polygon gave him both genuine blockchain benefits without the crippling costs.

The technical stack included USDC, a stablecoin pegged to the U.S. dollar as the medium of exchange. This solved another crucial problem: cryptocurrency volatility. If users had to bet in Ethereum or Bitcoin, their positions would be subject to wild price swings that had nothing to do with the events they were betting on. USDC provided stable value while maintaining cryptocurrency's advantages of speed and global accessibility.

For market mechanics, Polymarket would use automated market makers (AMMs), algorithmic systems that automatically provide liquidity and price shares based on supply and demand. This was borrowed from decentralized finance protocols like Uniswap. The beauty of AMMs was that markets could have liquidity even without professional market makers. The algorithm itself would always be willing to buy or sell shares at prices that reflected the current probability.

Learning from Augur's Mistakes

Coplan had studied Augur's failure meticulously, and every design decision for Polymarket reflected lessons learned from that cautionary tale.

User Experience First: Where Augur required users to download desktop software and understand complex verification mechanisms, Polymarket would be a simple web application. No downloads, no technical jargon, no cognitive overhead. You'd visit a website, connect a crypto wallet (or create one through the platform), deposit USDC, and start trading. That's it.

Curated Markets: Augur's pure decentralization had led to assassination markets and other problematic content that destroyed its reputation. Polymarket would take a different approach: the platform itself would control which markets got created. This was a concession to reality. Yes, it introduced centralization. But it prevented the platform from becoming a haven for illegal or deeply unethical betting.

Low Fees: By building on Polygon, Polymarket could offer trading with minimal costs. This was essential for attracting retail users who wanted to make small, frequent bets.

Focus on Resolution: One of Augur's biggest problems was dispute resolution, figuring out who had won when outcomes were ambiguous. Polymarket would employ a resolution team that used clear, verifiable sources to determine outcomes quickly. Again, this introduced centralization, but it solved a real problem.

Clean Interface: Augur's interface was cluttered and confusing, designed by engineers for engineers. Polymarket would prioritize clean, intuitive design that anyone could understand. Probability displayed prominently. Simple buy/sell mechanisms. Clear explanations of how everything worked.

The pattern was clear: Coplan was willing to sacrifice ideological purity for practical functionality. This would later become a source of criticism from crypto purists who felt Polymarket wasn't "decentralized enough." But it was also what allowed the platform to actually work.

Assembling Resources and Early Believers

By spring 2020, Coplan had a working prototype. But a prototype isn't a company. He needed capital, he needed users, and he needed credibility.

Polymarket launched its beta in June 2020. The timing was both fortunate and strategic. The pandemic had everyone's attention. Election season was heating up, the Trump-Biden race was already generating enormous interest. And crypto markets were beginning to recover from their 2018-2019 bear market, with fresh capital flowing into the space.

The early markets on Polymarket reflected the moment. COVID predictions dominated: Would there be more than 200,000 U.S. COVID deaths by year-end? Would schools reopen? Would Trump get COVID? The platform also created markets around the election: Who would win the presidency? Would there be a clear winner on election night? Would mail-in voting create disputes?

In just three months after launch, Polymarket saw over $1 million in trading volume. For a platform built by a solo founder in a bathroom, this was remarkable. The volume wasn't coming from nowhere, it suggested that Coplan had identified real demand. People wanted to trade on real-world outcomes, and they were willing to do it with real money.

But $1 million in volume was just a proof of concept. To scale, Coplan needed venture capital.

The First Funding Round

In October 2020, Polymarket closed a $4 million seed round led by Polychain Capital, one of the premier cryptocurrency venture firms. The round included some of the crypto world's most prominent names:

Naval Ravikant: The founder of AngelList and one of Silicon Valley's most influential thinkers had become a crypto enthusiast and angel investor. His participation signaled intellectual validation, this wasn't just another DeFi scheme; it was a serious attempt to solve an information problem.

Balaji Srinivasan: The former CTO of Coinbase and a prominent crypto advocate, Balaji was known for his futurist vision and technical depth. His investment suggested he saw real potential in prediction markets.

Meltem Demirors: CoinShares CSO and a respected voice in institutional crypto adoption, her involvement brought credibility with more traditional financial players.

Other participants included **1confirmation, ParaFi, Robot Ventures**, and **General Catalyst**. The latter was particularly significant, General Catalyst was a mainstream venture firm with a portfolio including Stripe, Airbnb, and Snapchat. Their involvement suggested Polymarket was being taken seriously beyond just the crypto bubble.

The $4 million wasn't enormous by venture capital standards, but for a three-month-old platform built in a bathroom, it was transformational. More important than the money was the network and credibility these investors brought. Naval alone had millions of Twitter followers and enormous influence in tech circles. His endorsement mattered.

Shayne Coplan's pitch to investors centered on a few key arguments:

Market Timing: The 2020 election and pandemic had created unprecedented demand for real-time, crowd-sourced forecasting. Traditional polls had proven unreliable. Expert predictions were all over the map. Prediction markets offered something different.

Information Value: This wasn't just gambling, it was information aggregation with real social value. Journalists, campaigns, businesses, and individuals could use Polymarket data to understand what was actually likely to happen, not just what polls or pundits claimed.

Technical Execution: By solving Augur's problems of user experience, market curation and low fees Polymarket had proven it could build something people would actually use. The $1 million in early volume demonstrated product-market fit.

Scalability: The blockchain infrastructure meant the platform could scale globally without massive capital expenditure. There were no servers to maintain in a traditional sense, no payment processing infrastructure to build out. The code could handle dramatically more volume with minimal additional cost.

Regulatory Strategy: By incorporating traditional compliance measures, KYC/AML processes, market oversight, cooperation with regulators Polymarket could avoid the fate of platforms that ignored laws entirely. This was crypto with guard rails.

The investors bought in. The funding announcement emphasized Polymarket's mission to fight fake news and hold accountable those "pumping disinformation in the news cycle."

Coplan explained his vision in the press release: "One of the biggest problems with social media and discourse on the internet today is the lack of accountability. Everyone has an opinion and isn't afraid to share it. At the moment there's little downside to being wrong; this makes it really hard for regular people to discern what's fact and what's fiction. 2020 has showcased just how bad the consequences of this can be."

This framing was deliberate. Coplan wasn't positioning Polymarket as a gambling site. He was positioning it as a solution to the misinformation crisis, a mechanism for discovering truth in an age of information chaos. Whether this framing was sincere or strategic (probably both), it resonated with investors and users alikc.

The Vision for Stage 2

The funding would support Polymarket's "stage 2" beta release, which aimed to remove technical complexities and make the platform more accessible to mainstream users. Specific goals included:

Unlimited Free Trading: Removing or dramatically reducing platform fees to encourage more frequent trading.

Fiat On-Ramps: Allowing users to deposit funds via debit or credit cards, not just cryptocurrency transfers. This would lower the barrier to entry for people unfamiliar with crypto.

Email Sign-In: Simplifying the onboarding process so users wouldn't need to understand crypto wallets or seed phrases to get started.

Team Expansion: Using the capital to hire engineers, designers, compliance staff, and market operators. Coplan couldn't run this alone anymore.

Market Expansion: Creating more markets across more categories of sports, entertainment, business, science, and international politics.

These improvements were designed to bridge the gap between crypto-native users and mainstream adoption. The challenge was maintaining the benefits of blockchain while hiding its complexity.

The Philosophical Foundation

Behind the technical decisions and business strategy was a deeper philosophical conviction. Coplan genuinely believed in the epistemic value of prediction markets, the idea that properly designed markets could reveal truth better than any alternative mechanism.

This belief was rooted in Friedrich Hayek's insights about distributed knowledge. No single person or institution could possess all relevant information about complex questions. But markets, by aggregating the dispersed knowledge of many participants, could produce surprisingly accurate probability estimates. When people had skin in the game, when being wrong cost them money they were incentivized to be right. The collective wisdom of self-interested traders, weighted by confidence (measured by bet size), could outperform experts, polls, and models.

Coplan had seen evidence of this in financial markets. Stock prices, for all their volatility, generally do a reasonable job of incorporating available information. Betting markets on elections had historically outperformed polls. Prediction markets in corporate settings had proven valuable for forecasting project completion dates and sales figures.

But prediction markets had never achieved mainstream adoption. They existed in narrow niches, limited by regulations, technology, and awareness. Coplan saw an opportunity to change that. With the right platform, at the right time, prediction markets could become a standard tool, something journalists consulted, campaigns monitored, businesses used, and individuals relied on.

This wasn't a get-rich-quick scheme. It was an attempt to build infrastructure for collective intelligence. The fact that it might also make him wealthy was a bonus, but not the primary motivation. At least, that's what Coplan told himself and others. And based on his willingness to work alone in a bathroom while nearly broke, it seems he meant it.

The Competitive Landscape

By late 2020, Polymarket wasn't alone in the prediction market space, but the competition was limited and flawed:

PredictIt: The academic research project operated with CFTC approval but was limited to small bet sizes ($850 per contract) and narrow market categories. It was more proof of concept than real market.

Augur: Still technically operational but essentially dead, with minimal volume and users.

Traditional Betting Sites: Betfair and other sports betting platforms sometimes offered political markets, but they were offshore, not blockchain-based, and didn't position themselves as information marketplaces.

Kalshi: Would later emerge as a competitor, but in 2020 was still navigating regulatory approval to operate legally in the U.S.

This landscape gave Polymarket room to grow. The platform wasn't competing against an established incumbent with network effects and user loyalty. It was competing against nothing, trying to create a market rather than capture one.

The Uncertainty Ahead

As 2020 drew to a close, Polymarket had momentum. Funding secured. Users growing. The 2020 election had generated enormous interest in political betting. The platform had proven it could create markets people cared about and attract real trading volume.

But enormous challenges loomed. The regulatory landscape was murky at best, hostile at worst. The platform would need to figure out how to operate globally while managing U.S. restrictions. It would need to build trust while operating in a space associated with gambling. It would need to grow fast enough to satisfy venture investors while building defensible advantages against competitors.

And most fundamentally, Polymarket would need to prove its core thesis: that prediction markets could become genuinely useful tools for understanding the future, not just gambling venues for crypto enthusiasts.

Coplan was no longer working in a bathroom. He had capital, a small team, and credibility. But the hardest part was just beginning. Taking a product from early adopters to mainstream adoption is where most startups fail. The next few years would determine whether Polymarket was a footnote in crypto history or the beginning of something transformative.

What happened next would exceed even Coplan's most optimistic projections but not before nearly destroying everything he had built.

PART II: BUILDING POLYMARKET

Chapter 4

Launch (2020)

Going Live

On June 1, 2020, Polymarket went live to the public. There was no splashy press release, no coordinated media campaign, no influencer endorsements. Just a tweet from Shayne Coplan announcing that the platform was open for business, and a simple website where anyone with a crypto wallet could start trading on the future.

The timing could not have been more perfect or more chaotic. America was three months into the COVID-19 pandemic. The country was locked down, with millions of people working from home, glued to their screens, refreshing news sites obsessively. George Floyd had been murdered just days earlier, on May 25th, and protests were erupting across every major city. The presidential election between Trump and Biden was heating up, with polls showing a tight race and enormous uncertainty about what would happen in November. The stock market was yo-yoing wildly. Everything felt unprecedented, unpredictable, urgent.

Into this maelstrom of uncertainty, Coplan offered something novel: a platform where people could put their money where their mouths were. Not just opinion polls where you clicked a button with no consequences. Not just Twitter arguments where everyone could claim to know what would happen. Real money, real stakes, real accountability.

The beta launch was modest. The interface was clean but basic, a far cry from the sophisticated platform Polymarket would become. Users needed to connect a crypto wallet (MetaMask was the most common), deposit USDC stablecoins, and then they could browse available markets and place bets. The user experience was smoother than Augur's notoriously clunky interface, but still required some technical literacy. You had to understand what a crypto wallet was, how to acquire USDC, and be comfortable transacting on blockchain.

Despite these barriers, people came. The first users were crypto natives, people already active in DeFi, familiar with Ethereum and its ecosystem, excited by the novelty of prediction markets. But they were also people genuinely curious about the future, tired of unreliable polls and bloviating pundits, intrigued by the idea that wisdom of crowds might work better than expert forecasts.

The First Markets

Polymarket began operations in June 2020, offering its users event-based binary options trading contracts, otherwise known as event markets. Users could place a bet on the probability of an event taking place and stand to win if their bet came to pass. Such bets varied from the U.S. presidential elections to the number of COVID cases.

The platform's inaugural markets reflected the moment's preoccupations. COVID dominated:

"Will there be more than 200,000 U.S. COVID deaths by December 31, 2020?" This was one of the first major markets, and it immediately demonstrated both the power and controversy of prediction markets. At the time, official death toll projections varied wildly. Some epidemiologists predicted catastrophic losses; others thought containment measures would work. The Polymarket consensus settled around a probability that proved remarkably prescient, though the human cost made the accuracy bittersweet.

"Will Donald Trump contract COVID-19 in 2020?" This market seemed almost frivolous when it launched in June. By October, when Trump announced he had tested positive, traders who had taken the "Yes" position reaped significant returns. The market had correctly identified something most observers missed: the President's exposure patterns and resistance to safety protocols created meaningful risk.

"Will schools reopen for in-person learning in Fall 2020?" Parents, teachers, and administrators across America were desperate for reliable information about this question. School districts were making billion-dollar decisions based on incomplete information. Polymarket aggregated insights from people with diverse knowledge, epidemiologists, teachers, parents in different regions, education policy experts into a probability estimate that proved more useful than any single official pronouncement.

"Presidential Election Winner 2024" The marquee market. Even in June 2020, five months before election day, this market was generating significant volume. Early trading had Biden as the favorite, consistent with national polls but with less certainty than polls suggested. The market's probability estimates would shift throughout the summer and fall, reacting to events, debates, and polling data in real time.

But Polymarket wasn't just politics and pandemic. Coplan understood that to build a real platform, you needed diversity of markets. So there were also:

- **"Will SpaceX successfully launch astronauts to the ISS?"** (They did, in May 2020, just before Polymarket launched)
- **"Will unemployment exceed 15% in 2020?"**
- **"Will there be a second stimulus check by December?"**
- **"Will TikTok be banned in the United States?"**
- **"Will the NBA resume its season in 2020?"**

Each market was a binary question with a clear resolution date and criteria. You bought "Yes" shares if you thought something would happen, "No" shares if you thought it wouldn't. The price of shares represented the market's collective probability estimate. If "Yes" shares were trading at $0.60, the market was saying there was a 60% chance the event would occur. If it happened, "Yes" shares paid out $1.00. If it didn't, they expired worthless.

This elegant simplicity, turning complex questions into binary markets with clear payouts was Polymarket's core innovation. Not the technology (blockchain-based prediction markets had existed before), but the execution: making it actually work at scale, with real users, on real events people cared about.

The Technical Architecture Comes Together

To understand why Polymarket worked when previous platforms had failed, you need to understand the technical decisions Coplan made.

Polygon (Matic) Blockchain: The choice to build on Polygon rather than Ethereum mainnet was crucial. Polymarket is a prediction markets platform on Polygon designed to allow users to trade and bet in real-time on outcomes of some of the most relevant real-world events. Ethereum's gas fees in 2020 could spike to $20-50 during periods of network congestion. Polygon offered the same security and smart contract capabilities but with transaction fees measured in fractions of a cent. This meant users could place small bets of $5, $10, $20 without fees eating up their potential profits.

USDC Integration: Every trade on Polymarket happened in USDC, a stablecoin pegged to the U.S. dollar and issued by Circle and Coinbase. This solved the volatility problem that plagued earlier crypto prediction markets. If you bought shares with Ethereum or Bitcoin, you were exposed to both the prediction market outcome and the cryptocurrency's price volatility. With USDC, a dollar was always a dollar. Your position value only changed based on the market's probability assessment, not crypto market swings.

Automated Market Makers (AMMs): This was perhaps the most technically sophisticated aspect of Polymarket. AMMs work by replacing the traditional order book with something called a liquidity pool, which is a smart contract that holds balances of two tokens. When someone makes a trade, they interact directly with this pool. The AMM uses a mathematical formula to update prices based on how much of each token is in the pool.

The constant product formula, where x multiplied by y equals k meant that Polymarket could always provide liquidity, even when there weren't natural buyers or sellers. The algorithm itself acted as counterparty to every trade. This was essential for a new platform with limited users. Without AMMs, many markets would have been too thin to trade. With AMMs, every market had instant liquidity from day one.

Smart Contracts for Settlement: Polymarket is built on Ethereum-based smart contracts and utilizes a protocol called UMA to record verifiable truths onto a blockchain. When a market resolved, payouts happened automatically. No central authority deciding who won, no payment processing delays, no disputes about whether you'd get paid. The code executed impartially, moving USDC from losing positions to winning positions based on the predetermined resolution criteria.

The Resolution Mechanism: One of Augur's biggest problems had been dispute resolution. When outcomes were ambiguous, the decentralized oracle system became a battlefield of competing factions, each trying to bias the result. Polymarket took a more pragmatic approach: a designated resolution team would determine outcomes based on reputable sources. This introduced centralization, but it worked. Markets resolved quickly, disputes were rare, and users trusted the process.

UMA Protocol: The Oracle Problem

The integration with UMA (Universal Market Access) protocol was particularly clever. UMA provided Polymarket with an optimistic oracle system, a mechanism for getting real-world data onto the blockchain in a trustworthy way.

Here's how it worked: When a market's resolution date arrived, someone (usually Polymarket's resolution team) would propose an outcome: "Yes, Trump did contract COVID" or "No, schools did not fully reopen." This proposal would go into a challenge period. If no one disputed it within a set timeframe (usually two hours), the outcome was accepted and the market settled automatically. If someone did dispute it, claiming the proposed outcome was wrong then UMA's more elaborate dispute resolution mechanism kicked in, involving token holders voting on the correct outcome.

In practice, disputes were extremely rare. Polymarket chose market questions with clear, verifiable outcomes and used reputable sources (New York Times, CDC data, official government announcements) as resolution criteria. The optimistic oracle meant most markets could settle quickly and automatically, while the dispute mechanism provided a backstop against errors or manipulation.

This was the kind of technical sophistication that separated Polymarket from amateur projects. Coplan hadn't just copied Augur's approach. He'd identified each failure point and designed solutions that balanced decentralization ideals with practical functionality.

Building Liquidity and Community

Technical excellence meant nothing without users and liquidity. In those first months, Coplan focused obsessively on both.

The early community formed on Discord and Twitter. These were crypto natives, yes, but also prediction market enthusiasts, data nerds, political junkies, and people who just enjoyed speculation. Some had been active on PredictIt or old InTrade. Others were new to prediction markets but intrigued by the concept. Many were drawn by the intersection of crypto and real-world events, this wasn't just another DeFi yield farming protocol; it was betting on things that mattered.

Coplan and his small team were extraordinarily active in the community. They solicited feedback on market design, explained how the platform worked, and most importantly, listened. When users reported bugs, they got fixed quickly. When users requested new markets, the team created them. This responsiveness built trust and loyalty.

Liquidity provision became a community activity. Some users acted as informal market makers, maintaining bid-ask spreads on popular markets to earn trading fees. Polymarket would sometimes seed initial liquidity in important markets to ensure they were tradable. And as volume grew, professional traders began to notice. These were people who traded on Betfair, PredictIt, or traditional financial prediction markets. They saw Polymarket as a new venue with potentially less efficient pricing, an opportunity to profit by providing liquidity and identifying mispriced probabilities.

The feedback loop was powerful: more liquidity attracted more traders, which improved pricing accuracy, which attracted media attention, which brought more users, which created more liquidity. In the platform's first three months after June launch, Polymarket saw over $1 million in trading volume. For a brand-new platform built in a bathroom and launched with no marketing budget, this was remarkable.

COVID's Sudden Relevance

The pandemic gave Polymarket an unexpected advantage: immediate relevance. In March 2020, as COVID transformed from distant concern to global catastrophe, everyone became an amateur epidemiologist. People were desperate for reliable information. When would this end? Would schools reopen? Would there be a second wave? Would vaccines work?

Traditional authorities, the CDC, WHO and government officials were providing contradictory information. The news media was simultaneously catastrophizing and downplaying. Social media was a cesspool of misinformation. Nobody knew what to believe.

Polymarket offered a different kind of answer. Not "here's what the experts say" but "here's what people with money at stake think." And crucially, those people with money at stake included actual experts, epidemiologists, healthcare workers and data analysts alongside informed amateurs, all forced to put probability estimates on their beliefs.

The COVID markets became Polymarket's proof of concept. On questions like vaccine development timelines, mask mandate implementations, and infection waves, Polymarket's consensus probabilities proved remarkably accurate. Not perfect, no forecasting method is but better than most expert predictions and dramatically better than media narratives.

Journalists began citing Polymarket. Not as a curiosity, but as a legitimate data source. "According to Polymarket traders, there's a 67% chance schools will remain closed through fall..." This media attention was invaluable. It legitimized the platform and brought non-crypto users who heard about it from mainstream sources.

Election Season Heats Up

But COVID markets, important as they were, represented only a fraction of Polymarket's potential. The real test would be the presidential election.

By summer 2020, election markets were exploding. The Biden vs. Trump race was generating enormous interest globally. Traditional polls showed

Biden with a comfortable but not overwhelming lead. But after 2016, nobody trusted polls anymore. People wanted better information, and they were willing to bet to get it.

Polymarket's presidential market became its flagship. Daily volume on "Presidential Election Winner 2024" exceeded all other markets combined. The price movements told a story. In early summer, Biden's probability peaked around 65%, higher than Trump but far from certain. After the first debate in late September, where Trump's performance was widely panned, Biden's probability spiked to 70%. But it never approached the 90%+ probabilities that some poll aggregators suggested.

This uncertainty, Polymarket giving Trump a fighting chance when many pundits declared the race over would later be vindicated by how close the actual election turned out to be. Though Biden won, it wasn't the blowout some predicted. Polymarket's probability estimates better reflected the true uncertainty.

Professional political traders took notice. Campaign operatives began monitoring Polymarket alongside traditional polls. Not officially, and rarely publicly, but the platform had become part of the information ecosystem that sophisticated political actors relied on.

Early Challenges

Success brought challenges. As volume grew, so did technical demands. The Polygon blockchain handled the load well, but Polymarket's servers and infrastructure needed constant upgrading. There were bugs, markets that didn't resolve correctly, prices that updated with lag, wallets that failed to connect. Coplan and his tiny team worked around the clock fixing issues.

Market manipulation was a concern from day one. Unlike traditional betting markets with stringent oversight, Polymarket operated in a regulatory gray zone with minimal monitoring. Could wealthy individuals or organized groups manipulate market prices by placing large coordinated bets? Theoretically, yes. In practice, it was harder than it seemed. The AMM design meant that moving prices significantly required enormous capital, more than most manipulators would risk. And other traders, seeing mispriced markets, would quickly arbitrage them back to fair value.

Still, there were suspicious patterns. Sudden large orders that seemed designed to manipulate rather than express genuine predictions. Wash trading, buying and selling to create false volume. Polymarket couldn't prevent all of this, but they monitored for obvious abuse and banned accounts that violated terms of service.

Another challenge was market selection. Since Polymarket's inception in 2020, it has offered over 900 separate event markets. Which events deserved markets? How would you phrase questions to ensure clear resolution? The team developed guidelines: events needed clear, verifiable outcomes; resolution criteria based on reputable sources; sufficient public interest; and reasonable timeframes (neither too immediate nor too far future).

Some requested markets were rejected as too ambiguous, too subjective, or too controversial. "Will extraterrestrials visit Earth?" No clear resolution criteria. "Will Kanye West become president?" Sure, technically possible but not worth platform resources. "Will a specific person die?" Ethical nightmare, legal liability, obviously no.

This editorial control was another departure from Augur's pure decentralization. Critics said it made Polymarket just another centralized platform cosplaying as crypto. Supporters said it made the platform actually usable. Coplan pragmatically chose function over ideology.

The Funding Announcement

By October 2020, Polymarket had proven itself. Over $1 million in volume, growing user base, media attention, and most importantly, demonstrated accuracy on important questions. It was time to raise capital to scale properly.

The $4 million seed round announcement came on October 27, 2020, perfectly timed to catch election fever. Naval Ravikant, Balaji Srinivasan, Polychain Capital, and other prominent crypto investors had bought in. The funding would be used to expand the team, improve technology, and most ambitiously, make Polymarket accessible to mainstream users not just crypto natives.

In the press release, Coplan articulated his mission: "One of the biggest problems with social media and discourse on the internet today is the lack of accountability. Everyone has an opinion and isn't afraid to share it. At the moment there's little downside to being wrong; this makes it really hard for regular people to discern what's fact and what's fiction. 2020 has showcased just how bad the consequences of this can be."

The positioning was brilliant. Polymarket wasn't gambling, it was accountability infrastructure. It wasn't speculation, it was truth-seeking. This framing would become central to how the platform marketed itself and defended against criticism.

Rob Hadick from Dragonfly, one of the investors, captured what made Coplan special: he "wants to be able to talk about it forever. This is his life. He lives it." During their first meeting, instead of a formal pitch, Coplan had proposed a walk around New York, during which he talked Hadick's ear off about prediction markets for two hours. That intensity, that all-consuming focus, convinced Hadick this wasn't just another entrepreneur chasing trends. This was someone building his life's work.

Election Night

November 3, 2020. Election day. Polymarket's greatest test.

Throughout the day, trading volume exploded. The presidential market saw more action in 24 hours than it had in the previous four months combined. Users were refreshing obsessively, watching probability numbers shift in real-time as voting results came in.

Polymarket didn't call the race incorrectly, but it didn't outperform traditional forecasts either. The market had shown Biden ahead going into election night, consistent with most polls. As results came in, the probabilities shifted dramatically. Trump led in several key states initially, Biden's probability dropping, then recovering as mail-in ballots were counted. The platform's real-time updating gave users a visceral sense of the race's fluidity in ways that traditional media couldn't capture.

The final outcome, Biden winning, but much closer than some polls suggested aligned reasonably well with Polymarket's pre-election probabilities. The platform had given Trump roughly a 35-40% chance in the final weeks, meaning a Trump victory wouldn't have been a shocking upset. In the event, Biden won, but several states were decided by razor-thin margins.

More importantly, Polymarket had proven it could handle high-volume, high-stakes events without technical failure. The infrastructure held. The markets stayed liquid. Users could trade throughout the night without significant outages or issues. For a platform less than six months old, this was a significant achievement.

What Launch Taught

By December 2020, Polymarket had been live for six months. In that time, it had processed over $10 million in total volume, attracted thousands of users, secured venture funding, and proven that blockchain-based prediction markets could work at scale.

But more importantly, those first six months established several crucial lessons:

Markets could aggregate information effectively. On questions where outcomes could be verified, Polymarket's consensus probabilities proved reasonably accurate, often more accurate than expert predictions or polls.

Users wanted this. The demand was real. People were hungry for better forecasting tools, for ways to express their beliefs with consequences, for alternatives to unreliable polls and punditry.

Crypto was enabling, not constraining. The blockchain infrastructure allowed Polymarket to operate globally, settle automatically, and provide transparency. These weren't just buzzwords, they were genuine advantages over traditional prediction markets.

Community matters. The early users weren't just customers; they were stakeholders, contributors, evangelists. They provided liquidity, suggested markets, caught bugs, and spread the word. Building this community was as important as building the technology.

Regulatory challenges loomed. Operating in a gray zone was fine for early growth, but Polymarket was offering something that looked suspiciously like gambling or unregistered securities. Eventually, regulators would notice.

That last lesson would prove prophetic. The success of 2020 had painted a target on Polymarket's back. By proving the concept worked, by generating real volume and mainstream attention, Coplan had also attracted the attention of the Commodity Futures Trading Commission.

The reckoning was coming. But for now, in the closing weeks of 2020, Polymarket was riding high. The bathroom office was behind them. The team was growing. Capital was in the bank. The platform had survived its first real test. Everything seemed possible.

Coplan posted on social media from his old bathroom workspace: "2020, running out of money, solo founder, HQ in my makeshift bathroom office. Little did I know Polymarket was going to change the world."

Whether that prediction would prove as accurate as Polymarket's election forecasts remained to be seen.

Chapter 5

Early Markets and Growth

The Post-Election Reality Check

December 2020. The election was over. Biden had won. The pandemic was still raging, but vaccine rollouts were beginning. And Polymarket had survived its first major test, not just survived, but proven its concept. The platform had processed millions in volume, maintained technical stability through election night chaos, and emerged with its reputation intact.

But the question now was: what comes next?

Elections are high-stakes, high-interest events that naturally attract betting. Every four years, hundreds of millions of people care deeply about the outcome. But those events are rare. If Polymarket was going to become a real business not just an election curiosity it needed to prove that prediction markets could work year-round, across diverse categories, drawing sustained engagement rather than episodic spikes.

Coplan and his growing team spent the early months of 2021 trying to answer that question. What markets would people trade on when there wasn't a presidential election? How do you build a platform that's valuable 365 days a year?

The answer, they discovered, was diversification and depth. Not just more markets, but better markets. Markets that mattered to specific communities, markets that filled information gaps, markets that couldn't be easily replicated elsewhere.

Building the Market Library

Throughout 2021, Polymarket dramatically expanded its market offerings. In late 2021 and early 2022, the team attempted to launch as many as 2,000 markets monthly, potentially to increase user engagement. This was an aggressive expansion strategy, almost overwhelming in its ambition.

The markets spanned a remarkable range:

Cryptocurrency Markets: When would Bitcoin hit $100,000? Would Ethereum move to proof-of-stake by the end of 2021? Would any exchange-traded Bitcoin ETF be approved? These markets attracted crypto natives who were already comfortable with the platform's blockchain infrastructure and had strong opinions (and inside knowledge) about crypto developments.

Sports Markets: Would Tom Brady retire after the 2021 season? Would the Olympics happen on schedule despite COVID? Would any team go undefeated in the NFL? Sports betting was already a massive industry, and Polymarket offered something traditional sportsbooks didn't: transparency, blockchain settlement, and the ability to trade positions before events concluded.

Entertainment and Pop Culture: Would there be a new James Bond movie in 2021? Would Kanye West actually release his album on time? Would any major celebrity couple divorce? These markets seemed frivolous, but they attracted a different demographic, people who followed pop culture closely and had insights others didn't.

Science and Technology: Would SpaceX successfully land Starship? Would commercial space tourism begin? Would any major tech company hit a trillion-dollar valuation? These markets attracted engineers, scientists, and tech industry insiders with genuine expertise.

Business and Economics: Would inflation exceed 5%? Would unemployment fall below a certain threshold? Would major companies announce layoffs? Business professionals and economists found these markets genuinely useful for stress-testing their assumptions.

Politics Beyond Elections: Would Trump be indicted? Would Biden's approval rating fall below 40%? Would any Supreme Court justice retire?

Political junkies wanted to bet on politics year-round, not just during election seasons.

COVID-19 Continued: The pandemic remained a dominant theme through 2021. Markets about vaccine efficacy, mandates, travel restrictions, and infection waves continued to generate significant volume. People were desperate for reliable information about when life would return to normal.

The diversity was strategic. By creating markets across categories, Polymarket could attract different communities, each bringing specialized knowledge and trading activity. A crypto trader might primarily follow Bitcoin markets but occasionally bet on political outcomes. A sports bettor might discover the platform through football markets but start trading on entertainment questions. Cross-pollination between communities created network effects.

The Platform Evolution

As markets expanded, the platform itself evolved rapidly. The October 2020 funding was being deployed to improve every aspect of user experience.

Onboarding Simplification: The biggest barrier to mainstream adoption was crypto complexity. Most people didn't have crypto wallets, didn't own USDC, and were intimidated by blockchain. Polymarket introduced email-based sign-up with simplified wallet creation in the background. Users could create accounts without understanding they were generating Ethereum keypairs. The wallet was abstracted away, it existed, but users didn't need to know or care.

Fiat On-Ramps: Partnerships with payment processors allowed users to purchase USDC directly with credit or debit cards. No longer did you need to first buy cryptocurrency on an exchange, transfer it to a wallet, and then deposit to Polymarket. You could go from having no crypto to placing your first bet in minutes.

Mobile Optimization: While Polymarket started as a desktop-first platform, by 2021 it was increasingly accessed via mobile devices. The interface was redesigned for smaller screens, touch interfaces, and on-the-go trading. Mobile was where mainstream adoption would happen.

API Development: Professional traders and data analysts wanted programmatic access. Polymarket developed APIs that allowed sophisticated users to build custom trading bots, analyze market data, and execute complex strategies. This attracted a class of serious traders who would provide liquidity and market efficiency.

Market Resolution Improvements: The UMA protocol integration was refined to make market resolution faster and more transparent. Clear criteria, reputable sources, and quick settlement became hallmarks of the platform. Trust in resolution was essential, users needed confidence they'd be paid correctly and promptly.

Educational Content: Polymarket created extensive documentation explaining how prediction markets work, how to interpret probabilities, and how to trade effectively. This content served dual purposes: educating new users and positioning the platform as intellectually serious rather than just another gambling site.

The Community Emerges

By mid-2021, Polymarket had developed a distinct community and culture. This wasn't just random gamblers, it was a self-selecting group of people interested in forecasting, probability, information markets, and crypto.

The Discord channel became the community hub. Thousands of users discussed markets, shared analysis, debated probabilities, and built relationships. Some emerged as informal opinion leaders, users whose market commentary others followed, whose trades others mimicked. This social layer added stickiness beyond just the trading mechanics.

Twitter became another crucial channel. Polymarket markets were increasingly cited in tweets about current events. "Polymarket now gives Trump a 35% chance of indictment in 2021" or "According to Polymarket, there's a 72% chance inflation exceeds 5%." These citations drove traffic and legitimacy. The platform was becoming part of the information ecosystem around major news events.

Professional traders began to take notice. These were people who made a living trading on political betting exchanges like Betfair or PredictIt. They saw Polymarket as a new venue with potentially less efficient pricing, opportunities to profit by identifying mispriced probabilities. Their participation improved market quality but also increased competition, making it harder for casual bettors to profit.

Data analysts and researchers discovered Polymarket as a research tool. Academic papers began citing Polymarket probabilities alongside traditional polling data. Journalists used it as a source for stories about public sentiment and expectations. This academic and journalistic attention brought credibility that pure gambling sites never achieved.

High-Profile Validation

The platform also caught the attention of notable figures like Vitalik Buterin, who endorsed the platform's potential in a 2021 blog post. This endorsement was enormously significant. Buterin, as Ethereum's co-founder, was one of the most respected voices in crypto. His approval signaled that Polymarket was doing something intellectually serious, not just another DeFi gimmick.

Buterin's support went beyond words. He participated in Polymarket's Series B funding round in May 2021, which raised $45 million and included Peter Thiel's Founders Fund. This funding represented a major step up from the $4 million seed round just seven months earlier. The valuation implied by the Series B suggested investors believed Polymarket could become genuinely large.

Buterin would later defend Polymarket against critics who argued that betting on tragic events like wars, disasters and deaths was morally problematic. His argument was sophisticated, prediction markets with "skin in the game" provide more accurate information than costless punditry. In a world drowning in misinformation, having a mechanism that financially punishes inaccurate predictions and rewards accuracy serves a social good. The fact that the mechanism looks like gambling doesn't negate its epistemic value.

This framing, prediction markets as information infrastructure rather than gambling became central to how Polymarket defended itself. And having Buterin, one of crypto's most thoughtful voices, making that argument publicly was invaluable.

Volume and Metrics

Despite being somewhat niche at the time, Polymarket's top-tier trading activity had already surpassed $1 million, demonstrating significant potential. This understates the achievement. By the end of 2021, Polymarket had processed tens of millions in cumulative volume across hundreds of markets.

The platform was still small compared to traditional prediction markets or betting exchanges. Betfair, the British betting exchange, processed billions in volume annually. Even PredictIt, limited by regulatory restrictions, had comparable volume on major political events. But Polymarket was growing faster, and critically, it was growing globally.

User metrics told a similar story. Thousands of active traders, with growth accelerating. The user base skewed young, male, tech-savvy, and internationally dispersed. These were early adopters, people comfortable with crypto, interested in prediction markets, willing to try something new. But they were also sophisticated and many had backgrounds in finance, technology, statistics, or political analysis.

Market liquidity remained a challenge. While major markets like presidential elections had deep liquidity, niche markets could be thin. A market about an obscure referendum or a minor celebrity might have wide bid-ask spreads and limited depth. The AMM system ensured you could always trade, but not always at favorable prices. Growing liquidity across all markets, not just the headline grabbers, would be essential for long-term success.

Notable Predictions and Accuracy

The platform's track record on accuracy was becoming impressive. While not perfect, Polymarket's consensus probabilities outperformed expert predictions and polling on numerous high-profile questions.

COVID Vaccine Timelines: Polymarket markets correctly anticipated that vaccines would be developed and approved faster than most experts predicted. When many epidemiologists were saying early 2022, Polymarket consensus said late 2020/early 2021, which proved correct.

Inflation Predictions: As inflation began accelerating in 2021, Polymarket markets gave higher probabilities to sustained inflation than many economists predicted. The Federal Reserve and Treasury insisted inflation would be "transitory." Polymarket was more skeptical, and ultimately more accurate.

Political Events: Markets about Congressional actions, Supreme Court decisions, and regulatory announcements generally outperformed pundit predictions. Not by enormous margins, but consistently enough to suggest the wisdom of crowds was real.

Tech Company Valuations: Markets about which companies would hit trillion-dollar valuations, which would announce major layoffs, and which would miss earnings proved remarkably prescient. Tech industry insiders were clearly trading on these markets with genuine information advantages.

These successes attracted media attention and drove user growth. Each time Polymarket correctly predicted something that experts or polls got wrong, it generated stories and social media discussion. "How did Polymarket know?" became a recurring question. The answer, aggregated information from diverse participants with skin in the game was Polymarket's core value proposition.

Challenges and Growing Pains

Success brought problems. As volume increased and markets expanded, several challenges emerged that would shape Polymarket's next phase.

Manipulation Concerns: Were large traders manipulating market prices? Could wealthy individuals or organized groups coordinate to distort probabilities? There were suspicious patterns, sudden large orders that seemed designed to move prices rather than reflect genuine beliefs. Polymarket's team monitored for abuse but had limited enforcement tools. Blockchain transparency meant suspicious trades were visible, but stopping them was difficult.

Wash Trading: Some users appeared to be trading with themselves to generate false volume or manipulate prices. This was easier to detect than prevent. Polymarket could ban accounts, but creating new accounts was trivial if someone was determined.

Market Selection Controversies: Which events deserved markets? Some users wanted markets on deaths of public figures, "assassination markets" that were both ethically problematic and potentially illegal. Polymarket refused these, but the line was often unclear. Markets about war casualties, natural disasters, and terror attacks raised similar ethical questions. Where was the boundary between legitimate forecasting and ghoulish profiteering?

Technical Scaling: As user numbers grew, the platform needed constant infrastructure improvements. Database optimization, server capacity, caching strategies, these technical details mattered enormously for user experience. Slow loading times or laggy price updates would drive users away.

Customer Support: With thousands of users, support inquiries multiplied. Disputes about market resolution, questions about deposits and withdrawals, technical problems, all required human attention. Scaling support operations was expensive and operationally complex.

Regulatory Uncertainty: The CFTC was watching. So was the SEC. So were international regulators. Operating at the intersection of prediction markets and futures trading, Polymarket faced unique regulatory challenges. The platform existed in a gray zone, not quite gambling (it claimed), not quite securities trading, not quite derivatives. But regulators were starting to pay attention, and attention from regulators rarely ends well.

The Data Value Proposition

As 2021 progressed, a new narrative emerged around Polymarket: the data itself was valuable, independent of trading profits.

Media organizations began citing Polymarket regularly. Not as a curiosity but as a legitimate data source alongside polls and expert analysis. "Polymarket gives Trump a 40% chance of 2024 nomination" appeared in mainstream news stories. This editorial validation was crucial for mainstream acceptance.

Political campaigns and consultants started monitoring Polymarket. Not publicly, no campaign wanted to admit they were watching betting markets but privately, strategists paid attention. The markets aggregated information that polls missed, especially about low-probability high-impact events.

Financial analysts used Polymarket markets about economic indicators and company performance as inputs to their models. Market probabilities about Federal Reserve decisions, GDP growth, and unemployment became part of the information diet for professional investors.

Academic researchers began publishing papers using Polymarket data. Studies comparing prediction market accuracy to polls, examining market efficiency, analyzing trader behavior, all used Polymarket as a data source. This academic attention brought intellectual credibility.

This data value created a second business model beyond transaction fees. Polymarket could potentially sell premium data access, analytical tools, or aggregated insights to professional users. Media organizations, hedge funds, political campaigns, and consulting firms might pay for enhanced access to market data and analytics.

The Competitors Stir

Polymarket's success didn't go unnoticed by competitors. Other platforms saw the opportunity and began developing their own prediction markets.

Kalshi was the most significant competitor. Unlike Polymarket, Kalshi was taking the regulatory-first approach, seeking CFTC approval to operate legally in the United States as a designated contract market. This was the opposite of Polymarket's strategy. Kalshi was slower, more restricted, but potentially more sustainable. The question was whether regulatory approval would strangle innovation or provide long-term competitive advantage.

Augur remained technically operational but had failed to recover from its early problems. Low volume, minimal users, and a reputation for unusability meant it wasn't a serious threat.

Traditional Betting Sites like Betfair and offshore sportsbooks were expanding into prediction markets. They had liquidity, regulatory frameworks, and established user bases. But they lacked blockchain transparency and were restricted by geography.

New Entrants were being incubated in crypto circles. The success of Polymarket inspired imitators. Some would use different blockchains, different market mechanics, or different regulatory strategies. Competition was inevitable.

For Coplan, this competitive landscape validated the market. If others were entering, it meant the opportunity was real. But it also meant Polymarket needed to move fast, build moats, and establish itself as the category leader before someone else did.

End of Year Assessment

By December 2021, Polymarket had accomplished more in 18 months than most startups achieve in five years. From bathroom office to legitimate venture-backed platform. From zero to millions in volume. From crypto curiosity to mainstream media citations.

But the company was at an inflection point. The early adopter phase was ending. Mainstream expansion would require different strategies, more marketing, more regulatory clarity, more infrastructure, more legitimacy. The scrappy startup needed to become a real company.

And looming over everything was the regulatory question. Operating in gray zones works until it doesn't. The CFTC had noticed Polymarket. Investigation was coming. How the company navigated that challenge would determine whether it became a lasting institution or a cautionary tale.

In October 2021, the Commodity Futures Trading Commission (CFTC) in the U.S. initiated an investigation into the platform. The reckoning that everyone knew was coming had arrived.

For now, though, the trajectory was upward. Users were growing. Volume was increasing. Media attention was expanding. Vitalik Buterin was endorsing them. Peter Thiel was investing. The vision of prediction markets as information infrastructure seemed increasingly plausible.

Coplan had taken his bathroom office project and built something real. Whether it could survive what came next would define his legacy and the future of prediction markets themselves.

The investigation was about to begin.

Chapter 6

The Funding Rounds

The Seed: Betting on Belief

October 2020. Polymarket had been live for just four months, but Shayne Coplan was already thinking years ahead. The platform had proven its concept, over $1 million in trading volume, thousands of users, media attention, and most importantly, demonstrated accuracy on COVID predictions and early election forecasting. But proving a concept and building a lasting company are entirely different challenges.

Coplan needed capital. Not just for servers and engineering talent, but to turn Polymarket from a crypto curiosity into genuine infrastructure. He needed to hire a team, improve the user experience, expand market offerings, and most critically, build the compliance and legal framework to survive in a hostile regulatory environment.

The seed round closed at $4 million, led by Polychain Capital, one of the premier cryptocurrency venture firms. But the investor list read like a who's who of crypto and tech elite: Naval Ravikant, Balaji Srinivasan, Meltem Demirors, 1confirmation, ParaFi, Robot Ventures, and General Catalyst.

Naval Ravikant's participation was particularly significant. The founder of AngelList and one of Silicon Valley's most influential philosophers had millions of Twitter followers who treated his investment decisions as signals. Naval didn't just invest in companies, he invested in ideas he believed would reshape how society functions. His backing suggested that Polymarket was intellectually serious, not just another DeFi yield farming scheme.

Balaji Srinivasan, the former CTO of Coinbase and a prominent futurist, brought both technical credibility and a network of connections throughout crypto. Balaji had long advocated for using markets and technology to route around legacy institutions. Polymarket fit perfectly into his worldview of building parallel systems that competed with and eventually replaced established powers.

General Catalyst was the outlier. While the other investors were crypto-native, General Catalyst was a traditional venture firm with a portfolio including Stripe, Airbnb, and Snapchat. Their involvement signaled that Polymarket's potential extended beyond the crypto bubble. This wasn't just a blockchain experiment; it was a legitimate business that mainstream investors could understand.

The pitch that won these investors over centered on several key arguments:

Timing: The 2020 election and pandemic had created unprecedented demand for real-time, crowd-sourced forecasting. Trust in traditional institutions, polls, experts, and the media was collapsing. People were desperate for better information.

Market Inefficiency: Traditional forecasting methods were demonstrably failing. Polls had been wrong in 2016 and would likely be wrong again. Prediction markets offered a fundamentally different approach: aggregating dispersed information through financial incentives.

Technical Execution: By solving Augur's problems of terrible user experience, high fees and unclear resolution Polymarket had built something people would actually use. The early volume proved product-market fit.

Global Opportunity: Crypto infrastructure meant Polymarket could scale globally without massive capital expenditure. No payment processors to negotiate with, no servers in each country, no traditional financial infrastructure.

Data Value: Beyond transaction fees, the platform was generating uniquely valuable data. Market probabilities could be sold to media organizations, political campaigns, hedge funds, and research institutions.

For Rob Hadick at Dragonfly, what sealed the deal wasn't a slick pitch deck, it was Coplan himself. At their initial meeting, Coplan eschewed a formal presentation and instead proposed a walk around New York. For two hours, he talked Hadick's ear off about prediction markets, barely pausing for breath. "He wants to be able to talk about it forever," Hadick would later recall. "This is his life. He lives it."

That intensity, that total commitment, was what distinguished founders who actually built things from those who just had ideas. Coplan wasn't exploring prediction markets as an interesting side project. He was consumed by them.

The funding was announced on October 27, 2020, with press coverage emphasizing Polymarket's mission to fight fake news and hold accountable those "pumping disinformation in the news cycle." This framing was deliberate and would become central to how the company positioned itself. Polymarket wasn't gambling, it was accountability infrastructure. It wasn't speculation, it was truth-seeking.

The Series A: Growing Pains and Quiet Capital

Between the October 2020 seed round and May 2024, Polymarket raised a Series A that went largely unannounced at the time. The Series A raised $25 million and was led by General Catalyst, with participation from Airbnb co-founder Joe Gebbia and Polychain.

The decision to keep this round quiet was strategic. By late 2021, the CFTC was investigating Polymarket. Making noise about raising capital while under regulatory scrutiny would have been foolish. Better to quietly secure the funding, keep building, and deal with the regulatory reckoning when it came.

The Series A capital funded crucial developments:

Team Expansion: Polymarket went from a handful of people to dozens. Engineers to improve infrastructure and build new features. Compliance professionals to navigate regulatory complexity. Customer support to handle growing user inquiries. Market operators to create and resolve markets. Designers to refine user experience.

Infrastructure Scaling: As volume grew, the platform needed constant upgrades. Database optimization, caching layers, API development, mobile optimization—all required significant engineering resources.

Market Development: Creating good prediction markets is harder than it looks. Questions need clear resolution criteria, verifiable sources, appropriate timeframes, and sufficient public interest. The team developed sophisticated processes for market creation and quality control.

Compliance Systems: Know Your Customer (KYC) and Anti-Money Laundering (AML) systems were implemented. Geographic restrictions were developed. Monitoring for suspicious trading patterns became more sophisticated. Legal counsel expanded to handle the inevitable regulatory challenges.

Joe Gebbia's involvement brought valuable insights from building Airbnb, another company that had operated in regulatory gray zones (short-term rental regulations) while scaling globally. His experience navigating hostile municipalities and building trust with skeptical users was directly applicable to Polymarket's challenges.

But the Series A came during a difficult period. The CFTC investigation that began in October 2021 hung over everything. Every decision had to account for regulatory risk. The platform was growing, but under a cloud of uncertainty.

The Series B: Thiel and Buterin

The Series B raised $45 million and saw participation from Vitalik Buterin, with Founders Fund leading the round. The announcement came in May 2024, simultaneously revealing the previously undisclosed Series A. Combined, the two rounds represented $70 million in new capital.

The Series B was transformative, not just for the capital but for who it brought to the table.

Peter Thiel's Founders Fund leading the round was a watershed moment. Thiel, the PayPal co-founder, early Facebook investor, and libertarian iconoclast, was one of the most influential investors in tech. Thiel sees the rise of crypto as a challenge to traditional financial systems. His fund's portfolio included Palantir, SpaceX, and OpenAI, companies pushing boundaries and challenging established powers.

Joey Krug, a Founders Fund partner, explained their enthusiasm: "Polymarket has finally made the vision for prediction markets a reality, an opportunity that we have been passionate about for years. Internally at Founders Fund we developed a habit of checking Polymarket at times of breaking news. The tangible benefits of using Polymarket as a complement to consuming news on social and mainstream media was obvious. It became clear to us that Polymarket was the winner in this market."

This was crucial: sophisticated investors were using Polymarket themselves, finding it genuinely useful, and then investing based on that firsthand experience. This wasn't speculative capital chasing returns; it was conviction capital backing something they believed in.

Vitalik Buterin, Ethereum's co-founder, participating was equally significant. Buterin wasn't just any investor, he was crypto's most respected intellectual, a philosopher-coder whose opinions carried enormous weight. His endorsement came with a philosophical defense of prediction markets that would prove essential as criticism mounted.

Buterin had written in 2021 about the epistemic value of prediction markets. His argument was sophisticated: in a world drowning in misinformation, having mechanisms that financially punish inaccuracy and reward truth serves a social good. Yes, prediction markets look like gambling. But that appearance obscures their deeper function as information aggregation systems.

The timing of the Series B was fascinating. It came just days after the CFTC proposed a ban on political betting markets, which would affect competitors like Kalshi but not the already-banned-in-the-US Polymarket. Joey Krug noted, "A lot of the reason why certain people don't like prediction markets in the US kind of dates back to pretty puritanical thinking about betting. In the short- to mid-term it's good for Polymarket because they are targeting non-US markets. In the long run, it will be good if Americans can participate in this market too."

The message was clear: regulatory hostility in the U.S. was temporary. Eventually, prediction markets would gain acceptance. Polymarket was playing the long game, building internationally while waiting for American policy to catch up.

Despite having no revenue at the moment, the funding valued the company at a lower level than previous discussions. The company had been eyeing a valuation of almost $1 billion before the CFTC action. The regulatory settlement had depressed Polymarket's valuation, but investors were betting that the setback was temporary.

Other participants in the Series B included existing investors 1confirmation and ParaFi, along with Dragonfly Capital and Eventbrite co-founder Kevin Hartz. The roster suggested both conviction from existing backers (they were doubling down) and new believers attracted by Polymarket's traction.

Strategic Hires: Building Legitimacy

Alongside the Series B, Polymarket announced key hires designed to signal seriousness about regulatory compliance and market expansion.

Richard Jaycobs joined as head of market expansion. Jaycobs previously served as president of the Cantor Exchange and CEO of The Clearing Corporation, traditional finance credentials that brought credibility with regulators and institutional investors. His 30-year career in financial derivatives exchanges gave Polymarket expertise it desperately needed.

Even more significantly, in May 2022, Polymarket had appointed J. Christopher Giancarlo as chairman of its advisory board. Giancarlo, nicknamed "CryptoDad," had served as chairman of the CFTC from 2017 to 2019. Having the former head of the very agency that had fined Polymarket $1.4 million join the company was a clear signal: Polymarket was serious about compliance and believed it could eventually operate legally in the United States.

These hires demonstrated a sophisticated strategy. Polymarket wasn't fighting regulators head-on. It was building relationships, hiring people who understood regulatory thinking, and positioning itself as a responsible actor rather than a crypto cowboy operation.

The Unicorn Round: $200 Million at $1 Billion

In June 2025, reports emerged that Polymarket was finalizing a $200 million funding round that would value the company at approximately $1 billion, according to sources familiar with the matter. This raise was set to be led by Peter Thiel's Founders Fund, which was already an investor in Polymarket.

The timing was strategic. The funding round came after the prediction platform announced a partnership with Elon Musk's social media platform X in early June. The partnership aimed to merge Polymarket's prediction markets with AI-driven insights from X's Grok chatbot, potentially enhancing the platform's predictive capabilities.

The unicorn valuation of $1 billion was a milestone that conferred legitimacy in Silicon Valley and beyond. It meant Polymarket wasn't just a successful startup; it was a category-defining company. The "unicorn" label attracted talent, media attention, and additional capital.

The platform had experienced explosive growth during the 2024 US presidential election, with trading volume topping $2.5 billion in November as bettors used cryptocurrency to wager on election outcomes and a host of other events. This volume validated the business model and demonstrated that prediction markets could generate massive engagement on major events.

The $200 million round also came after Polymarket had already secured $100 million in funding earlier in 2025, including a $50 million capital injection. The company was raising capital aggressively, recognizing that the window of opportunity was open but might not stay that way forever.

The Ultimate Validation: ICE Investment

Then came the deal that changed everything.

In October 2025, Polymarket secured up to a $2 billion investment from Intercontinental Exchange, which valued the company at $8 billion. This was no ordinary venture round. Intercontinental Exchange, ICE is the owner of the New York Stock Exchange, one of the most established institutions in global finance.

The symbolism was extraordinary. Just five years after Coplan started Polymarket in a bathroom office, the company behind the NYSE was investing billions. The crypto upstart that regulators had fined and investigated was now partnered with Wall Street's establishment.

The $8 billion pre-money valuation made Shayne Coplan, who owns approximately 11% of the company, the world's youngest self-made billionaire at age 27. From broke dropout to billionaire in half a decade, it was the kind of trajectory that seemed impossible outside of fairytales.

But the ICE deal was about more than just money. ICE and Polymarket agreed to partner on tokenization initiatives in the future, suggesting that the two companies saw opportunities to blend traditional finance with blockchain technology. ICE brought regulatory expertise, institutional relationships, and mainstream credibility. Polymarket brought crypto infrastructure, prediction market technology, and a growing global user base.

The deal also came after crucial regulatory progress. In July 2025, both the Justice Department and CFTC had dropped their investigations without filing charges. That same month, Polymarket acquired QCEX, a CFTC-licensed derivatives exchange and clearinghouse, for $112 million, giving it legal grounds to operate in the United States.

These pieces fit together into a coherent strategy: resolve regulatory issues, acquire necessary licenses, partner with established financial institutions, and return to the U.S. market from a position of strength rather than as a supplicant.

The Funding Journey: Lessons and Implications

In total, Polymarket raised $2.3 billion over 7 funding rounds from 26 investors. The journey from $4 million seed to $2 billion from ICE represented one of the most dramatic funding progressions in recent tech history.

Several lessons emerge from this funding trajectory:

Conviction Capital Matters: The investors who backed Polymarket early, Naval, Balaji, Polychain weren't chasing returns. They believed in the concept of prediction markets as information infrastructure. That conviction sustained the company through regulatory challenges.

Regulatory Risk Depresses Valuations: The CFTC settlement clearly impacted Polymarket's valuation in 2022-2023. But investors who could see past short-term regulatory uncertainty to long-term potential were rewarded enormously.

Mainstream Validation is Gradual: The progression from crypto-native investors (Polychain) to mainstream VC (General Catalyst) to traditional finance (ICE) shows how legitimacy compounds. Each round made the next possible.

Strategic Hires Signal Seriousness: Bringing in executives from traditional finance and former regulators demonstrated that Polymarket wasn't just another reckless crypto project. It was building institutional quality.

Timing is Everything: Raising the Series B right after election betting was banned in the U.S. seemed counterintuitive but was brilliant. It signaled confidence and long-term thinking when others might have panicked.

Products Trump Pitches: What really attracted capital wasn't Coplan's pitch decks, it was that sophisticated investors were using Polymarket themselves and finding it valuable. Product-market fit drove funding, not salesmanship.

Patience Pays: From 2020 to 2025, Coplan could have sold the company multiple times. Instead, he kept building, raised capital strategically, and ultimately created something worth billions rather than millions.

The funding rounds tell a story of a company that started as a crypto experiment, faced existential regulatory threats, pivoted to international markets, proved its model worked at scale, and ultimately achieved legitimacy with Wall Street's blessing. It's a story of vision, persistence, and strategic capital deployment.

But funding rounds are just fuel. The real story is what Polymarket built with that capital and whether the vision of prediction markets as information infrastructure would actually work at scale. The billions in funding gave Coplan the resources to find out. Whether he would succeed remained an open question as the company entered its next phase of growth.

Chapter 7

Product Evolution

From MVP to Mainstream

When Polymarket launched in June 2020, it was a minimum viable product in the truest sense. The interface was functional but basic. The onboarding required crypto literacy. The feature set was limited to core trading mechanics. It worked, but barely. For crypto natives accustomed to clunky DeFi interfaces, this was acceptable. For mainstream users, it was a non-starter.

Over the next four years, Polymarket would undergo a radical transformation. Not just incremental improvements, but a complete reimagining of what a prediction market platform could be. The journey from crypto experiment to consumer product reveals how Shayne Coplan and his team learned to balance ideological purity with practical usability, decentralization dreams with centralized convenience, and crypto complexity with mainstream accessibility.

This evolution happened in waves, each responding to user feedback, competitive pressure, and the team's growing ambitions. By 2024, Polymarket bore little resemblance to its 2020 incarnation, except in its core mission of aggregating information through markets.

Wave One: Removing Friction (2021)

The first major evolution focused on eliminating barriers to entry. Every unnecessary step in the user journey was a potential abandonment point. The early data was brutal: many users who started the onboarding process never completed it. They got confused by crypto wallets, intimidated by blockchain terminology, or frustrated by the complexity of acquiring USDC.

Simplified Onboarding: The original process required users to install MetaMask or another crypto wallet, understand seed phrases and private keys, acquire cryptocurrency on an exchange, and manually transfer USDC to Polymarket. For crypto natives, this was routine. For everyone else, it was impossibly complex.

Polymarket redesigned onboarding from first principles. Email-based sign-up with simplified wallet creation handled in the background became the default path. Users could create accounts without understanding they were generating Ethereum keypairs. The wallet existed, it had to, for blockchain transactions but it was abstracted away behind a familiar email/password interface.

This was controversial among crypto purists who believed users should control their own keys. "Not your keys, not your crypto" was gospel in crypto circles. But Coplan understood that ideological purity was killing adoption. Most users didn't want to be their own bank, they wanted to place bets on election outcomes without a computer science degree.

Fiat On-Ramps: Partnerships with payment processors allowed users to purchase USDC directly with credit or debit cards. This was transformative. No longer did you need to first buy cryptocurrency on Coinbase, transfer it to a wallet, bridge it to Polygon, and then deposit to Polymarket. You could go from having no crypto to placing your first bet in minutes.

The technical challenge was significant. Payment processors were wary of crypto businesses, especially ones that looked like gambling. Polymarket needed robust KYC/AML systems, fraud prevention, and compliance infrastructure. The company hired specialized compliance staff and built systems to satisfy both payment processors and evolving regulatory requirements.

Mobile Optimization: While Polymarket started as a desktop-first platform, by 2021 it was increasingly accessed via mobile devices. The interface was completely redesigned for smaller screens, touch interfaces, and on-the-go trading. This wasn't just responsive design, it was rethinking core functionality for mobile use patterns.

Mobile users behaved differently. They wanted quick glances at market odds, rapid position checks, and simple trading. They weren't conducting deep analysis or managing complex portfolios. The mobile experience needed to reflect this: larger touch targets, simplified navigation, prominent display of key information, and streamlined trading flows.

Wave Two: Professional Tools (2022)

As Polymarket grew, it attracted a more sophisticated user base. Professional traders who made living betting on political outcomes saw the platform as a new venue with potentially inefficient pricing. These users needed different tools than casual bettors.

API Development: Polymarket developed comprehensive APIs that allowed programmatic access to market data and trading functionality. Professional traders could build custom trading bots, automated strategies, and sophisticated analysis tools. The API documentation was extensive, covering market discovery, order placement, position management, and real-time data streams.

The Order Book API allowed market makers and traders to programmatically create and manage orders. Orders could be placed off-chain and matched by the Operator, with only final settlement happening on-chain. This hybrid approach combined the speed of centralized systems with the transparency and finality of blockchain settlement.

Advanced Charting: Casual users wanted simple probability displays. Professional traders wanted detailed historical data, volume analysis, and technical indicators. Polymarket added sophisticated charting tools showing price movements over time, trading volume patterns, and order book depth. These tools were hidden behind an "advanced" toggle so as not to overwhelm casual users, but power users could access institutional-grade analytics.

Portfolio Management: As users accumulated positions across dozens of markets, portfolio management became essential. New features showed aggregate exposure, unrealized gains/losses, and risk metrics. Users could filter positions by category, sort by profitability, and get comprehensive snapshots of their trading performance.

Limit Orders: The original implementation only supported market orders, buy or sell at current prices. Professional traders demanded limit orders, the ability to specify a price and have the order execute only if that price is reached. This required significant infrastructure development but was essential for sophisticated trading strategies.

Wave Three: Content and Context (2023)

By 2023, Polymarket had proven that prediction markets worked at scale. The next challenge was helping users make better predictions. Raw market odds were valuable, but context and analysis could make them more useful.

Educational Content: Polymarket created extensive documentation explaining how prediction markets work, how to interpret probabilities, common cognitive biases, and effective trading strategies. This content served dual purposes: educating new users and positioning the platform as intellectually serious rather than just another gambling site.

The education initiative included "Polymarket Learn", a comprehensive guide covering everything from basic probability concepts to advanced market mechanics. Blog posts explained current events that were driving market movements. Video content showed how to use the platform and interpret market signals.

Market Context and News Integration: Instead of just displaying odds, Polymarket began integrating relevant news, background information, and analysis directly into market pages. When viewing a market about Federal Reserve interest rate decisions, users would see recent economic data, Fed statements, and expert commentary, all curated to provide context without overwhelming.

This curation was editorial work disguised as product features. A small team monitored news sources, identified relevant information, and linked it to appropriate markets. The line between platform and media publication blurred. Polymarket wasn't just facilitating bets; it was helping users understand the events they were betting on.

Community Insights: Leveraging its active Discord community, Polymarket began surfacing community analysis and discussion within the platform itself. Top comments, analysis threads, and community debates appeared alongside market data. This social layer added depth and helped users learn from each other.

The community also influenced market creation. Through polls and feedback channels, the community could suggest new features, such as alert systems for specific market changes, which would then be implemented based on popular demand. This participatory model ensured users felt ownership over the platform's evolution.

Wave Four: Mobile Apps and Native Experiences (2024)

The mobile web experience was good, but dedicated apps offered opportunities for deeper engagement and better user experience. In 2024, Polymarket launched native iOS and Android applications.

The iOS app launched in September 2024 and quickly gained traction during the election season. Users praised how the app allowed them to track developments in real time, including cabinet appointments, forecasted policy changes, and event odds as they unfolded, with insights adapting to breaking news, market intel, and major events.

The Android app followed shortly after, available on Google Play. The apps let users get their news from the future, seeing who was leading on the world's largest prediction market, where odds changed in real time, reflecting breaking news, new polls, and major events.

Push Notifications: Mobile apps enabled push notifications, alerts when markets hit certain probabilities, when your positions gained or lost significant value, or when major news affected markets you cared about. This turned Polymarket from a destination you visited into an ambient information source that kept you updated.

Native Performance: Apps loaded faster, felt more responsive, and integrated better with phone operating systems than mobile web could. Biometric authentication (Face ID, fingerprint) made logging in seamless. Native UI elements felt familiar and reduced friction.

Limitations: Notably, the apps were primarily viewing tools rather than full trading platforms. Regulatory concerns meant that, initially, you couldn't place trades directly through the apps, you could monitor markets, track positions, and consume information, but actual trading required the web interface. This was frustrating for users but reflected the legal caution Polymarket maintained post-CFTC settlement.

The iOS app was rated 4.80 out of 5 stars based on 28 thousand ratings, suggesting strong user satisfaction despite trading limitations.

Category Expansion: From Politics to Everything

Perhaps the most significant product evolution was the dramatic expansion of market categories. What began as primarily political and COVID markets evolved into a comprehensive prediction marketplace covering virtually any topic with verifiable outcomes.

Politics: Always the core category, but dramatically expanded beyond just elections. Markets covered cabinet appointments, legislative outcomes, impeachment probabilities, Supreme Court decisions, approval ratings, and international political events. Every major political story generated markets.

Sports: Polymarket expanded aggressively into sports betting, championship winners, MVP awards, individual player performance, coaching changes, and franchise moves. Sports betting was already a massive industry, and Polymarket offered transparent, blockchain-based alternatives to traditional sportsbooks.

Cryptocurrency: Natural fit given the user base. Markets about Bitcoin price targets, Ethereum upgrades, exchange-traded fund approvals, regulatory decisions, and DeFi protocol outcomes. Crypto traders found these markets genuinely useful for hedging and speculation.

Pop Culture: Celebrity relationships, award show winners, album release dates, movie box office performance, reality TV outcomes. These markets seemed frivolous but attracted engaged communities and steady volume.

Business and Economics: Earnings announcements, merger approvals, layoff predictions, IPO timing, economic indicators, Federal Reserve decisions. Professional investors used these markets to gauge consensus expectations and hedge positions.

Science and Technology: Space launches, clinical trial results, technology milestones, product announcements, research breakthroughs. Tech enthusiasts and industry insiders brought specialized knowledge to these markets.

Weather and Natural Events: Hurricane paths, temperature records, snowfall totals. Meteorology meets prediction markets, useful for both speculation and practical hedging.

Since Polymarket's inception in 2020, it has offered over 900 separate event markets, demonstrating the breadth of coverage achieved.

Market Creation: Art and Science

Creating good prediction markets is harder than it looks. Questions need clear resolution criteria, verifiable sources, appropriate timeframes, and sufficient public interest. The team developed sophisticated processes for market creation and quality control.

Resolution Criteria: Every market needed unambiguous success conditions. "Will inflation exceed 5%?" required specifying which inflation measure (CPI, PCE, etc.), which reporting period, and which data source. Ambiguity killed trust, users needed confidence that markets would resolve fairly based on objective criteria.

Timing Windows: Markets needed appropriate timeframes. Too short and there wasn't enough time for information to be incorporated into prices. Too long and capital was tied up indefinitely. The optimal timeframe varied by category, election markets worked months in advance, while markets about Federal Reserve decisions worked best days before announcements.

Source Selection: Resolution sources had to be reputable and uncontroversial. New York Times reporting, government statistics, official announcements, sources that all users would accept as authoritative. Choosing resolution sources carefully prevented disputes and maintained trust.

Market Curation: Unlike Augur's permissionless approach where anyone could create any market, Polymarket maintained centralized control over market creation. This prevented assassination markets, legally problematic bets, and low-quality spam. The tradeoff was less decentralization for more quality and lower legal risk.

Data Products and Institutional Tools

As Polymarket's data became increasingly valuable, the company developed products specifically for institutional users, media organizations, and researchers.

Data API: Premium access to historical data, real-time feeds, and analytical tools. Hedge funds, political campaigns, and media organizations paid for enhanced data access. This created a second revenue stream beyond transaction fees.

Embeddable Widgets: Media organizations could embed live Polymarket odds directly into articles and broadcasts. During the 2024 election, numerous news sites displayed Polymarket probabilities alongside traditional polling data. These widgets kept users on partner sites while driving traffic back to Polymarket.

Analytical Dashboards: Tools for analyzing market movements, identifying unusual trading patterns, and understanding the relationship between events and odds changes. These weren't just for Polymarket's internal use, they became products sold to sophisticated users.

Research Partnerships: Collaborations with academic institutions studying prediction markets, collective intelligence, and forecasting accuracy. Polymarket provided data to researchers in exchange for academic validation and intellectual credibility.

Nate Silver: The Ultimate Endorsement

In 2024, Polymarket announced that Nate Silver, founder of polling analysis firm FiveThirtyEight, had joined as an advisor. This was extraordinary validation. Silver was America's most famous election forecaster, known for correctly predicting presidential outcomes while many polls failed.

Silver's endorsement carried weight beyond just another advisor announcement. He represented the statistical establishment that Polymarket was challenging. His involvement suggested that prediction markets and traditional polling weren't competitors but complements, different tools for understanding uncertainty.

Silver brought methodological rigor, statistical expertise, and media credibility. His presence signaled that Polymarket was serious about accuracy, not just volume. It also helped differentiate Polymarket from pure gambling sites. Silver wouldn't associate with a mere betting platform, but he would with a forecasting tool.

User Experience Philosophy

Through all these evolutions, certain principles remained constant in Polymarket's design philosophy:

Simplicity for Casual Users: The default experience remained clean and simple. Complexity was hidden behind optional "advanced" toggles. New users weren't overwhelmed with features they didn't need.

Power for Professionals: Advanced users could access institutional-grade tools, APIs, and analytics. The platform scaled from complete beginners to professional traders.

Mobile-First Thinking: Even before native apps, the web experience prioritized mobile. Most users accessed Polymarket on phones, and the design reflected that reality.

Speed and Responsiveness: Odds updated in real-time. Trades executed instantly. The platform felt alive and reactive. Lag or delays would have been fatal.

Trust Through Transparency: Blockchain settlement, clear resolution criteria, and public market data built trust. Users could verify everything independently.

The Continuous Evolution

Product development never stopped. Even as Polymarket achieved mainstream recognition during the 2024 election, the team continued shipping improvements weekly. New markets, better analytics, improved mobile experiences, enhanced social features, and refined algorithms for market making and price discovery.

The roadmap extended years into the future. Polymarket wasn't done evolving, it was just getting started. Features in development included more sophisticated social trading (following other traders' positions), improved portfolio analytics, predictive AI that could suggest interesting markets, and integration with external data sources to automate certain types of predictions.

The partnership announced with X (formerly Twitter) and integration with the Grok AI chatbot suggested future directions, combining prediction markets with artificial intelligence to create something new. Not just betting on outcomes, but AI-augmented forecasting that blended machine learning with human wisdom.

From Product to Platform

By 2025, Polymarket had evolved from a product into a platform. It wasn't just a place to bet on outcomes, it was infrastructure that other applications could build on. The APIs allowed developers to create tools, bots, and services that enhanced or extended Polymarket's functionality.

Data providers used Polymarket to gauge public sentiment. Media organizations embedded Polymarket odds in their coverage. Political campaigns monitored markets to understand voter perceptions. Researchers studied market efficiency and forecasting accuracy. Developers built trading bots and analysis tools.

This platform approach created network effects. Each new use case attracted new users, which improved liquidity, which made markets more efficient, which attracted more use cases. The flywheel was spinning.

The product that started as Shayne Coplan alone in a bathroom had become genuine infrastructure, something that thousands of people and organizations relied on daily. The evolution from minimum viable product to essential platform took just five years. What would the next five bring?

The answer would depend on factors beyond product development: regulation, competition, and whether Polymarket's core thesis, that prediction markets could become mainstream forecasting tools, would prove correct at scale.

PART III: THE REGULATORY RECKONING

Chapter 8

Regulatory Gray Zones

The law, Shayne Coplan would learn, is never as clear as engineers want it to be.

In the summer of 2020, as Polymarket's trading volumes began their first sustained climb, the young founder sat in a video conference with a battery of lawyers whose hourly rates exceeded what most Americans earned in a day. They were walking him through the labyrinth of U.S. financial regulation, and with each passing minute, the picture grew murkier rather than clearer.

"So we're not a securities exchange," Shayne said, trying to summarize what he'd heard over the past hour.

"Correct," one of the lawyers said.

"And we're not offering securities."

"Also correct, under most interpretations."

"But we might be offering commodity derivatives?"

"That's where it gets complicated."

Complicated was an understatement. What Shayne had built, what he believed was a revolutionary tool for aggregating information and discovering truth, existed in a regulatory space that Congress had never imagined and that regulators were only beginning to understand. The laws governing financial markets in America were written for a world of stocks, bonds, corn futures, and currency swaps. Nobody had contemplated what to do about a decentralized blockchain platform where people could bet on literally anything from presidential elections to the next Federal Reserve interest rate decision to whether aliens would be discovered by 2025.

This was Polymarket's fundamental challenge: it was too new for the law.

The Commodity Futures Trading Commission's Long Shadow

To understand Polymarket's regulatory predicament, you have to understand the Commodity Futures Trading Commission, an agency that most Americans have never heard of but which wields enormous power over markets.

The CFTC was born in 1974, carved out from the Department of Agriculture to regulate the growing complexity of commodity futures markets. For decades, it had a clear mandate: oversee exchanges where farmers hedged their crops, airlines locked in fuel prices, and traders speculated on everything from pork bellies to crude oil. The agency operated largely outside the public eye, a technocratic regulator dealing with arcane financial instruments.

Then came 2008.

The financial crisis thrust the CFTC into the spotlight. Suddenly, the exotic derivatives that had nearly collapsed the global economy fell under its jurisdiction. The Dodd-Frank Act of 2010 massively expanded the agency's authority, giving it regulatory power over swaps, options on commodities, and crucially for Polymarket "event contracts."

Event contracts were a relatively new concept in U.S. law. The Commodity Exchange Act defined them broadly as agreements where payouts depended on the occurrence or non-occurrence of an event. A bet on whether it would rain tomorrow? Event contract. A market on whether GDP would exceed 3% growth? Event contract. A prediction market on who would win the Super Bowl? Definitely an event contract.

And event contracts, the CFTC had decided, were illegal unless specifically authorized.

This interpretation sent shockwaves through the nascent prediction markets industry. Platforms that had operated in a regulatory gray zone suddenly found themselves potentially in violation of federal law. The CFTC wasn't prohibiting all event contracts, it recognized their potential value but it wanted control. Any platform offering event contracts to U.S. users needed to either register as a designated contract market (essentially becoming a regulated exchange) or obtain explicit approval for each type of contract.

For a scrappy startup built on the ethos of decentralization and permissionless innovation, this was anathema.

The Precedents: How Others Had Navigated the Maze

Shayne and his team studied every company that had come before them, looking for a path through the regulatory wilderness.

Intrade had been the cautionary tale. The Irish prediction markets platform had operated successfully for years, allowing users worldwide including Americans to bet on everything from elections to Oscar winners. At its peak, Intrade was the go-to source for election forecasting, regularly cited by mainstream media. Then, in 2012, the CFTC brought charges against the company for offering commodity options transactions to U.S. customers without CFTC approval. Intrade agreed to block U.S. users and pay a fine. A year later, citing financial difficulties partly stemming from the regulatory restrictions, Intrade shut down entirely.

The message was clear: the CFTC could kill your company.

PredictIt had taken a different approach. Operated by Victoria University of Wellington in New Zealand, PredictIt had secured a "no-action letter" from the CFTC in 2014. This letter essentially said the CFTC wouldn't take enforcement action against PredictIt as long as it operated within strict parameters: a maximum of 5,000 traders per market, an $850 limit on how much any individual could invest in any single contract, and a focus on political and financial event contracts for research purposes.

These restrictions made PredictIt more of an academic experiment than a serious financial marketplace. Liquidity was limited, price discovery was imperfect, and the platform couldn't scale. But it was legal.

Augur represented the crypto-native approach. Launched in 2018, Augur was a fully decentralized prediction market platform built on Ethereum. Its creators argued that because no central entity controlled the platform, it ran on smart contracts that no one could shut down; traditional regulation didn't apply. Users could create markets on anything, with no geographic restrictions and no central authority to regulate.

The CFTC had never explicitly blessed this approach, but neither had it taken action against Augur. The agency seemed uncertain how to regulate a platform that genuinely had no owner, no corporate entity, and no off-switch. Augur existed in the regulatory gray zone by being impossible to regulate through traditional means.

Each precedent offered lessons, but none provided a clear path forward for Polymarket. Shayne wanted to build something bigger than PredictIt's restricted sandbox but more user-friendly than Augur's fully decentralized maze. He wanted scale, liquidity, and mainstream adoption. But he also wanted to move fast.

The Calculus: Growth vs. Compliance

Inside Polymarket's growing team, a debate raged about how to handle U.S. regulation.

The cautious approach would have been to seek a no-action letter from the CFTC before launching in the United States, or to proactively block U.S. users from the start. This would provide legal certainty but would cut off access to the world's largest market for financial products and the country where prediction markets had the most cultural relevance.

The aggressive approach would be to launch globally, including in the U.S., and deal with regulatory questions if and when they arose. This was the Silicon Valley playbook: ask for forgiveness rather than permission. Uber had disrupted taxi regulations in city after city by operating first and negotiating later. Airbnb had done the same with hotel laws. Coinbase had built a massive cryptocurrency exchange before regulators fully understood what they were dealing with.

Why shouldn't Polymarket follow the same path?

The arguments for moving fast were compelling. First, the regulatory status of prediction markets remained genuinely unclear. Different lawyers gave different opinions on whether Polymarket's specific structure using cryptocurrency, operating on blockchain, with no central counterparty fit within existing CFTC jurisdiction. If the law was ambiguous, why assume the most restrictive interpretation?

Second, being first mattered enormously. Prediction markets exhibited strong network effects: the more traders you had, the better your prices became, which attracted more traders. If Polymarket blocked U.S. users from the start while competitors didn't, they might lose the market permanently.

Third, there was the philosophical argument. Shayne genuinely believed prediction markets served a social good. They aggregated information, provided early warning signals, and offered a corrective to biased polling and punditry. If overregulation prevented these markets from existing, society lost valuable information. Sometimes, the lawyers told him, you have to force regulators to confront questions they'd rather avoid.

But there were counterarguments too. The CFTC had proven it would pursue prediction markets platforms aggressively. The fines could be substantial, the agency could seek civil monetary penalties of up to the greater of $1 million or triple the monetary gain for each violation. Criminal prosecution was even possible for willful violations.

More importantly, a regulatory battle could distract from building the product. Shayne wanted to focus on improving the platform, adding features, and growing the user base. Fighting the CFTC would consume time, money, and attention.

In those early days, Polymarket threaded the needle. The platform's terms of service stated that users in prohibited jurisdictions shouldn't use the service. The company wasn't explicitly marketing to U.S. customers. But neither was it implementing robust geo-blocking technology that would actually prevent American users from accessing the platform.

It was a calculated risk, and everyone involved knew it.

Understanding the Legal Landscape: Why This Was So Complicated

The regulatory confusion surrounding Polymarket wasn't just bureaucratic obstinacy. The platform genuinely raised novel legal questions that existing frameworks struggled to address.

Start with the most basic question: What exactly was Polymarket offering?

If you asked a user, they might say "a place to bet on events" or "a prediction market." But legal categories don't map neatly onto common sense descriptions. Was a position in a Polymarket prediction market a security? A commodity derivative? A swap? A gaming wager? Each classification triggered different regulatory regimes.

The Securities Analysis: Under the Howey Test, the Supreme Court standard for what constitutes a security, an investment contract exists if there's an investment of money in a common enterprise with profits derived from the efforts of others. Polymarket arguably didn't fit this definition. When you bought shares in "Trump wins the 2024 election," you weren't investing in a common enterprise, and your profits didn't depend on anyone else's efforts. The outcome was determined by reality itself, not by a promoter or company. Most legal experts agreed Polymarket wasn't offering securities.

The Commodity Derivative Analysis: This was trickier. The Commodity Exchange Act defines commodity very broadly to include "all services, rights, and interests in which contracts for future delivery are presently or in the future dealt in." Courts had interpreted this to include nearly anything. Prediction market contracts certainly looked like derivatives, their value derived from an underlying event.

But were they commodity derivatives specifically under CFTC jurisdiction? That required the underlying "commodity" to be something traded in interstate commerce. Supreme Court elections and Oscar winners weren't commodities in any traditional sense. However, the CFTC had taken the position that even event contracts with no traditional commodity underlying fell under its authority if they served a price discovery or hedging function.

The Gaming/Gambling Analysis: Separate from federal commodity law, there was the question of whether prediction markets constituted illegal gambling. This was primarily a state law issue, and it was a minefield. Different states had wildly different gambling laws. Some prohibited essentially all wagering outside of licensed casinos. Others exempted "games of skill" from gambling restrictions. Still others had specific carve-outs for fantasy sports or horse racing.

Prediction markets advocates argued their platforms weren't gambling because they served a hedging function. If you owned a restaurant and wanted to hedge against the risk that a recession would hurt your business, you might buy shares in "U.S. enters recession in 2024" on Polymarket. If the recession happened, your restaurant would suffer but your Polymarket position would pay out, offsetting some of the damage. That's hedging, not gambling.

Skeptics pointed out that 99% of Polymarket users weren't hedging anything. They were speculating, which looked a lot like gambling.

The Decentralization Defense: Polymarket's blockchain architecture added another layer of complexity. The platform argued it didn't actually operate a market, it merely provided software that allowed users to interact with smart contracts on the Polygon blockchain. Those smart contracts were immutable and ran automatically. Polymarket couldn't stop trades, reverse transactions, or control the markets once they were created.

If that was true, if Polymarket was just a software interface rather than a market operator then traditional financial regulation might not apply. You can't regulate an automated smart contract the same way you regulate the New York Stock Exchange.

But regulators were deeply skeptical of this argument. They'd heard similar claims from cryptocurrency companies trying to evade oversight. The CFTC's position was straightforward: if you create the software, maintain the interface, promote the platform, and profit from its operation, you're responsible for compliance regardless of how decentralized the technology is.

The International Dimension: Playing Jurisdictional Arbitrage

One of Polymarket's most important strategic decisions was where to incorporate and base its operations.

The company was structured with a corporate entity outside the United States. This provided some legal distance from U.S. jurisdiction and, in theory, made it easier to serve international users without automatically subjecting the company to all U.S. regulations. Many cryptocurrency and blockchain companies had adopted similar structures, think of Binance, BitMEX, or Bitmex, all of which operated globally while maintaining corporate structures offshore.

This approach had both advantages and risks. On the plus side, it meant U.S. regulations weren't automatically applicable to all of Polymarket's operations. The company could argue that it was serving a global market and shouldn't be bound by the rules of any single country.

On the downside, it didn't provide immunity from U.S. enforcement if the CFTC decided Polymarket was effectively doing business in America. Regulators had proven adept at piercing corporate veils and pursuing foreign entities that served U.S. customers. BitMEX's founders had eventually faced criminal charges in the United States despite the company being based in Seychelles.

The international structure did clarify one thing: Polymarket was thinking globally from day one. Unlike PredictIt, which was explicitly a U.S.-focused platform operating under a special exemption, Polymarket envisioned serving users worldwide. American traders might be valuable, but they weren't essential to the business model.

This global focus would prove critical when the regulatory hammer eventually fell.

The Warning Signs: When the CFTC Started Paying Attention

By late 2020, it was clear that Polymarket was on the CFTC's radar.

The first indication came through back channels. Lawyers who worked on financial regulatory matters began hearing from contacts at the CFTC that the agency was looking at decentralized prediction markets. Polymarket wasn't named specifically, but in a space with only a handful of significant players, the implication was clear.

Then came the informal inquiries. The CFTC reached out to law firms known to represent cryptocurrency companies, asking questions about how prediction markets were structured and operated. These weren't formal investigations, not yet but they were information-gathering exercises that often preceded enforcement actions.

Inside Polymarket, the team began preparing for potential regulatory scrutiny. They hired additional legal counsel with specific expertise in CFTC matters. They reviewed their terms of service and user agreements. They discussed various scenarios: a formal investigation, a subpoena for documents, a request for a voluntary interview, a settlement offer.

The question wasn't if the CFTC would act, but when and how.

Some team members advocated for a preemptive approach: reach out to the CFTC proactively, explain how Polymarket worked, and try to negotiate a path forward before any enforcement action. This might show good faith and potentially lead to a more favorable outcome.

Others argued the opposite. Contacting the CFTC might trigger an investigation that otherwise wouldn't happen. Better to let sleeping dogs lie and hope the agency focused its limited resources elsewhere.

Shayne was caught between these positions. He wanted to do the right thing, but he wasn't entirely sure what the right thing was. The law remained genuinely unclear. Different legal experts gave different opinions. And while the CFTC had broad authority, it also had to choose its battles carefully.

By early 2021, Polymarket's growth had made the decision for them. The platform was processing millions of dollars in trading volume monthly. Media outlets were citing Polymarket's odds in articles about politics and current events. The company had raised significant venture capital funding. They were no longer a small experiment flying under the radar, they were becoming a real business.

And real businesses attract regulatory attention.

The Philosophical Divide: Regulatory Innovation vs. Consumer Protection

Behind the legal technicalities lay a deeper conflict about how financial markets should work in the 21st century.

Shayne and many of his supporters came from the cryptocurrency and blockchain world, where "permissionless innovation" was gospel. This philosophy held that innovation happened fastest when builders could experiment freely without seeking approval from gatekeepers. The internet had flourished because you didn't need the FCC's permission to launch a website. Open-source software had revolutionized technology because you didn't need Microsoft's approval to write code.

Why should financial innovation be different? If people wanted to trade predictions about future events using cryptocurrency, and they were doing so voluntarily with eyes open, who was harmed? The regulations the CFTC was enforcing had been written for a different era and a different type of market. Applying them to blockchain-based prediction markets was like trying to regulate automobiles under laws written for horses and buggies.

The CFTC saw things very differently. The agency's mission was protecting market integrity and preventing fraud, manipulation, and abuse. Financial regulations existed for good reasons. The derivatives that nearly destroyed the economy in 2008 had been allowed to grow in poorly regulated shadow markets. The CFTC wasn't going to let that happen again.

From the regulator's perspective, prediction markets posed real risks. They could be manipulated, a wealthy individual could move market prices by placing large trades, potentially influencing public perception of an election or other event. They could facilitate insider trading if someone with privileged information traded on that information in prediction markets. They could serve as vehicles for money laundering, with illicit funds disguised as trading gains.

And yes, they could simply be illegal gambling masquerading as sophisticated financial products.

Both sides had legitimate points, but they were speaking past each other. Shayne saw unnecessary bureaucratic obstacles to valuable innovation. The CFTC saw a company trying to operate a derivatives market without proper oversight.

This wasn't a conflict that could be resolved through better arguments or more persuasive rhetoric. It would be settled through the legal process through investigations, negotiations, and ultimately enforcement actions.

As 2021 progressed, that process was already beginning.

The Compliance Calculation: What Polymarket Knew and When

Later, critics would ask: Did Polymarket knowingly violate the law?

The honest answer is complicated. The company certainly knew it was operating in a regulatory gray zone. Internal documents and communications would likely show extensive discussions about CFTC jurisdiction, about the risks of serving U.S. users, about the potential for enforcement action.

But knowing you're in a gray zone isn't the same as knowing you're breaking the law. Shayne and his team believed or at least convinced themselves that their interpretation of the regulations was defensible. They had lawyers who supported their position. They could point to aspects of Polymarket's structure that distinguished it from the platforms the CFTC had previously pursued.

The fact remained, however, that they were allowing U.S. users to access the platform and trade on event contracts without CFTC authorization. Whether that was illegal was a legal conclusion the CFTC would reach, not Polymarket.

As the months passed and Polymarket grew, the risk calculation shifted. Every new user, every million dollars in trading volume, every media mention made the platform more visible and more likely to attract regulatory attention. The potential penalties grew proportionally.

Some inside the company began to worry. The early scrappiness of a startup operating in a regulatory gray zone was evolving into something more troubling: a substantial business with real money at stake potentially in violation of federal law.

The question was no longer whether Polymarket would face regulatory scrutiny. The question was what the company would do when that scrutiny arrived.

The answer would come in January 2022, with a settlement that would reshape Polymarket's entire business model and set the stage for everything that followed.

Chapter 9

The CFTC Settlement (January 2022)

The email arrived on a Tuesday morning in November 2021, and everyone who saw it knew what it meant.

The Commodity Futures Trading Commission's Division of Enforcement was formally requesting documents and information regarding Polymarket's operations. The request was polite in the way that government communications are always polite, professional, measured and entirely devoid of emotion. But beneath the bureaucratic language was an unmistakable force: produce these records, answer these questions, and do it quickly.

The investigation everyone had feared was now official.

Shayne Coplan read the email three times in his apartment, the Manhattan skyline visible through the windows behind his laptop. He was 23 years old, his company was processing tens of millions of dollars in monthly trading volume, and the federal government was now formally investigating whether he'd broken the law.

He picked up his phone and called the lawyers.

The Investigation Unfolds: October-December 2021

What followed was the kind of experience that ages founders rapidly. Suddenly, instead of focusing on product development, user growth, and fundraising, Shayne found himself spending hours each day in conference calls with attorneys, reviewing documents, and preparing for potential testimony.

The CFTC's investigation was methodical and comprehensive. Enforcement attorneys wanted to understand every aspect of how Polymarket operated: the technical architecture, the corporate structure, the user onboarding process, the marketing strategy, and most critically what the company had done to prevent U.S. users from accessing the platform.

The answer to that last question was uncomfortable: very little.

Document production began immediately. The CFTC wanted emails, Slack messages, board meeting minutes, legal memos, marketing materials, and user data. Polymarket's legal team worked around the clock, reviewing thousands of pages of internal communications, flagging privileged materials, and preparing document dumps that would satisfy the regulators while protecting the company's legal position as much as possible.

Some of what the attorneys found was helpful. Internal messages showed the team had consulted lawyers extensively about regulatory issues. Shayne had clearly taken the question seriously and sought expert guidance. The company had included geographic restrictions in its terms of service. These facts might support an argument that Polymarket hadn't willfully violated the law.

Other documents were more problematic. There were messages celebrating user growth without distinguishing between U.S. and international users. Marketing materials that clearly appealed to American traders interested in U.S. political events. Technical specifications showing that while Polymarket had terms of service restricting U.S. users, the actual technological barriers to American users accessing the platform were minimal, a simple checkbox asking users to confirm they weren't in a prohibited jurisdiction.

Any competent prosecutor would argue this was a fig leaf, not a genuine effort at compliance.

The CFTC also wanted to understand the numbers. How many U.S. users had accessed Polymarket? How much trading volume came from American traders? What percentage of the company's revenue was attributable to U.S.-based activity?

These were difficult questions to answer with precision. Blockchain transactions were pseudonymous by design. Polymarket didn't collect extensive identity documents from users, that was part of the platform's appeal. Users accessed the site through cryptocurrency wallets, not traditional accounts with government-issued ID verification.

But the CFTC had tools for piercing anonymity. They could analyze IP addresses, correlate on-chain wallet addresses with known entities, and subpoena user data from payment processors and exchanges where users purchased the USDC stablecoin they used on Polymarket. The picture that emerged was clear: a substantial portion of Polymarket's users were accessing the platform from the United States.

Inside the company, debates raged about how to respond. Some advocated for a vigorous defense. They could argue that Polymarket's decentralized structure meant the company wasn't actually operating a market in the traditional sense. They could challenge whether prediction markets really fell under CFTC jurisdiction. They could question whether the agency had authority over a platform structured as Polymarket was.

These arguments had merit, but they also had risks. Fighting the CFTC meant litigation that could drag on for years, cost millions of dollars, and generate hostile media coverage. It meant Shayne might have to testify publicly about company operations. It meant discovery that could expose sensitive business information. And it meant the very real possibility of losing, which could result in larger penalties and potentially criminal referrals.

The alternative was settlement: acknowledge the violation, pay a fine, agree to restrictions, and move on. It was the pragmatic choice, even if it felt like surrender.

The Charges: Offering Unregistered Event-Based Binary Options

By December 2021, the CFTC's position had crystallized. The agency's enforcement division had concluded that Polymarket had violated the Commodity Exchange Act and CFTC regulations by operating an illegal, unregistered facility that allowed users to trade event-based binary options.

The legal theory was straightforward. According to the CFTC, the contracts Polymarket offered, binary options that paid out based on whether specific events occurred were "swaps" under the Commodity Exchange Act. More specifically, they were event contracts that fall under the CFTC's exclusive jurisdiction.

Any entity offering such contracts to U.S. persons was required to either:

1. Register as a designated contract market (DCM) and comply with extensive regulatory requirements, or
2. Obtain CFTC approval for specific contracts through a lengthy application process

Polymarket had done neither.

The charging document, which would eventually become public as part of the settlement, laid out the case methodically. From approximately July 2020 through the present, Polymarket had operated a facility, the online platform and related smart contracts that allowed users to trade binary options based on event outcomes. These included markets on:

- Political events (election outcomes, confirmation votes, impeachment proceedings)

- Economic indicators (inflation rates, GDP growth, unemployment figures)
- Public health developments (COVID-19 case counts, vaccine approvals)
- Entertainment and pop culture (award show winners, celebrity news)
- Cryptocurrency prices and developments

Users purchased positions for prices between $0.01 and $0.99 per share. If the event occurred, shares paid out $1.00. If it didn't occur, shares became worthless. This was textbook binary option structure.

The CFTC's investigation had documented that U.S. users had accessed the platform and conducted substantial trading activity. The agency noted that while Polymarket's terms of service included restrictions on U.S. users, these were "ineffective" because:

- The platform implemented no meaningful geolocation or IP blocking technology
- Users could access the site by simply checking a box claiming they weren't in a prohibited jurisdiction
- No identity verification was required beyond connecting a cryptocurrency wallet
- The company took no active steps to identify and block U.S. users who accessed the platform

Furthermore, the CFTC argued that Polymarket had actively solicited U.S. users through various means, including social media marketing that targeted American audiences and media outreach that resulted in coverage in U.S. publications.

The charges were narrowly technical, failure to register, operation of an unlawful facility, offering swaps to non-eligible contract participants but the implications were profound. If these allegations were proven in court, Polymarket could face civil monetary penalties potentially running into tens of millions of dollars. The company could be shut down entirely. Individual executives, including Shayne, could face personal liability.

Settlement began to look not just prudent, but essential.

Negotiating the Terms: A Delicate Dance

Settlement negotiations between regulatory agencies and companies they're investigating follow predictable patterns, but each case has unique dynamics. Polymarket's negotiations, which took place primarily in December 2021 and early January 2022, were complicated by several factors.

First, there was the question of how much Polymarket would pay. The CFTC enforcement division typically seeks penalties that are significant enough to punish the violation and deter future wrongdoing, but not so large they destroy the company. The agency has broad discretion in penalty calculations, considering factors like the seriousness of the violation, the duration of the conduct, the company's cooperation with the investigation, and whether there was willful intent to break the law.

Polymarket's lawyers argued for leniency. The company was a small startup that had operated in a genuine gray area of the law. Management had consulted attorneys and tried to understand their obligations. There was no evidence of fraud, manipulation, or consumer harm. The company had cooperated fully with the investigation. And importantly, Polymarket was willing to immediately cease serving U.S. users and implement robust compliance measures going forward.

The CFTC's enforcement attorneys were less sympathetic. Polymarket had generated substantial revenue from U.S. users while avoiding the regulatory compliance costs that legitimate exchanges bore. The "gray area" argument was convenient but not entirely convincing, the company had to have known it was pushing boundaries. And the violation was ongoing and deliberate, not a one-time mistake.

After weeks of back-and-forth, the parties settled on $1.4 million. By the standards of CFTC penalties, this was relatively modest. The agency had imposed fines of tens or hundreds of millions of dollars against major financial institutions for various violations. But for a startup, $1.4 million was significant, real money that would come out of the company's limited runway.

The more consequential negotiation involved the forward-looking restrictions. The CFTC insisted that Polymarket immediately cease allowing U.S. users to access the platform. This meant implementing technological barriers that would actually work: IP-based geoblocking, enhanced identity verification, and active monitoring to detect and prevent U.S. users from circumventing restrictions.

Polymarket's team pushed back on the strictness of these requirements. Perfect geoblocking was technologically challenging and expensive to implement. Users with VPNs could circumvent IP-based restrictions. The company argued it could include clearer terms of service restrictions and rely primarily on user representations about their location.

The CFTC was unmoved. If Polymarket wanted to settle rather than face continued enforcement action, the company needed to actually block U.S. users, not just pretend to block them while winking at easy workarounds.

There was also discussion of whether Polymarket should be required to wind down existing positions held by U.S. users or whether those could remain open. The CFTC ultimately agreed that existing positions could resolve naturally, but no new trading by U.S. persons would be permitted.

Another key term: Polymarket would neither admit nor deny the CFTC's findings. This is standard in regulatory settlements, it allows the company to resolve the matter without creating evidence that could be used against it in private litigation. Shayne wouldn't have to publicly acknowledge breaking the law, even though he was paying a penalty for doing so.

Finally, there was the question of publicity. The CFTC would issue a press release announcing the settlement. This was non-negotiable, enforcement actions are public by design, serving both to punish the specific violator and to warn others in the industry. But Polymarket negotiated the right to issue its own statement simultaneously, framing the settlement on its own terms.

By early January 2022, the deal was done. All that remained was the formal announcement.

The Announcement: January 3, 2022

The CFTC's press release went live at 8:30 AM Eastern Time on January 3, 2022. The headline was direct: "CFTC Orders Polymarket to Cease Offering Event-Based Binary Options Contracts and Pay $1.4 Million Penalty."

The release summarized the case in the matter-of-fact language that government agencies favor:

> The Commodity Futures Trading Commission today issued an order filing and settling charges against Polymarket LLC (Polymarket) for operating an unregistered facility for the trading of binary options contracts based on future events, also known as event markets. The order requires Polymarket to cease offering its markets to persons located in the United States unless and until it is properly registered with the

> Commission, and to pay a $1.4 million civil monetary penalty.

The release quoted the Director of the Division of Enforcement: "Today's action should make clear that the offer of event-based binary options contracts to U.S. persons without registration violates the Commodity Exchange Act and CFTC regulations. Polymarket did not have Commission approval to operate a facility for the trading of event contracts, nor was it registered with the CFTC to do so. This order makes clear that these markets, regardless of the label, must comply with the Commodity Exchange Act and CFTC regulations."

For anyone familiar with regulatory enforcement, the message was clear: we caught you, you paid, don't do it again, and let this be a warning to everyone else.

Within minutes, the press picked up the story. Bloomberg, Reuters, CoinDesk, and The Block all published articles within the first hour. The coverage was straightforward reporting, startup pays penalty for regulatory violations but the implications were significant for the prediction markets industry.

Polymarket's Response: Reframing the Narrative

Polymarket had prepared carefully for this moment. The company's statement, released minutes after the CFTC announcement, struck a different tone than the regulator's.

The statement opened with Shayne's perspective:

> "We made the decision to proactively work with the CFTC to resolve this matter and bring Polymarket into compliance with U.S. regulations. While we believed we were operating in an area where the regulatory landscape was still

> developing, we recognize the CFTC's authority and their interpretation of how existing rules apply to prediction markets."

This was carefully worded. "Proactively work with" suggested cooperation rather than enforcement. "Resolve this matter" implied mutual problem-solving. "Regulatory landscape was still developing" maintained the gray-area narrative without directly contradicting the CFTC's position.

The statement continued:

> "Prediction markets serve an important function in aggregating information and providing valuable signals about future events. We remain committed to this mission and will continue to operate Polymarket for users around the world. We're implementing enhanced compliance measures to ensure we meet regulatory requirements going forward."

This was the key message: we're not shutting down, we're just geographically restricting. Polymarket would survive this setback.

The statement acknowledged the $1.4 million penalty but didn't dwell on it. Instead, it emphasized the company's cooperation with regulators and its commitment to compliance. It mentioned the investors who supported the company and the users who found value in prediction markets.

Nowhere in the statement did Polymarket admit wrongdoing. Nowhere did it acknowledge that the company had violated the law. The framing was entirely forward-looking: we're working with regulators, we're implementing changes, we're committed to operating responsibly.

The PR strategy was sound, but it couldn't change the fundamental fact: Polymarket had been forced to cut off access to the U.S. market, which many considered essential for a prediction markets platform focused heavily on American politics.

Industry Reaction: Competitors, Critics, and Supporters

The settlement sent ripples through the small but growing prediction markets industry.

Kalshi, a New York-based prediction markets platform that had taken a completely different regulatory approach, issued a carefully worded statement through its CEO. Kalshi had spent years working within the regulatory system, obtaining proper CFTC authorization to offer event contracts on specific topics. The process had been expensive and time-consuming, but it gave Kalshi legal certainty and access to U.S. users without restriction.

From Kalshi's perspective, Polymarket's settlement vindicated their compliance-first strategy. "This demonstrates the importance of working with regulators from day one," a Kalshi spokesperson said. "Prediction markets can serve a valuable function, but they need to operate within established legal frameworks."

The subtext was obvious: we did it the right way, they tried to cut corners, and they got caught.

PredictIt, operating under its no-action letter with strict limitations, also watched with interest. The platform had long chafed under the restrictions imposed by its agreement with the CFTC, the caps on investment amounts and trader numbers meant PredictIt could never scale to compete with unrestricted platforms. But those restrictions now looked like the price of legal operation in the United States.

Augur, the fully decentralized prediction market protocol, had a more complex reaction. Augur's supporters argued that the Polymarket settlement proved their point: you couldn't have a truly permissionless prediction market with a centralized company that regulators could target. Only full decentralization, no company, no central point of control could resist regulatory pressure.

Critics countered that Augur's approach had its own problems. The platform was difficult to use, liquidity was limited, and there were serious questions about market integrity when no one was responsible for ensuring fair outcomes. Decentralization for its own sake wasn't a solution if it made the product unusable.

In the broader cryptocurrency and blockchain community, reactions split along predictable lines. Crypto-libertarians saw the settlement as government overreach, another example of regulators stifling innovation to protect incumbent financial institutions. They argued that people should be free to trade predictions about future events without government permission.

More mainstream voices in the industry took a different view. Responsible cryptocurrency companies needed to work within legal frameworks, not flaunt them. Polymarket's settlement showed what happened when you pushed too hard against regulatory boundaries. The lesson was: move fast, but not so fast you end up paying $1.4 million in penalties.

Media coverage generally played the story straight. This was a regulatory enforcement action against a startup that had violated the law, interesting for those who followed the prediction markets space, but not a major scandal. Some articles noted the irony that Polymarket had predicted various future events but apparently hadn't predicted its own regulatory troubles.

A few commentators raised deeper questions. What did it mean for democracy and information aggregation if prediction markets could only operate under heavy restrictions or offshore? Were U.S. regulations preventing Americans from accessing valuable tools for understanding political reality? The settlement might resolve Polymarket's legal issues, but it didn't resolve the underlying tension between regulatory caution and innovation.

The Implementation Challenge: Actually Blocking U.S. Users

Settling with the CFTC was one thing. Actually preventing U.S. users from accessing Polymarket proved considerably more complicated.

The company moved quickly to implement geoblocking technology. This meant identifying users' geographic locations through IP addresses and preventing connections from U.S.-based IP addresses from accessing the platform. Within days of the settlement announcement, users attempting to access Polymarket from American IP addresses received an error message explaining that the service wasn't available in their region.

But IP-based geoblocking has obvious limitations. Virtual Private Networks (VPNs) allow users to mask their true location, making it appear they're accessing the internet from a different country. Any moderately sophisticated user could subscribe to a VPN service for a few dollars per month and easily circumvent Polymarket's geographic restrictions.

The CFTC was aware of this problem, of course. The settlement agreement required Polymarket to implement "reasonable" measures to prevent U.S. users from accessing the platform. The key word was "reasonable", the company wasn't expected to achieve perfect enforcement, but it needed to make a genuine effort.

This meant Polymarket had to do more than basic IP blocking. The company implemented monitoring systems to detect suspicious patterns that might indicate VPN usage. They blocked access from known VPN providers' IP ranges. They added additional verification steps for users whose behavior suggested they might be circumventing geographic restrictions.

But there were limits to how aggressive Polymarket could be. The platform's entire appeal was ease of use and minimal friction. Requiring extensive identity verification, passport scans, proof of residence, the kind of Know Your Customer (KYC) documentation that traditional financial institutions demand would destroy the user experience and drive users to competitors.

The result was an uncomfortable equilibrium. Polymarket implemented enough restrictions to satisfy the CFTC that it was making a good-faith effort at compliance. But determined U.S. users who really wanted to access the platform could still find ways to do so. The company would claim it was blocking U.S. users; regulators would understand that enforcement wasn't perfect but was adequate; and everyone would live with the ambiguity.

This raised an interesting question: How many U.S. users continued accessing Polymarket after the settlement through VPNs and other workarounds? Polymarket's public statements emphasized compliance and geo-blocking. Behind the scenes, the numbers told a more complex story. Trading volumes didn't collapse after U.S. users were supposedly blocked. Activity in markets about American political events remained robust. Someone was trading on these markets, and much of that someone appeared to be in or connected to the United States.

This ambiguity would come back to haunt the company years later.

The Strategic Pivot: Embracing the Global Market

The CFTC settlement forced Polymarket to make a crucial strategic decision: Was the company's future in the United States or internationally?

Before the settlement, the answer would have been obvious. The U.S. was the world's largest financial market, had the most liquidity, and was home to the political events that drove the most trading interest. Cutting off American users seemed like a potentially fatal blow.

But Shayne and his team reframed the restriction as an opportunity. Polymarket would become the global prediction market platform. Instead of fighting endless regulatory battles in the United States, they would focus on markets where the regulatory environment was clearer or more favorable.

In Europe, Asia and Latin America there were billions of people interested in prediction markets who weren't subject to CFTC jurisdiction. Many of them cared about U.S. political events and would trade on those markets regardless of their own location. And as cryptocurrency adoption grew globally, Polymarket could tap into an increasingly international user base that transcended geographic boundaries.

The company doubled down on marketing to international users. It added support for multiple languages. It created markets on events that mattered to non-American audiences: European elections, Asian economic developments, global sporting events beyond U.S.-centric sports.

This strategy had several advantages. First, it gave Polymarket room to grow without constant regulatory scrutiny. The company could experiment with new market types, new features, and new approaches without worrying about whether each change would trigger another CFTC investigation.

Second, it positioned Polymarket as the platform for global events at a time when the world was becoming increasingly interconnected. The COVID-19 pandemic had shown how events in one country instantly affected the entire world. Climate change, technological developments, and geopolitical conflicts all demanded global perspectives. Polymarket could serve that need.

Third, and perhaps most importantly, it gave the company a narrative that wasn't "startup forced offshore by regulators." Instead, the story became "global platform that happens to have geographic restrictions in one market." This was a subtle but important distinction for future fundraising and partnership opportunities.

The geographic restriction also had an unexpected benefit: it made Polymarket more credible in some circles. The company had been investigated by federal regulators, had settled the case, and was now operating in compliance with that settlement. This wasn't a rogue operation flouting the law, it was a business that had faced regulatory scrutiny and emerged with a clear path forward.

The Cost: More Than Money

The $1.4 million penalty was the headline number, but the true cost of the CFTC settlement went far beyond the fine.

There were the legal fees, easily six figures for the months of investigation, negotiation, and settlement implementation. There was the opportunity cost of executive time spent dealing with regulatory issues rather than building the product. There was the disruption to company morale as the team dealt with the stress and uncertainty of a government investigation.

More subtle were the reputational costs. Some users and potential partners viewed the settlement as proof that Polymarket had been operating irresponsibly. The stain of regulatory enforcement, even with no admission of wrongdoing, created lingering questions about the company's judgment and compliance culture.

For Shayne personally, the settlement was a formative experience. He was in his early twenties, running a company that had attracted federal investigation. The weight of that, the lawyers, the negotiations, the threat of larger penalties or worse consequences matured him rapidly. Friends who saw him during this period noticed a change. The enthusiastic young founder had become more guarded, more calculated, more aware of risks.

But there was also defiance. Shayne believed deeply in what Polymarket was doing. He thought prediction markets served a valuable social function and that regulation limiting them was counterproductive. The settlement hadn't changed his mind about the mission, if anything it had reinforced his conviction that he was challenging an established order that was resistant to innovation.

This conviction would drive Polymarket's next phase. The company had survived regulatory enforcement. Now it would prove that prediction markets could thrive even under restrictions. And in doing so, it would build toward the moment, years later, when Polymarket's predictions would prove more accurate than traditional polls and pundits vindicating Shayne's vision even as new controversies emerged.

Chapter 10

The Geo-Block Paradox

Three months after the CFTC settlement, Polymarket's engineering team gathered for their weekly metrics review. The numbers on the screen told a story that everyone in the room understood but nobody wanted to say out loud.

Trading volume: up 47% since January.

Active users: up 38%.

Markets on U.S. political events: among the highest volume on the platform.

This shouldn't have been possible. Polymarket had implemented geoblocking technology that prevented U.S. IP addresses from accessing the site. The company had paid $1.4 million specifically to settle charges that it had improperly allowed Americans to trade on its platform. And yet, three months later, the platform was more active than ever, with robust trading on markets that were overwhelmingly of interest to American users.

Welcome to the geo-block paradox: the phenomenon where restricting access to a platform in a major market somehow leads to increased attention, user growth, and trading activity. It was counterintuitive, frustrating to regulators, and absolutely central to understanding Polymarket's trajectory from 2022 onward.

The VPN Economy: How Users Circumvented Restrictions

The first thing to understand about internet geo-blocking is that it has never really worked.

Virtual Private Networks, VPNs were originally developed for corporate security, allowing remote workers to securely access company networks. But they had an unintended consequence: by routing internet traffic through servers in different countries, VPNs allowed users to mask their true geographic location.

For someone in New York wanting to access Polymarket after the CFTC settlement, the process was trivial:

1. Subscribe to a VPN service (ExpressVPN, NordVPN, ProtonVPN—dozens of options, many costing less than $10/month)
2. Connect to a server in a country where Polymarket was allowed (UK, Canada, anywhere in Europe)
3. Access Polymarket's website, which would now see the connection as coming from the VPN server's location, not New York
4. Trade freely on any market

The entire process took less than five minutes for someone with even basic technical literacy. And cryptocurrency's pseudonymous nature meant that once users were on the platform, their trading activities left no obvious fingerprint identifying them as American.

Polymarket's technical team was well aware of this loophole. They implemented measures to detect and block known VPN IP addresses. They monitored for suspicious patterns, users whose IP addresses changed frequently or matched known VPN providers. They added additional verification steps for accounts that exhibited behaviors consistent with location masking.

But it was an arms race they couldn't win. VPN providers constantly added new servers. Users could chain multiple VPNs together. Sophisticated users employed residential proxy networks that made their connections appear to come from ordinary home internet connections rather than data centers.

The fundamental problem was architectural. Polymarket was built on the premise of permissionless, pseudonymous access. Users connected cryptocurrency wallets, no email required, no government ID, no phone verification. This design was core to the platform's appeal: seamless, private access to prediction markets. But it also meant the company had very limited ability to verify users' true identities or locations.

Compare this to traditional financial platforms. When you open an account with Charles Schwab or Coinbase, you provide extensive documentation: Social Security number, proof of address, government-issued photo ID. These platforms can confidently verify that you are who you claim to be and where you're located. The cost is friction, account opening takes days or weeks, requires uploading documents, and involves verification calls.

Polymarket had deliberately chosen the opposite model. The entire onboarding experience was designed to be frictionless: connect wallet, fund account, start trading. This made the platform accessible and user-friendly, but it also made geographic enforcement nearly impossible.

The Streisand Effect: How Restrictions Increased Attention

The geo-blocking didn't just fail to keep U.S. users away, in some ways it actually attracted them.

This was a classic example of the Streisand Effect, named after the singer Barbra Streisand's attempt to suppress photographs of her Malibu home, which only drew far more attention to them. When you tell people they can't access something, you make it more interesting.

Before the CFTC settlement, Polymarket was known primarily within cryptocurrency and prediction markets niches. The settlement changed that. Major media outlets covered the story: a startup fined for allowing Americans to bet on elections and other events, now blocked from serving U.S. users. For many readers, this was the first time they'd heard of Polymarket.

The narrative was irresistible: a platform that let you bet on political outcomes, something that felt intuitively valuable during polarized election cycles had been shut down by regulators protecting established interests. It had a whiff of forbidden fruit, of accessing something the government didn't want you to have.

Reddit threads and Twitter discussions about the settlement inevitably included comments like: "Wait, so there's a platform where you can bet real money on who wins elections, and they won't let Americans use it? That seems backwards." Followed by: "Can't you just use a VPN?" And: "Here's a link to the step-by-step guide I wrote."

The cryptocurrency community, already skeptical of government regulation and enthusiastic about circumventing geographic restrictions, rallied around Polymarket. Using a VPN to access the platform became a minor act of civil disobedience, a way of asserting that markets should be free and information should flow without government interference.

Polymarket didn't explicitly encourage this behavior, that would have violated the settlement agreement and invited new enforcement action. But the company didn't need to encourage it. The combination of regulatory restriction and easy workarounds created a dynamic that fed on itself.

Media coverage helped too. Articles about Polymarket after the settlement often included paragraphs like: "While U.S. users are technically prohibited from accessing the platform following the CFTC settlement, observers note that determined users can circumvent these restrictions using widely available VPN services." This wasn't the journalists' way of encouraging violation of the settlement terms, it was simply accurately reporting the technical reality. But it had the effect of informing readers exactly how to access the platform.

By mid-2022, Polymarket had more name recognition in the United States than it had before the CFTC settlement. The restriction had become free marketing.

The Metrics That Couldn't Be Ignored

Inside Polymarket, the growth numbers created a complex situation. On one hand, the company was thriving. Trading volumes were up, the platform was gaining mainstream attention, and venture capitalists were increasingly interested. On the other hand, a significant portion of that success appeared to be coming from users who weren't supposed to be accessing the platform at all.

How much of Polymarket's trading volume came from U.S. users accessing the platform via VPNs? This was a question the company was careful not to answer too precisely, even internally.

The challenge was that determining users' true locations was technically difficult and potentially dangerous. If Polymarket developed sophisticated systems to identify probable U.S. users based on trading patterns, time zones, linguistic markers, or other signals, what would the company do with that information? Block those users and watch trading volume collapse? Report them to the CFTC? Ignore them and hope regulators never asked?

The safest approach was studied ignorance. Polymarket could honestly tell regulators: "We've implemented geo-blocking technology as required by our settlement agreement. We monitor for VPN usage and block known VPN IP addresses. We cannot, however, detect every method users might employ to mask their location, and we have no way to verify with certainty that users are not in prohibited jurisdictions."

This was technically true. But it also conveniently avoided confronting the elephant in the room: that U.S. users were clearly still accessing the platform in large numbers.

Some data points were unavoidable. Markets on obscure U.S. state legislative races attracted substantial trading volume, unlikely if the traders were primarily Europeans or Asians. Trading patterns showed spikes during U.S. business hours and drops during American nighttime, suggesting traders in U.S. time zones. The sophistication of trading on U.S. political markets suggested people with deep knowledge of American politics, again more consistent with U.S. users than international ones.

But these were circumstantial indicators, not proof. Polymarket could plausibly argue that Americans living abroad, international users with strong interest in U.S. politics, and non-U.S. political operatives and analysts accounted for the activity.

The ambiguity was sustainable because both Polymarket and the CFTC had reasons not to look too closely. The company wanted to keep growing. The CFTC had achieved its enforcement goal, making clear that unregistered event markets violated the law and didn't necessarily want to engage in endless cat-and-mouse games with a startup that was at least making good-faith efforts at compliance.

Legal Strategies: Walking the Line

Polymarket's legal team developed a careful strategy for navigating the post-settlement landscape. The approach had several key elements:

1. Document Everything

Every decision related to compliance was documented. When the engineering team implemented new VPN detection measures, the compliance team noted it. When they discussed whether to block additional IP ranges, the reasoning was recorded. If the CFTC ever questioned the company's efforts, Polymarket wanted a paper trail showing active, ongoing compliance work.

2. Implement "Reasonable" Measures

The settlement required "reasonable efforts" to prevent U.S. users from accessing the platform. The key word was "reasonable", the standard wasn't perfection, it was good-faith effort. Polymarket focused on meeting this standard: IP blocking, VPN detection, terms of service restrictions, user representations about location. The fact that determined users could circumvent these measures didn't mean the measures were inadequate; it meant perfect enforcement was impossible.

3. Avoid Active Facilitation

The company was scrupulous about not helping U.S. users circumvent restrictions. No employee discussed VPN usage in official communications. The company didn't create guides for accessing the platform from prohibited jurisdictions. Customer support requests from obviously U.S.-based users were declined with references to the geographic restrictions.

This created an absurd dynamic where both parties understood what was happening but couldn't acknowledge it. A user would email: "I'm traveling internationally and trying to access my account, but I'm getting an error message." Support would respond: "Our service is not available in the United States. If you are accessing from a prohibited jurisdiction, we cannot assist you." Neither party would mention VPNs, but both understood the subtext.

4. Focus on the International Story

Publicly, Polymarket emphasized its global growth. The company highlighted users in Europe, Asia, and Latin America. It expanded language support, created markets relevant to international audiences, and positioned itself as a worldwide platform that happened to have restrictions in one market.

This framing was important for future regulatory conversations. If Polymarket ever needed to explain its continued growth despite U.S. restrictions, the answer was ready: "We're a global platform serving users in dozens of countries. The fact that we're successful internationally demonstrates that prediction markets have worldwide appeal."

5. Prepare for Potential Future Scrutiny

The legal team knew that if Polymarket became too successful, or if evidence emerged of widespread U.S. user activity, the CFTC might take a renewed interest. They prepared defensive strategies: arguments about the limits of geo-blocking technology, comparisons to how other platforms handled similar challenges, expert opinions on what "reasonable efforts" meant in practice.

The hope was these defenses would never be needed. But preparing them was prudent, especially as the platform's profile continued to rise.

The Competitive Landscape: How Geo-Blocking Changed Market Dynamics

Polymarket's geographic restrictions created interesting competitive dynamics in the prediction markets space.

Kalshi, operating legally in the United States with CFTC approval, should have had a significant advantage. American users who wanted to trade prediction markets without using VPNs or worrying about violating terms of service could use Kalshi with complete legal clarity.

But Kalshi had its own restrictions. The CFTC approval process meant the platform could only offer markets on specific types of events that the agency had authorized. The user experience was more traditional financial platform than crypto-native marketplace. And the regulatory compliance costs meant Kalshi needed to charge higher fees and maintain more restrictive policies.

The result was that Kalshi attracted a different user base: more institutional, more risk-averse, more focused on the specific markets the platform was authorized to offer. Polymarket, despite its restrictions, remained the choice for users who wanted broader market selection, lower fees, and the cryptocurrency-native experience.

PredictIt continued to operate under its no-action letter, with severe restrictions on market size and user positions. These limitations prevented it from competing seriously with either Kalshi or Polymarket in terms of liquidity and price discovery. PredictIt remained primarily an academic and research tool rather than a serious trading venue.

Augur and other fully decentralized platforms had their own challenges. The promise of regulatory resistance through decentralization remained appealing in theory but difficult in practice. These platforms struggled with user experience issues, limited liquidity, and questions about market integrity. Being unstoppable didn't matter if no one wanted to use you.

The competitive landscape thus created a peculiar situation: Polymarket, supposedly blocked from the U.S. market, maintained significant advantages over platforms that could legally serve American users. This was possible only because of the geo-block paradox, the combination of easy circumvention and increased attention that made the restrictions less limiting than they appeared.

The Users: Why They Stayed (Or Came)

Understanding the geo-block paradox requires understanding the users who continued accessing Polymarket despite the restrictions.

The Political Junkies: These users were deeply engaged with American politics and frustrated by the limitations of traditional election forecasting. They believed prediction markets provided more accurate signals than polls or pundit predictions. For them, using a VPN to access Polymarket was a minor inconvenience worth the superior information.

The Cryptocurrency Natives: Many users came from the cryptocurrency community, where using VPNs to access geo-restricted services was routine. They were comfortable with pseudonymous transactions, familiar with blockchain wallets, and philosophically opposed to geographic restrictions on internet services. For them, Polymarket's crypto-native design was more important than legal clarity.

The Traders: Professional and semi-professional traders saw opportunities in Polymarket's markets that weren't available elsewhere. The platform offered deeper liquidity, tighter spreads, and more diverse markets than competitors. If they had an edge, superior analysis, faster information, better models Polymarket was where they could profit from it. VPN usage was a cost of doing business.

The Information Seekers: Some users accessed Polymarket primarily to see market prices, not to trade. They believed prediction market prices provided valuable information about event probabilities. Checking Polymarket odds became part of their routine for understanding politics, sports, or other topics. Even if they rarely traded, they wanted access to the price signals.

The Principle-Driven: A subset of users accessed Polymarket specifically because they objected to the restrictions. They believed prediction markets served a social good, that U.S. regulations were misguided, and that circumventing those restrictions was justified. For them, trading on Polymarket was a form of protest.

These user segments overlapped, and many individuals fit multiple categories. But collectively, they represented a user base that was motivated enough to overcome the friction of VPN usage and determined enough to continue despite legal ambiguity.

Platform Growth Despite (Or Because Of?) Restrictions

By the end of 2022, Polymarket's growth trajectory was clear. The platform was significantly larger than it had been before the CFTC settlement, by almost every metric:

- Monthly trading volume had more than doubled
- Active user counts had increased substantially
- Market diversity had expanded, more topics, more niches, more continuous activity
- Media mentions and mainstream awareness had grown exponentially
- The platform had attracted additional venture capital funding at a higher valuation

How much of this growth was despite the geographic restrictions versus because of them?

The honest answer was: both. Polymarket had lost some users who weren't willing to use VPNs or who were uncomfortable accessing a platform they were technically prohibited from using. The company had also lost potential mainstream adoption from users who wanted clear legal status and weren't willing to work around restrictions.

But the company had gained something perhaps more valuable: a narrative, a mystique, and a sense of being the platform that established interests didn't want you to access. The restriction had made Polymarket noteworthy in a way that simply being "another prediction markets platform" never would have.

There was also the timing factor. The CFTC settlement came in early 2022, just as interest in prediction markets was beginning to surge. The 2024 presidential election cycle was starting to heat up. Economic uncertainty, continuing pandemic effects, and geopolitical tensions made people hungry for better forecasting tools. Polymarket was positioned perfectly to capture this growing interest.

The geographic restrictions might have limited growth somewhat, but they didn't prevent it. And in some ways, they may have accelerated it by generating attention and creating a compelling story.

The Sustainability Question: How Long Could This Last?

By late 2022, some observers were asking: how long could Polymarket maintain this dynamic?

The optimistic view was that the company had found a sustainable equilibrium. It had settled with the CFTC, implemented compliance measures, and was growing internationally. Yes, some U.S. users were accessing the platform via VPNs, but the company was making reasonable efforts to prevent this, which was all the settlement required. Polymarket could continue on this path indefinitely, gradually becoming the global standard for prediction markets while remaining blocked from its home country.

The pessimistic view was that the current situation was unstable. As Polymarket grew larger and more prominent, it would attract renewed regulatory scrutiny. If the CFTC determined that the company wasn't doing enough to prevent U.S. user access or if evidence emerged of widespread violation of the geographic restrictions enforcement could resume. The next penalty might be larger, the next settlement might be stricter, and the company might face restrictions that couldn't be worked around.

There was also the question of what happened when Polymarket's predictions proved dramatically more accurate than traditional forecasting methods. If the platform consistently outperformed polls and pundits on major events, elections, economic indicators, geopolitical developments it would become impossible to ignore. At that point, either regulators would find a way to legitimize prediction markets in the U.S., or they would crack down harder to prevent Americans from accessing these valuable information sources.

The middle view, held by many close to the company, was that Polymarket was buying time. The current equilibrium wouldn't last forever, but it didn't need to. If the company could grow large enough, prove its value clearly enough, and build a strong enough user base, it would eventually have the leverage to negotiate better terms, either through regulatory change, political pressure, or sheer market dominance that made restrictions untenable.

Shayne Coplan appeared to hold this middle view. In interviews and public statements during 2022-2023, he emphasized the platform's international growth while occasionally hinting at hopes for eventual U.S. re-entry. "We're building the infrastructure for prediction markets globally," he said in one interview. "The regulatory landscape is still evolving, and we're optimistic that over time, there will be paths for more participation in different markets."

This was carefully worded, optimistic without being committal, acknowledging regulatory constraints while suggesting they might not be permanent.

The Ethical Dimension: Responsibility and Complicity

The geo-block paradox raised uncomfortable ethical questions that the company didn't fully resolve.

Was Polymarket complicit in users' violation of the CFTC settlement terms? The company hadn't encouraged VPN usage, but it also hadn't made it particularly difficult. The platform's design, permissionless, pseudonymous, crypto-native made circumvention easy. Was this a bug or a feature?

Did the company have an obligation to do more to prevent U.S. user access, even if it meant fundamentally changing the platform's design? Implementing robust identity verification and location confirmation would require users to provide documentation, undergo checks, and accept friction in the user experience. This would make the platform less appealing but more compliant. Was this trade-off justified?

What about users who were violating not just Polymarket's terms of service but potentially U.S. law? If a platform knows its terms are being systematically violated but doesn't take aggressive action to prevent it, is it responsible for those violations?

These weren't just theoretical questions, they went to the heart of what Polymarket was and what it should become. The company's response was essentially to implement measures that satisfied regulatory requirements while maintaining a product design that served its users' needs. If users chose to circumvent restrictions, that was their decision, not the company's responsibility.

This position was defensible but not entirely comfortable. It meant living with the knowledge that the platform's success was partly built on users acting against the spirit (if not always the letter) of the settlement agreement.

Some employees struggled with this ambiguity. The company culture emphasized building useful products and serving users, but also valued operating responsibly and respecting regulations. When those goals conflicted, when serving users meant turning a blind eye to likely violations the ethical path wasn't always clear.

Looking Ahead: The Seeds of Future Controversy

The geo-block paradox wasn't just a curious phenomenon in Polymarket's history, it was planting seeds that would eventually grow into serious problems.

By creating a situation where the company's success depended partly on inadequate enforcement of geographic restrictions, Polymarket was building a vulnerability. If regulators ever decided to investigate whether the platform was truly complying with its settlement agreement, the evidence would be uncomfortable. High trading volumes on U.S. political markets, user behavior patterns consistent with American traders, and the general knowledge that VPN circumvention was widespread would all suggest that Polymarket hadn't effectively prevented U.S. user access.

The company's defense would be that it had implemented reasonable measures and that perfect enforcement was technologically impossible. This defense might work, or it might not. But the ambiguity meant Polymarket was operating with perpetual risk, the possibility that at any time, the CFTC might decide the company's efforts had been insufficient.

This risk would remain theoretical through 2022 and 2023 as the platform grew and gained credibility. But it would become very real in 2024, when Polymarket's predictions about the presidential election proved dramatically accurate, attracting massive attention and, eventually, renewed federal scrutiny.

The FBI raid that would open this book, agents showing up at Shayne Coplan's apartment in November 2024, seizing devices, investigating potential violations had its roots in the geo-block paradox of 2022. The company had found a way to grow despite restrictions, but that growth had come with lasting vulnerabilities.

In mid-2022, those consequences still seemed distant. For now, Polymarket was thriving, prediction markets were gaining legitimacy, and the geographic restrictions seemed like an obstacle the company had successfully navigated. The paradox had worked in Polymarket's favor.

How long that favor would last remained to be seen.

PART IV: THE ASCENT

Chapter 11

2022-2023: Building Momentum

The graph on Shayne Coplan's monitor showed a hockey stick curve that would make any startup founder's heart race. Monthly trading volume on Polymarket had grown from $20 million in January 2022 to over $50 million by December, and the trajectory was only accelerating into 2023. By mid-2023, some months were seeing north of $100 million in volume.

But numbers alone don't tell the whole story of how Polymarket transformed from a crypto curiosity into a platform that mainstream media, professional traders, and eventually political campaigns would take seriously. The period from early 2022 through the end of 2023 was when Polymarket built the foundation for everything that would follow, the credibility, the user base, the technological infrastructure, and the track record of accurate predictions that would make it indispensable by 2024.

This was the momentum phase, when a startup with a controversial regulatory history became the most important prediction market platform in the world.

January-March 2022: Post-Settlement Reset

The first quarter after the CFTC settlement was about proving Polymarket could survive the restrictions. Many observers had predicted the geographic blocking would cripple the company. Without U.S. users or at least, without being able to officially serve them how could a prediction market platform focused heavily on American politics sustain itself?

The answer came quickly: international growth and VPN circumvention, though the company would only acknowledge the former.

Shayne and his team focused obsessively on user experience during this period. If accessing Polymarket required a VPN, every other aspect of the platform needed to be frictionless. The onboarding flow was streamlined to take less than two minutes from landing page to first trade. The user interface was redesigned to be more intuitive, with clearer market categories and better search functionality.

The engineering team also worked on scaling infrastructure. The smart contracts underlying Polymarket's markets needed to handle increased transaction volume without slowdowns or failures. The Polygon blockchain integration was optimized to reduce transaction costs and confirmation times. Backend systems were upgraded to support the growth the company anticipated.

This was unglamorous work, the kind of technical infrastructure improvement that users never notice when it works correctly but rage about when it fails. But it was essential. If Polymarket was going to attract serious traders and institutional interest, it needed to be reliable at scale.

The company also expanded its team significantly. Key hires in this period included:

- A head of growth with experience scaling consumer applications
- Additional engineers focused on backend infrastructure and smart contract security
- A content strategist to develop educational materials about prediction markets
- Customer support staff to handle the increasing volume of user inquiries
- Data analysts to better understand trading patterns and market dynamics

By March 2022, the post-settlement panic had subsided. Polymarket was not only surviving but growing. The foundation was set for the momentum to come.

April-June 2022: The First Major Predictions

Polymarket's credibility as a forecasting tool was built on getting predictions right, especially when conventional wisdom got them wrong. The second quarter of 2022 provided several opportunities to demonstrate this.

The French Presidential Election (April 2022) was Polymarket's first major test of political forecasting outside the United States. The market dynamics were fascinating: Emmanuel Macron was the favorite, but Marine Le Pen's odds fluctuated significantly based on polling data and debate performances.

Polymarket's final prices before voting began had Macron at a 72% chance of victory, slightly more confident than most polls suggested. When Macron won with 58.5% of the vote, Polymarket's odds proved well-calibrated. More importantly, the platform had provided real-time probability updates throughout the campaign, giving observers a continuous read on the race rather than intermittent snapshots from polling.

International media coverage of the election increasingly cited Polymarket odds alongside traditional polls. This was a significant shift. Just a year earlier, prediction market prices were niche data points for political junkies. Now they were appearing in Financial Times articles and Reuters coverage.

Inflation Predictions became another area where Polymarket demonstrated value. The Federal Reserve and most economists had been arguing throughout 2021 and early 2022 that inflation was "transitory", a temporary spike that would resolve without aggressive intervention. Polymarket's markets told a different story.

In spring 2022, when the Fed was still maintaining its transitory inflation narrative, Polymarket odds on "U.S. inflation above 7% in 2022" were trading above 80%. The consensus of traders, synthesizing information from commodity markets, labor data, supply chain reports, and monetary policy analysis was that inflation would remain elevated. They were right. By June 2022, U.S. inflation hit 9.1%, forcing the Fed to begin aggressive interest rate increases.

This was Polymarket's value proposition in action: aggregating dispersed information faster and more accurately than institutional forecasters. Traders with money at stake weren't committed to any particular narrative. They just wanted to be right, and being right meant incorporating all available information, not just what supported a preferred story.

The Roe v. Wade Decision (June 2022) provided another high-profile moment. After Politico published a leaked draft opinion suggesting the Supreme Court would overturn Roe v. Wade, Polymarket's markets on the decision became intensely active.

Before the leak, markets had given roughly 35-40% odds to Roe being overturned. After the leak, odds spiked immediately to over 80%. When the official decision came down in late June, overturning Roe as the leaked draft had indicated, Polymarket had accurately priced the probability throughout.

More interestingly, the platform saw enormous engagement from users who weren't typical traders. The Roe markets attracted activists on both sides, legal analysts, journalists, and ordinary people trying to understand what would happen. Trading volume was high, but so was view count, many people were checking market prices without trading, using Polymarket as an information source.

This foreshadowed a pattern that would become crucial: Polymarket's influence extended beyond its active traders to a much larger audience of information consumers.

July-September 2022: Going Mainstream

The third quarter of 2022 was when Polymarket crossed from crypto-native niche to mainstream awareness.

Part of this was media coverage. Articles about Polymarket appeared in The New York Times, Washington Post, Wall Street Journal, Bloomberg, and The Economist. The tone of coverage was shifting from "weird cryptocurrency prediction market gets in trouble with regulators" to "this platform's odds might be more reliable than polls."

Nate Silver, the renowned statistician and founder of FiveThirtyEight, mentioned Polymarket odds in his election forecasting discussions. This was significant, Silver had long been skeptical of prediction markets, arguing that they often just reflected polling averages rather than providing independent signals. But he acknowledged that Polymarket's liquidity and trader sophistication were creating markets that sometimes spotted trends before polls did.

The platform also began attracting "whale" traders, individuals or entities placing large positions worth tens or hundreds of thousands of dollars. These weren't retail users making $50 bets for entertainment. These were sophisticated traders treating Polymarket as a serious financial market.

The presence of whales improved market quality in some ways and created concerns in others. Larger traders meant more liquidity and tighter spreads, making markets more efficient. But they also meant individual actors could potentially move prices, raising manipulation concerns that would become more prominent later.

World Cup Predictions in the lead-up to the November tournament gave Polymarket another mainstream hook. Sports betting was familiar to general audiences in a way that political prediction markets weren't. When Polymarket's World Cup markets showed different odds than traditional sportsbooks, sports media covered it as a curiosity but the curiosity brought new users.

The platform saw user growth accelerate through the summer and into fall. The onboarding funnel that had been optimized earlier in the year was converting visitors efficiently. New users who came for one high-profile market often stayed to explore others.

By September 2022, Polymarket had achieved something remarkable: it had become the default answer to "what are the odds?" questions for a growing segment of journalists, analysts, and politically engaged citizens. When someone wanted to know the probability of a future event, checking Polymarket was becoming habitual.

October-December 2022: The Midterm Elections Test

The 2022 U.S. midterm elections represented the biggest test yet of Polymarket's forecasting ability and its most significant opportunity for mainstream validation.

The narrative heading into the midterms was clear: Republicans were expected to make substantial gains, potentially winning both the House and Senate. President Biden's approval ratings were underwater, inflation was high, and historical patterns suggested the president's party would suffer losses in midterms.

Traditional polls supported this narrative. Most polling averages showed Republicans with significant advantages in key races. Political pundits were nearly unanimous in predicting a "red wave."

Polymarket's markets told a more nuanced story. While Republican odds were elevated, they weren't as overwhelming as pundit consensus suggested. The platform gave Republicans strong odds of taking the House but much more uncertain odds for the Senate. Key Senate races in Georgia,

Pennsylvania, Arizona and Nevada showed tight probabilities that fluctuated based on late-breaking developments.

The company's infrastructure was tested as never before. On election night, Polymarket saw unprecedented traffic. Traders were updating positions in real-time as results came in. The platform needed to handle massive simultaneous transaction volume without crashes or slowdowns.

The technical team had prepared extensively. Additional server capacity had been provisioned. Smart contract executions had been optimized. Monitoring systems tracked every aspect of platform performance. When election night arrived, Polymarket handled the load smoothly, a crucial success that proved the platform could scale to handle major events.

The Results and Vindication

When votes were counted, Polymarket's predictions proved more accurate than the pundit consensus and competitive with the best polling averages:

- Republicans won the House, as Polymarket had predicted was likely (around 75% probability going into election night)
- Democrats held the Senate, which Polymarket had rated as roughly 55-60% probable in the final days, closer to a coin flip than the red wave narrative suggested
- Most individual Senate races resolved close to Polymarket's final probabilities

This wasn't perfect calibration, no forecasting method is but it was good. More importantly, Polymarket had avoided the trap of overconfident predictions. When races were genuinely uncertain, the market prices reflected that uncertainty rather than forcing false confidence.

The coverage after the midterms marked a turning point. Articles that might have been skeptical of prediction markets instead treated

Polymarket's odds as serious forecasting data. "Polymarket saw it coming" became a common framing. The platform had provided value when it mattered most.

By the end of 2022, monthly trading volume was hitting $60-70 million. The user base had more than doubled since the beginning of the year. And most importantly, Polymarket had established itself as a credible forecasting tool that deserved to be taken seriously.

January-March 2023: Institutional Interest Begins

The new year brought a qualitative shift: institutional interest in Polymarket's data and technology.

Hedge funds and trading firms began reaching out to discuss data partnerships. They wanted access to real-time market prices, historical data, and APIs that would let them incorporate prediction market signals into their own trading models. Some saw Polymarket as a valuable alternative data source, information that wasn't available from traditional vendors and might provide an edge.

Political campaigns and consulting firms also started paying attention. While they couldn't officially acknowledge using betting markets for strategic decisions, several campaigns began having staffers monitor Polymarket odds. If a candidate's odds were dropping, it signaled that informed traders believed something about the campaign wasn't working. This could prompt strategy adjustments faster than waiting for polling data.

Media organizations were most explicit about their interest. Several major publications discussed partnerships where they would display Polymarket odds in their election coverage. The New York Times, CNN, and others had traditionally relied on polling averages and their own political analysts.

Now they were considering integrating prediction market data as another signal.

Shayne and his team were cautious about these institutional partnerships. They didn't want Polymarket to be seen as captured by particular political or media interests. But they also recognized that institutional adoption was essential for long-term legitimacy. The challenge was maintaining the platform's independence while building partnerships that expanded its influence.

The company formalized its approach through a new **Data & Research division.** This team would handle institutional inquiries, develop API access for approved partners, and create research reports analyzing market trends and accuracy. The goal was to position Polymarket not just as a trading platform but as an information infrastructure provider.

This strategic evolution was significant. Polymarket was becoming more than a place to trade predictions, it was becoming a source of truth about probabilities, a real-time aggregator of collective intelligence that institutions needed to understand reality.

April-June 2023: Product Evolution and New Markets

With the platform's credibility established and institutional interest growing, Polymarket focused on expanding its market offerings and improving the product experience.

New Market Categories launched in quick succession:

- **Technology and AI**: Markets on when major AI milestones would be achieved, which companies would reach trillion-dollar valuations, when specific products would launch
- **Climate and Weather**: Predictions about temperature records, climate policy milestones, extreme weather events

- **Financial Markets:** Enhanced offerings on stock market performance, cryptocurrency prices, economic indicators
- **Entertainment:** Deeper markets on award shows, celebrity news, streaming platform performance
- **Science:** Markets on Nobel Prize winners, breakthrough announcements, space exploration milestones

The diversity of markets served multiple purposes. It attracted different user demographics, created more opportunities for information discovery, and demonstrated that prediction markets could work for virtually any future event with a definable outcome.

The Mobile Strategy became a priority. While Polymarket had always been mobile-responsive, the company developed dedicated mobile apps for iOS and Android. Mobile users behaved differently than desktop traders, they checked odds frequently throughout the day, made smaller trades, and were more likely to share markets on social media.

The mobile app launch required navigating app store policies, which added complexity. Both Apple and Google had restrictions around gambling and betting apps. Polymarket's position was that it offered prediction markets, not gambling, and was already blocked from U.S. users. After negotiations with both app stores, the apps were approved but with geographic restrictions enforced at the app store level, another layer of geo-blocking that, like the others, could be circumvented by determined users.

API Development for Professional Traders was another major product initiative. Sophisticated traders wanted programmatic access to place orders, monitor prices, and manage positions. Polymarket built a comprehensive API that enabled algorithmic trading, automated market making, and integration with external analysis tools.

This attracted a new category of users: quantitative traders and developers who built bots and trading systems on top of Polymarket's infrastructure. These users generated substantial volume and improved market efficiency, though they also raised questions about whether automated trading gave unfair advantages over retail users.

July-September 2023: The Competition Heats Up

Polymarket's success inevitably attracted competition. The third quarter of 2023 saw several new entrants and intensified rivalry with existing platforms.

Kalshi was the most significant competitor. Operating legally in the U.S. with CFTC approval, Kalshi had been steadily expanding its offerings and improving its platform. The company secured additional regulatory approvals for new market types and began an aggressive marketing campaign positioning itself as the "legal" alternative to offshore prediction markets.

The contrast between Kalshi and Polymarket was sharp: regulated versus crypto-native, restricted versus permissionless, U.S.-focused versus global. Both platforms had advantages, and both were growing. But Polymarket's lead in volume, liquidity, and brand recognition was substantial.

New blockchain-based platforms also emerged. Several projects announced plans to build decentralized prediction markets similar to Polymarket but with different technical approaches or governance models. Most of these remained vaporware or attracted minimal usage. Building a successful prediction market required not just technology but liquidity, trust, and network effects, all of which Polymarket had built over years.

Traditional betting platforms began exploring prediction market features. Established sports betting companies saw the attention Polymarket was getting and wondered if they should offer political or event betting alongside sports. However, they faced their own regulatory challenges, sports betting was legal in many U.S. states, but event betting on politics was not.

The competitive landscape validated Polymarket's approach. The company had moved first, built aggressively, and established a dominant position that would be difficult to displace. Competitors could chip away at market share in specific niches, but Polymarket had become the category leader.

October-December 2023: Preparing for 2024

As 2023 wound down, everyone at Polymarket knew what was coming: the 2024 U.S. presidential election would be the biggest event in the platform's history.

The company began preparing months in advance. Infrastructure investments accelerated. The engineering team modeled worst-case scenarios for traffic and transaction volume, then built systems capable of handling several multiples of those projections. There would be no room for failure when the world was watching.

The policy team also prepared. The 2024 election would attract unprecedented attention to Polymarket, which meant renewed scrutiny of how the platform operated. Were U.S. users still accessing it? Was trading activity influencing public perception of the race? Could markets be manipulated by well-funded actors trying to shape narratives?

These questions would need answers. The company developed communication strategies, prepared talking points, and briefed the legal team on potential scenarios. Everyone understood that success in covering the 2024 election could cement Polymarket's position permanently, but any major failure, technical crashes, obvious manipulation, evidence of regulatory violations could be existential.

The 2024 Markets Launch

Polymarket opened markets for the 2024 presidential election in late 2023, more than a year before the vote. Early trading was dominated by speculation about who would win the Republican and Democratic nominations, with Donald Trump and Joe Biden as the respective favorites.

These early markets attracted immediate attention. Even before primaries began, millions of dollars in volume flowed through 2024 election markets. Political media covered the odds daily. Campaign operatives watched them obsessively, even if they wouldn't admit it publicly.

By December 2023, the 2024 presidential election market on Polymarket had become one of the most liquid prediction markets in history. The spread between buying and selling prices was tight, suggesting efficient price discovery. The depth of the order book meant large trades could execute without dramatically moving the market.

This was what Polymarket had been building toward: a market so liquid, so efficient, and so closely watched that it became essential infrastructure for understanding the election. Not the only source of information, but an indispensable one that synthesized dispersed knowledge into a single, actionable probability.

The Metrics That Mattered

By the end of 2023, Polymarket's growth was undeniable across every dimension:

Trading Volume: Monthly volume had grown from $20 million in January 2022 to over $150 million by December 2023, more than 7x growth in two years.

User Base: Active monthly users had increased by over 300%, with particularly strong growth in Europe, Asia, and Latin America (officially, at least, the geographic distribution of traders remained somewhat ambiguous).

Market Diversity: The platform hosted thousands of active markets at any given time, covering dozens of categories beyond politics.

Media Mentions: References to Polymarket in major publications had increased exponentially. The platform was cited regularly in election coverage, economic analysis, and technology reporting.

Mainstream Recognition: Polymarket had transcended its crypto origins to become recognizable to general audiences. It was becoming the Kleenex of prediction markets, the brand name that represented the entire category.

Accuracy Track Record: Retrospective analysis of major markets showed strong calibration. Events that Polymarket priced at 70% likely happened approximately 70% of the time. This wasn't perfect, no forecasting method is but it was good enough to be useful.

These metrics told a story of a platform that had successfully navigated regulatory challenges, built credibility through accurate predictions, and positioned itself for the biggest moment yet to come.

The Culture and Community

Numbers alone don't capture what Polymarket had become by late 2023. The platform had developed a distinctive culture and community that set it apart from both traditional financial markets and typical cryptocurrency projects.

The Traders: A core group of sophisticated traders had emerged who took prediction markets seriously as a domain for skill and profit. These traders shared analysis, debated methodology, and competed for alpha (excess returns). Some became known personalities in the community, with others following their positions and reasoning.

The Researchers: Academics and data scientists began treating Polymarket as a valuable research subject. Papers analyzed market efficiency, information aggregation, and the accuracy of crowd wisdom. The platform became a real-world laboratory for testing economic theories about prediction markets.

The Information Consumers: Far more people viewed Polymarket odds than actually traded. These users treated the platform as a news source, a way to quickly understand the probability of events without wading through pundit speculation or biased reporting.

The Believers: A subset of users and community members saw prediction markets as genuinely important for society. They believed that better forecasting tools could improve decision-making, reduce misinformation, and help people understand uncertainty. For them, Polymarket wasn't just a trading platform, it was infrastructure for a more rational world.

This culture gave Polymarket something valuable beyond its technology or liquidity: a sense of mission and community that would sustain the platform through future challenges.

Looking Ahead to 2024

As 2023 ended, the momentum Polymarket had built over two years was undeniable. The company had survived regulatory enforcement, proven its forecasting value, attracted institutional interest, and built a global user base.

But everyone involved understood that 2024 would be the real test. If Polymarket's odds on the presidential election proved accurate when traditional polls failed, the platform would achieve a level of legitimacy that could never be taken away. Prediction markets would move from niche curiosity to essential tool for understanding political reality.

If, however, the platform's predictions proved badly wrong, or if technical failures disrupted election coverage, or if manipulation became obvious, the reputational damage could be catastrophic. Two years of momentum could collapse in a single night.

Shayne Coplan felt the weight of this moment. He was 25 years old, running a platform that would help millions of people understand the most important election of their lives. The infrastructure was ready. The team was prepared. The markets were liquid and efficient.

Now it was just a matter of getting it right when it mattered most.

The momentum phase was ending. The high-stakes execution phase was beginning.

Chapter 12

The Polymarket Ecosystem

By mid-2023, Polymarket was no longer just a platform, it had become an ecosystem. Like successful technology companies before it, Amazon, Twitter and Ethereum Polymarket had reached the point where third-party developers, data analysts, professional traders, and media organizations were building services, tools, and businesses on top of its infrastructure.

This was the sign that Polymarket had achieved product-market fit beyond its wildest projections. The platform wasn't just serving users; it was enabling an entire economy of participants who each played distinct roles in making prediction markets more efficient, more liquid, and more valuable as sources of information.

Understanding this ecosystem is essential to understanding Polymarket's power and influence. The company itself employed fewer than fifty people by 2023, yet thousands of participants were contributing to market quality, information discovery, and the platform's growing mainstream credibility.

The Whales: Professional Traders and Large Position Holders

At the top of the food chain were the whales, traders who regularly placed positions worth tens or hundreds of thousands of dollars.

Profile: "The Analyst"

One of the most successful whales, known in the community only by his pseudonymous wallet address, had reportedly made over $2 million in profit from Polymarket trading by late 2023. His approach was methodical: deep research into political races, economic indicators, and other events, combined with careful position sizing and risk management.

The Analyst didn't trade on intuition or partisan preference. He built models. For political races, this meant aggregating polling data, analyzing fundraising reports, studying historical patterns, and identifying market inefficiencies where Polymarket's prices diverged from his calculated probabilities. When he found an edge, markets that were mispriced by his analysis he would place large bets and wait for prices to correct.

His trading style was patient. He rarely day-traded based on news events, preferring to build positions early when he believed markets hadn't yet incorporated available information. Sometimes this meant enduring drawdowns when his positions initially moved against him, but his edge played out over time.

Other whales in the ecosystem followed different strategies:

The News Trader specialized in ultra-fast reaction to breaking information. He monitored news feeds, Twitter, and other sources constantly, ready to trade within seconds of relevant announcements. When Russia invaded Ukraine in February 2022, he was among the first to buy shares in various related markets before prices could adjust. His edge was speed and the ability to quickly assess implications.

The French Trader became something of a legend in late 2024, though his activities were more controversial. He reportedly placed enormous positions on Donald Trump winning the presidential election, positions so large they moved market prices and generated media coverage. Whether he had genuine information advantages or was simply making a calculated bet became the subject of intense speculation. His actions would later attract regulatory scrutiny.

The Arbitrageur didn't try to predict outcomes so much as exploit price differences across markets. If Polymarket showed Biden at 52% to win the election while another platform showed 48%, he would simultaneously buy on one platform and sell on the other, locking in risk-free profit when prices converged. His trading made markets more efficient by ensuring prices stayed aligned across platforms.

What all whales shared was sophistication. These weren't casual users making emotional bets. They treated Polymarket as a serious financial market where skill and analysis could generate consistent returns. Their presence meant substantial liquidity, large orders could execute without dramatically moving prices and their trading activity helped correct mispriced markets.

But whales also created concerns. When a single trader could move market prices with large positions, questions arose about whether Polymarket odds truly reflected the wisdom of crowds or just the opinions of a few wealthy actors. This tension would become more prominent as the platform grew.

Market Makers: The Liquidity Providers

While whales captured attention with large directional bets, market makers played a less visible but equally essential role in the ecosystem.

Market makers provided liquidity by continuously offering to buy and sell shares at specified prices. If you wanted to buy shares in "Trump wins 2024" at any given moment, market makers ensured there were shares available to buy without waiting for another user to place a matching sell order.

How Market Making Worked on Polymarket

Unlike traditional exchanges where designated market makers have special obligations and privileges, Polymarket's market making was permissionless. Anyone could act as a market maker using the platform's automated market maker (AMM) mechanism or by manually placing limit orders.

The AMM pools functioned similarly to decentralized exchanges like Uniswap. Users could deposit liquidity (USDC) into pools for specific markets, and the AMM algorithm would automatically price shares based on the ratio of funds in the pool. As traders bought or sold shares, prices would adjust, and liquidity providers would earn fees on trades.

Manual market makers took a more active approach. They would analyze markets, calculate fair prices with appropriate bid-ask spreads, and place limit orders on both sides of the market. When their orders were executed, they profited from the spread while providing liquidity to other traders.

Profile: The Algorithmic Market Maker

One particularly sophisticated market maker operated entirely through automated systems. His bots monitored hundreds of Polymarket markets simultaneously, adjusting prices microsecond by microsecond based on trading activity, news events, and external data sources like polls or prediction models.

His infrastructure was impressive: servers co-located for minimal latency, custom-built APIs for rapid order placement, machine learning models for price optimization, and risk management systems that automatically hedged positions across correlated markets.

This automated market making was profitable, the spread between his buy and sell prices generated consistent returns but it also provided enormous value to the ecosystem. Because his bots were always active, traders could execute orders at any time without waiting for counterparties. Markets stayed liquid even during slow trading periods.

The presence of sophisticated market makers meant that Polymarket could maintain relatively tight spreads, the difference between buying and selling prices comparable to professional financial markets. This was crucial for institutional adoption. Sophisticated users wouldn't trade on markets with 5% spreads when they could find 1% spreads elsewhere.

Data Analysts and Researchers: Mining Information from Markets

A thriving ecosystem of analysts emerged around Polymarket, treating the platform's data as a valuable resource for understanding the world.

Independent Analysts

Several individuals built followings by providing regular analysis of Polymarket odds. They wrote newsletters, posted threads on Twitter, or published Substack articles explaining what market prices revealed about upcoming events.

These analysts served several functions:

- **Interpretation**: Explaining what probability numbers meant in practical terms
- **Context**: Comparing Polymarket odds to polls, expert forecasts, and historical patterns
- **Education**: Teaching audiences how to read prediction markets and understand their limitations
- **Signal Extraction**: Identifying when market movements indicated genuine information versus noise

One popular analyst focused exclusively on comparing Polymarket odds to polling averages in political races. His daily charts showing the two forecasting methods side-by-side became essential reading for political junkies. When Polymarket and polls diverged, he would investigate why, were traders seeing something polls missed, or were markets being inefficient?

Academic Researchers

Universities increasingly treated Polymarket as a valuable research laboratory. Economics departments studied market efficiency and information aggregation. Political science departments analyzed whether prediction markets outperformed polling. Computer science departments examined the technical architecture and smart contract design.

Several published papers used Polymarket data:

- "Information Aggregation in Cryptocurrency Prediction Markets" analyzed how quickly markets incorporated new information compared to traditional forecasting methods
- "The Wisdom of Crypto Crowds: Evidence from Polymarket" examined whether the platform's predictions were well-calibrated across different event types
- "Market Microstructure in Decentralized Prediction Markets" studied trading patterns and market maker behavior

This academic attention served multiple purposes. It provided intellectual legitimacy, treating prediction markets as serious subjects of study rather than gambling curiosities. It generated insights that helped improve market design. And it created a pipeline of researchers who understood prediction markets and could advocate for their value in policy discussions.

Proprietary Research Teams

Some hedge funds and trading firms built internal teams dedicated to analyzing prediction market data. They treated Polymarket odds as alternative data, information not widely available from traditional vendors that might provide trading edges.

These teams developed sophisticated approaches:

- Correlation analysis between prediction market prices and traditional asset prices
- Event studies examining how quickly different information sources updated after news

- Machine learning models incorporating prediction market data alongside fundamental analysis
- Risk management frameworks using prediction markets to hedge tail risks

The fact that professional investors were allocating resources to analyzing Polymarket indicated the platform had become serious financial infrastructure.

Media Organizations: Using Markets for Coverage

By 2023, numerous media organizations had integrated Polymarket data into their coverage workflows.

Real-Time Election Dashboards

Several major publications built dashboards displaying Polymarket odds alongside polling averages, fundraising data, and expert ratings. These dashboards updated continuously, giving readers real-time probability estimates for election outcomes.

The New York Times' experimental election forecast in 2023 included a section showing Polymarket odds with appropriate caveats about their meaning and limitations. This was significant, the Times had long been skeptical of prediction markets, viewing them as glorified gambling with no advantage over careful statistical analysis. The inclusion suggested institutional acceptance was growing.

CNN's politics team began referencing Polymarket odds in on-air coverage during special events. When unexpected news broke, commentators would check "what the markets are saying" alongside traditional expert analysis. This mainstreamed prediction market data in ways that would have been unthinkable a few years earlier.

Data Journalism Projects

Some journalists built entire stories around Polymarket data. They would analyze trading patterns around specific events, identify large position changes, or examine historical accuracy.

One investigation tracked every market prediction Polymarket had made over a two-year period, calculating overall calibration. The findings were nuanced: markets were generally well-calibrated but showed systematic biases in certain categories. Political markets tended to overestimate incumbent advantages. Cryptocurrency markets showed excessive volatility. But overall accuracy was competitive with expert forecasts.

Another project examined who was winning and losing on Polymarket. While the platform didn't release user-level data, blockchain analysis allowed some reconstruction of trading patterns. The investigation found that a small number of sophisticated traders captured most profits, while the majority of users lost money, consistent with any speculative market.

Ethical Debates

The increasing media reliance on Polymarket created editorial challenges. Should news organizations cite betting odds as legitimate forecasting data? Did this normalize gambling? Could markets be manipulated by actors trying to influence media narratives?

These questions didn't have simple answers. Media organizations developed varying policies. Some cited Polymarket freely while noting limitations. Others avoided prediction market data entirely, viewing it as inappropriate for serious journalism. Most fell somewhere in between, using markets as one data point among many.

The Community: Culture and Social Dynamics

Beyond professional participants, Polymarket developed a vibrant community culture that shaped how the platform functioned.

Discord and Telegram Groups

Unofficial community spaces emerged where traders discussed strategies, analyzed markets, and shared information. The largest Discord server had thousands of members engaged in continuous conversation about trading opportunities.

These communities developed their own norms and culture:

- **Anti-partisan ethos**: Successful traders emphasized that political preferences should never influence trading decisions. "Vote with your heart, trade with your head" became a common saying.
- **Information sharing**: Despite being in competition, traders often shared research and analysis. Someone might post polling data or news that others had missed, improving collective market understanding.
- **Mentorship**: Experienced traders helped newcomers understand market mechanics, avoid common mistakes, and develop better analytical frameworks.
- **Skepticism of mainstream narratives**: The community prided itself on seeing through media hype and conventional wisdom. If pundits were unanimous about something, traders looked for contrarian opportunities.

This culture attracted a particular demographic: analytically minded, often libertarian-leaning, skeptical of institutions, and comfortable with cryptocurrency and technology. Many were software engineers, quantitative analysts, or entrepreneurs who saw Polymarket as an intellectually stimulating alternative to traditional finance.

Social Media Presence

Polymarket developed a significant social media following, particularly on Twitter (later X). The platform's official account posted daily market highlights, interesting price movements, and educational content about how prediction markets worked.

More importantly, organic communities emerged. Traders posted screenshots of successful predictions, shared analysis of market movements, and debated the meaning of odds changes. Hashtags like #Polymarket and #PredictionMarkets became aggregation points for discussion.

Some traders became micro-celebrities, building followings by consistently sharing good analysis or making bold, accurate predictions. Their reputations, earned through a track record of being right gave them influence in market discussions.

The "Degen" Subculture

A subset of users embraced the "degen" (degenerate gambler) label with ironic self-awareness. They made wild, longshot bets on highly unlikely outcomes, celebrated lucky wins, and shared stories of spectacular losses.

This subculture was somewhat at odds with Polymarket's positioning as a serious information aggregation tool. Company leadership was ambivalent about it, the entertainment value and social media engagement helped growth, but the gambling associations risked undermining mainstream credibility.

The tension reflected broader questions about what Polymarket was: A serious financial market for information discovery? A form of entertainment and gambling? Both? Neither? The answer varied depending on who was using it and why.

Developers and Technical Contributors

Polymarket's open API and blockchain transparency enabled a developer ecosystem that extended the platform's capabilities.

Trading Bots and Automation

Developers built sophisticated trading systems on top of Polymarket's infrastructure:

- **Arbitrage bots** that exploited price differences between related markets
- **Momentum trading algorithms** that detected significant price movements and followed trends
- **Mean reversion systems** that bet against extreme price movements
- **News-triggered trading** that automatically placed orders based on specific keywords or events in news feeds

These bots were controversial. They improved market efficiency by quickly correcting misprices, but they also meant that retail users were competing against automated systems with faster reaction times and more sophisticated analysis.

Analytics Dashboards

Several developers built third-party websites that analyzed Polymarket data in ways the official platform didn't:

- Historical price charts with technical indicators
- Portfolio tracking tools showing profit/loss across all positions
- Market comparison tools showing odds across multiple prediction platforms
- Alert systems notifying users of significant price movements

These tools filled gaps in Polymarket's native interface and attracted users who wanted more sophisticated analytical capabilities.

Data APIs and Research Tools

Some developers created services specifically for researchers and institutions:

- Clean data exports of historical market prices
- Statistical analysis tools for measuring market calibration
- Integration plugins allowing Polymarket data to flow into standard analytics platforms like Jupyter notebooks or R

This infrastructure made Polymarket more valuable to academics and institutional users who needed reliable, well-formatted data for their work.

The Ethereum and Polygon Communities

Polymarket's blockchain foundation connected it to broader cryptocurrency communities, particularly Ethereum and Polygon.

Polygon's Showcase Application

Polygon, the layer-2 scaling solution where Polymarket operated, featured the platform prominently as a showcase for what could be built on its infrastructure. Polymarket demonstrated that blockchain could support real-world applications with genuine utility beyond speculative token trading.

This relationship was mutually beneficial. Polygon provided Polymarket with fast, low-cost transactions essential for a high-frequency trading platform. Polymarket provided Polygon with a high-profile success story that attracted other developers to build on the network.

DeFi Integration

Polymarket connected to the broader decentralized finance (DeFi) ecosystem in various ways:

- Users could earn yield on USDC holdings in DeFi protocols, then deploy that capital to Polymarket
- Some traders used DeFi lending platforms to leverage their Polymarket positions
- Arbitrage opportunities existed between Polymarket and other DeFi prediction protocols

These integrations made Polymarket part of the larger DeFi landscape rather than an isolated application.

The Network Effects: Why the Ecosystem Mattered

The strength of Polymarket's ecosystem created powerful network effects that made the platform increasingly dominant:

Liquidity Attracts Liquidity: Professional market makers and large traders were attracted by existing liquidity, and their participation increased liquidity further, creating a virtuous cycle.

Data Drives Discovery: As more analysts and researchers used Polymarket data, they publicized the platform's insights, attracting new users and generating more data.

Tools Lower Barriers: Third-party tools and educational content made Polymarket more accessible, bringing in users who might have found the native platform intimidating.

Credibility Compounds: Each accurate prediction increased credibility, which attracted media coverage, which brought new users, which improved market quality, which led to more accurate predictions.

Community Reinforces Culture: A strong community culture attracted like-minded users and repelled those who didn't fit, creating coherent norms that supported the platform's mission.

These network effects meant that competing prediction market platforms faced enormous challenges. Even if they built better technology or offered superior features, they would struggle to match Polymarket's liquidity, community, and ecosystem of third-party services. The platform had achieved escape velocity.

The Dark Side: Manipulation and Abuse

Not every ecosystem participant contributed positively. The same openness and permissionlessness that enabled innovation also created opportunities for manipulation and abuse.

Wash Trading Concerns

Some observers suspected that certain accounts engaged in wash trading, buying and selling shares to themselves to create the appearance of volume and move prices. This was difficult to prove definitively because blockchain pseudonymity obscured connections between wallets, but suspicious patterns existed.

The motivation for wash trading varied: manipulating prices to influence media narratives, creating the appearance of market liquidity, or simply trying to trigger other traders' algorithms to follow perceived trends.

Pump and Dump Schemes

In low-liquidity markets, coordinated groups could artificially move prices. They would collectively buy shares in a longshot outcome, driving the price up, then sell to later arrivals attracted by the movement. This was classic pump-and-dump behavior adapted to prediction markets.

Information Asymmetry Exploitation

Some traders had structural advantages that bordered on unfairness. Political operatives with inside knowledge of campaign strategies could trade on information not available to others. Journalists with advanced knowledge of stories they would publish could front-run market reactions. The line between informational edge and insider trading was murky.

Polymarket had limited tools to prevent these abuses. The platform could monitor for obvious manipulation patterns and suspend accounts, but sophisticated bad actors could obscure their activities. The tension between maintaining permissionless access and preventing abuse had no perfect solution.

Looking Forward: The Ecosystem as Competitive Moat

By the end of 2023, Polymarket's ecosystem had become its greatest strategic asset, a competitive moat that would be nearly impossible for rivals to replicate.

Building technology was hard but achievable. Any competent team could create a prediction market platform with similar features. But building an ecosystem, the whales, market makers, analysts, developers, media relationships, community culture, and institutional credibility required years of organic growth that couldn't be manufactured or copied.

This ecosystem would prove crucial during the 2024 election cycle, when Polymarket's accuracy would thrust the platform into mainstream consciousness. The infrastructure was already in place: the liquidity to handle enormous trading volume, the analysts to interpret market signals, the media relationships to amplify Polymarket's forecasts, and the community to defend the platform's credibility.

Shayne Coplan hadn't just built a product. He had catalyzed an ecosystem that was now largely self-sustaining and self-reinforcing. That ecosystem, more than any specific feature or technical innovation, was why Polymarket would dominate prediction markets for the foreseeable future.

It was also why the platform would attract such intense scrutiny, both legitimate regulatory oversight and, some would argue, politically motivated investigation after its triumph in forecasting the 2024 election. When you build something powerful enough to challenge established institutions' monopoly on forecasting and narrative-setting, those institutions push back.

The ecosystem had made Polymarket powerful. Soon, that power would be tested.

Chapter 13

Technology and Innovation

The beauty of Polymarket's technology was that most users never thought about it. They saw markets, clicked buttons, placed trades, and received payouts. The complexity happening beneath that simple interface, the blockchain transactions, smart contract executions, oracle resolutions, and automated market making algorithms remained invisible.

This invisibility was intentional and difficult to achieve. Shayne Coplan and his engineering team had spent years solving problems that most users would never know existed. Every millisecond of latency removed, every edge case handled, every potential vulnerability patched represented countless hours of work that manifested only in the absence of problems.

Understanding Polymarket's technical innovation requires looking beyond the user interface to the infrastructure that made prediction markets work at scale. This was where the company's true competitive advantage lived—not in marketing or community building, but in solving hard technical problems that kept markets liquid, secure, and reliable even during the highest-stakes moments.

The Blockchain Architecture: Why Polygon?

Polymarket's most fundamental technical decision was building on the Polygon blockchain rather than Ethereum mainnet or creating a proprietary system.

The choice of Polygon, a layer-2 scaling solution for Ethereum was driven by practical constraints. Prediction markets required high transaction throughput at low cost. Users needed to place orders, update positions, and settle markets without paying prohibitive fees or waiting minutes for confirmations.

Ethereum mainnet couldn't support this. During peak usage periods in 2020-2021, Ethereum transaction fees regularly exceeded $50, sometimes reaching over $100 for complex smart contract interactions. Confirmation times could stretch to several minutes or longer when the network was congested. For a prediction market platform where users might trade frequently based on breaking news, these limitations were fatal.

Polygon solved these problems through a proof-of-stake sidechain that processed transactions off the main Ethereum chain while maintaining security guarantees through periodic checkpoints back to Ethereum. This architecture enabled:

- **Transaction costs under $0.01**: Low enough to be negligible for most trades
- **Confirmation times of 2-3 seconds**: Fast enough to feel instantaneous
- **Throughput of thousands of transactions per second**: Sufficient for peak trading periods
- **Ethereum security**: Assets could be bridged back to Ethereum mainnet if needed

The Polygon choice also connected Polymarket to the broader Ethereum ecosystem. Users could bridge USDC stablecoins from Ethereum to Polygon easily. Developers familiar with Ethereum could build on Polymarket without learning new tools. And the platform benefited from Ethereum's established security auditing practices and developer resources.

The Technical Tradeoffs

Building on Polygon rather than a fully independent blockchain meant accepting certain limitations. Polymarket inherited Polygon's technical constraints and governance decisions. If Polygon experienced downtime or technical issues, Polymarket would be affected. The platform also paid some level of rent to the Polygon ecosystem through gas fees and dependency on Polygon's infrastructure.

But the benefits outweighed these tradeoffs. Time-to-market was faster because the core blockchain infrastructure already existed. Security was stronger because Polygon had been battle-tested. And integration with the cryptocurrency ecosystem was seamless because users already had wallets and stablecoins compatible with the platform.

By 2023, the Polygon choice looked prescient. Other prediction market platforms that had built on Ethereum mainnet or on alternative blockchains struggled with higher costs, slower transactions, or fragmented liquidity. Polymarket's technical foundation supported its growth when competitors' infrastructure held them back.

Smart Contract Design: The Market Mechanics

At the heart of Polymarket's technology were the smart contracts that created, maintained, and resolved prediction markets.

Binary Outcome Markets

Most Polymarket markets were binary, they had exactly two outcomes (Yes or No). This simplicity was elegant but required careful technical design.

Each market was represented by a smart contract that held USDC collateral and minted two complementary tokens: YES and NO. If you bought one YES token for $0.65, you were betting the event would occur. Someone else simultaneously bought the corresponding NO token for $0.35. Together, YES + NO always equaled $1.00.

When the market resolved, one token type paid out $1.00 and the other became worthless. If the event occurred, YES tokens paid out. If it didn't, NO tokens paid out. The smart contract handled this automatically, no human intervention required.

This design had several advantages:

- **Balanced liquidity**: Every buyer of YES tokens created corresponding NO tokens for others to buy
- **Clear probability signals:** The price of YES tokens represented the market's probability estimate (65% in the example above)
- **Automatic settlement:** Smart contracts enforced payouts with no counterparty risk
- **Composability**: YES and NO tokens could be traded, transferred, or used in other DeFi protocols

The AMM Implementation

Polymarket implemented automated market maker (AMM) pools similar to those pioneered by Uniswap and other decentralized exchanges. These pools provided continuous liquidity without requiring manual market making.

The AMM algorithm used a constant product formula adjusted for binary outcomes. As users bought YES tokens, the price of YES tokens increased and NO tokens decreased, maintaining the relationship that YES + NO = $1.00. The exact pricing formula incorporated fees and slippage calculations to ensure liquidity providers earned returns.

This meant users could always trade, there was always liquidity available from the AMM, even if no other human traders were active. The price might be worse for large orders (due to slippage), but the market never completely dried up.

Order Book Integration

Alongside AMM pools, Polymarket implemented a traditional order book where users could place limit orders: "I'll buy 1000 YES tokens at $0.60" or "I'll sell 500 NO tokens at $0.42."

This hybrid approach, AMM for continuous liquidity, order book for precise price execution gave Polymarket advantages over purely AMM-based systems. Sophisticated traders could place limit orders and avoid slippage, while casual users could trade instantly against AMM pools.

The technical challenge was integrating these two systems seamlessly. When should trades execute against the order book versus the AMM? How should the systems interact to maintain consistent pricing? Polymarket's engineers built matching logic that optimized execution across both sources of liquidity.

The Oracle Problem: Resolving Markets with Truth

The hardest technical problem in prediction markets is oracle resolution: determining what actually happened and settling markets accordingly.

This sounds simple but is actually profoundly difficult. Who decides whether an event occurred? What if there's disagreement about outcomes? How do you prevent manipulation or bias in resolution decisions?

Polymarket's Resolution System

Polymarket used a multi-tiered resolution process:

1. **Automated Resolution (when possible):** For some markets, outcomes could be determined automatically from verifiable data sources. If a market asked "Will Bitcoin close above $50,000 on December 31?", the platform could query price APIs and resolve automatically.

2. **UMA Protocol Integration:** For most markets, Polymarket integrated with UMA Protocol, a decentralized oracle system. When a market needed resolution, UMA's mechanism allowed token holders to propose outcomes. Other participants could

dispute proposals by putting up bonds. If disputed, the question went to a wider vote among UMA token holders.

3. **Internal Review**: Polymarket's team provided an additional review layer for particularly sensitive or high-stakes resolutions. This centralized component was controversial but pragmatic—for markets involving millions of dollars, multiple verification sources were essential.

The resolution criteria were specified in advance when markets were created. "Donald Trump wins the 2024 presidential election" required a specific definition: What counted as winning? Did electoral college votes determine the outcome, or official certification, or something else? Clear resolution rules prevented disputes.

Edge Cases and Controversies

Despite careful design, resolution controversies occasionally emerged:

- Markets that became impossible to resolve due to ambiguous outcomes
- Events that technically occurred but not in the way market creators anticipated
- Disputes about interpretation of resolution criteria
- Time zone and timing ambiguities for markets with specific deadlines

Each controversy required judgment calls that could never satisfy everyone. Polymarket developed extensive documentation and precedent to guide resolution, but edge cases continued to arise.

The technical challenge was building systems that handled both the straightforward 99% of cases and the contentious 1% that generated user complaints and potential legal liability.

Scaling Infrastructure: Handling Peak Load

The 2022 midterm elections provided Polymarket's first real test of infrastructure scalability. The platform needed to handle:

- 100x normal trading volume in concentrated time periods
- Thousands of simultaneous users placing orders
- Rapid market price updates propagating to all clients
- Database queries for portfolio values and market data
- API requests from third-party applications and bots

The Architecture Evolution

Polymarket's infrastructure evolved significantly from its early days:

Frontend: The user interface was built as a React application that ran in users' browsers. This client-side architecture offloaded rendering and computation to users' devices rather than Polymarket's servers. State management used Redux to efficiently handle complex trading data.

Backend: A Node.js backend provided APIs for market data, user authentication, and order placement. This layer abstracted away blockchain complexity, users didn't need to understand smart contracts or gas fees to trade.

Database: PostgreSQL databases stored market metadata, order book state, and user information. The team implemented extensive caching layers (Redis) to reduce database load during traffic spikes.

Blockchain Interface: Custom services monitored Polygon blockchain state, indexed contract events, and submitted transactions. These services handled the translation between Polymarket's internal representation and blockchain reality.

CDN and Caching: Static assets and market data were served through content delivery networks with aggressive caching policies. This meant most data requests never hit Polymarket's servers.

Load Balancing: Multiple redundant servers behind load balancers ensured no single point of failure. If one server crashed, traffic automatically routed to others.

The Election Night Test

On election night 2022, Polymarket's infrastructure performed flawlessly. Peak traffic exceeded projections by 3x, but response times remained under 200 milliseconds for most requests. No outages occurred. Trading continued uninterrupted as results came in.

This success required months of preparation: load testing, performance profiling, database optimization, and infrastructure provisioning. The engineering team had identified bottlenecks and eliminated them systematically.

The smooth election night performance built confidence internally and externally. Polymarket could handle the big moments when they mattered most.

Security: Protecting Assets and Data

Running a platform where millions of dollars in user funds were at stake meant security had to be paramount.

Smart Contract Security

Polymarket's smart contracts underwent multiple professional security audits by firms like Trail of Bits and OpenZeppelin. These audits examined the code for vulnerabilities that could allow:

- Theft of user funds
- Market manipulation through contract exploits
- Unauthorized market resolution
- Denial of service attacks

The audit process was iterative. Auditors would identify potential issues, engineers would fix them, and auditors would verify the fixes. Critical contracts were audited multiple times as the code evolved.

Beyond formal audits, Polymarket offered bug bounties, rewards for security researchers who found and reported vulnerabilities. Serious bugs could earn rewards of $50,000 or more, creating incentives for white-hat hackers to help secure the platform.

Operational Security

Smart contract security was necessary but not sufficient. The team also needed to secure:

- Private keys controlling critical contracts
- Database access credentials
- API keys for external services
- Employee accounts and permissions

Polymarket implemented multi-signature wallets for contract upgrades and fund management. This meant multiple team members had to approve critical actions, preventing any single compromised account from catastrophically affecting the platform.

The company also used hardware security modules, encrypted backups, and rigorous access control policies. Employees underwent security training and followed best practices for password management and two-factor authentication.

User Security

On the user side, Polymarket leveraged cryptocurrency wallet security. Users controlled their own private keys through wallets like MetaMask or WalletConnect. Polymarket never held user funds directly, they remained in user-controlled wallets until trades executed.

This non-custodial approach reduced Polymarket's security burden and regulatory exposure. The company couldn't lose or steal user funds because it never held them. But it also meant users bore responsibility for securing their own wallets and private keys.

The Incident That Never Happened

By late 2023, Polymarket had never experienced a major security breach or hack, a remarkable achievement in the cryptocurrency space where exploits are common. The company's cautious, security-first approach had prevented the kind of catastrophic failure that destroyed other platforms.

This clean security record became a competitive advantage. Users trusted Polymarket with substantial funds because the platform had proven it could protect them.

Performance Optimization: Milliseconds Matter

In prediction markets, speed can be the difference between profit and loss. When news breaks, traders race to update positions before prices adjust. Polymarket's technical team obsessed over latency, optimizing every step of the execution pipeline.

Frontend Performance

The user interface was aggressively optimized:

- Code splitting ensured users only downloaded JavaScript needed for features they used
- Images were compressed and served in modern formats like WebP
- Critical rendering paths were optimized so content appeared as fast as possible
- Prefetching loaded likely next pages before users clicked

These optimizations meant the interface felt instant and responsive even on slower devices and connections.

API Latency

Backend services were tuned for minimal latency:

- Database queries were optimized with proper indexing and query structure
- Caching eliminated repeated computation for frequently accessed data
- Connection pooling reduced overhead of database connections
- Asynchronous processing handled slow operations without blocking fast ones

The engineering team monitored latency continuously, setting up alerts for any degradation. The p99 latency, the time within which 99% of requests completed was tracked as carefully as average latency.

Blockchain Interaction

Submitting transactions to the blockchain and waiting for confirmations was often the slowest part of trading. Polymarket optimized this through:

- Gas price optimization to ensure fast confirmation without overpaying
- Nonce management to submit multiple transactions without conflicts
- Websocket connections for instant notification of transaction confirmations
- Transaction batching where possible to reduce on-chain overhead

The goal was making blockchain-based trading feel as fast as traditional web applications. Users shouldn't feel they're waiting for blockchain confirmations, transactions should appear instant.

Data Infrastructure: The Knowledge Engine

Beyond trading infrastructure, Polymarket built sophisticated data systems that made the platform more valuable to researchers, media, and institutional users.

Historical Data

Every trade, every price change, every market creation was permanently recorded. This historical data enabled:

- Backtesting trading strategies
- Analyzing market accuracy over time
- Academic research on prediction market efficiency
- Regulatory compliance and audit trails

The challenge was storing, indexing, and querying this data efficiently. Polymarket built custom indexing systems that made historical queries fast even across years of data.

Analytics Pipeline

Real-time analytics aggregated trading data to provide insights:

- Volume by market category
- User growth and retention metrics
- Market accuracy measurements
- Liquidity depth and spread analysis

These analytics informed product decisions and helped identify issues before they became critical.

API Design

The public API gave external developers access to Polymarket data. The API needed to be:

- **Fast:** Response times under 100ms for most queries
- **Reliable:** 99.9% uptime even during peak usage
- **Well-documented:** Clear documentation with examples
- **Rate-limited:** Protection against abuse without hindering legitimate use

A well-designed API extended Polymarket's reach by enabling third-party tools and integrations.

Innovation: What's Next

By late 2023, Polymarket's technical team was exploring several innovation frontiers:

AI Integration: Could machine learning models help identify mispriced markets, detect manipulation attempts, or improve resolution accuracy? Early experiments showed promise.

Cross-chain Expansion: While Polygon worked well, could Polymarket expand to other blockchains to access different user bases and liquidity pools?

Advanced Market Types: Beyond binary markets, could the platform support more complex structures like multi-outcome markets, conditional markets, or continuous futures-style contracts?

Institutional Infrastructure: Professional trading firms wanted deeper integration, FIX protocol support, more sophisticated order types, better risk management tools. Building this infrastructure could open institutional adoption.

Mobile Optimization: The mobile apps worked, but could they be dramatically better? Could mobile-first design unlock new user segments?

These innovations would have to wait until after the 2024 election. For now, the focus was ensuring existing infrastructure could handle the biggest prediction market event in history without failure.

The Technical Foundation of Success

Technology alone doesn't make a successful company, but it's necessary. Polymarket's technical excellence, the reliability, security, performance, and scalability of its infrastructure enabled everything else.

The whales and market makers could only provide liquidity because the platform's technology supported high-frequency trading at low cost. Media organizations could only integrate Polymarket data because the APIs were reliable and well-documented. The community could only trust the platform because security had been proven through years without major incidents.

Shayne Coplan understood that in prediction markets, trust was everything. Users needed to trust that markets would resolve fairly, that funds were secure, that the platform would work during critical moments. Building that trust required technical excellence, not marketing slogans.

By late 2023, Polymarket's technical foundation was as solid as any cryptocurrency platform in existence. The infrastructure was ready. The security was proven. The performance was optimized.

Now it just needed to work flawlessly during the most watched election in American history, with billions of dollars in trading volume, millions of users watching in real-time, and the entire world paying attention.

No pressure.

PART V: THE 2024 ELECTION

Chapter 14

The Most Consequential Market

The market opened on November 8, 2023, exactly one year before the 2024 presidential election. The question was simple: "Who will win the 2024 U.S. presidential election?"

Within hours, over $1 million had been wagered. Within days, it was $10 million. By the summer of 2024, this single market would surpass $1 billion in total trading volume, making it the largest prediction market in history. By election day, the number would exceed $3.6 billion.

This was the market Polymarket had been building toward since its founding. Every technical improvement, every relationship with media organizations, every lesson learned from previous elections, all of it had been preparation for this moment. The 2024 presidential election market would either cement Polymarket's position as essential infrastructure for understanding American politics or expose the platform as overhyped speculation with no real forecasting value.

There was no middle ground.

Setting Up the Infrastructure: Preparing for the Deluge

Shayne Coplan knew the 2024 election market would be different in scale and scrutiny from anything Polymarket had handled before. The 2022 midterms had been a test. The presidential race would be the Super Bowl, World Cup, and Olympics combined.

Planning began in late 2023. The engineering team modeled traffic scenarios based on previous elections, then multiplied by conservative factors of 5-10x to account for Polymarket's growth and increased mainstream awareness. They provisioned server capacity that seemed excessive, knowing that election night would push every system to its limits.

But infrastructure was only part of the challenge. The team also needed to consider:

Market Structure and Rules

The main presidential election market was binary: one candidate would win, the other would lose. But defining "win" precisely was essential. The market resolution criteria specified:

"This market will resolve to 'Yes' for the candidate who wins the majority of Electoral College votes as certified by Congress in January 2025. In the event of any disputes, contingencies, or extraordinary circumstances, resolution will follow the candidate who is officially inaugurated as President on January 20, 2025."

These detailed criteria prevented ambiguity. The 2000 Bush v. Gore situation, with its contested Florida recount and Supreme Court intervention, showed why precision mattered. If 2024 produced similar controversy and there were reasons to think it might—Polymarket needed ironclad resolution rules.

Related Markets

Beyond the main presidential winner market, Polymarket created dozens of related markets:

- Individual state outcomes (Pennsylvania, Georgia, Arizona, Wisconsin, Michigan, Nevada, North Carolina)
- Popular vote winner
- Electoral college vote totals
- Timing of result certainty ("Will the winner be known by November 10?")
- Specific scenarios ("Will there be a contested result?", "Will Trump concede if he loses?")

This constellation of markets served multiple purposes. It provided trading opportunities beyond the main event. It allowed more granular analysis, you could trade on specific swing state outcomes rather than just the overall winner. And it created arbitrage relationships that improved price discovery across all markets.

If Pennsylvania markets showed Trump with 65% odds but the main election market showed him with only 55% odds, sophisticated traders could exploit this discrepancy. This arbitrage activity helped keep all related markets aligned with each other.

Handling Nomination Uncertainty

In early 2024, there was still technical uncertainty about who the nominees would be. Joe Biden and Donald Trump were overwhelming favorites, but neither had been officially nominated. Polymarket created separate markets for "Who will be the Republican nominee?" and "Who will be the Democratic nominee?" that would resolve at their respective conventions.

This created some complexity. The general election market had to account for scenarios where different candidates might emerge. Biden's age and health generated persistent speculation about whether he would actually be the nominee. On the Republican side, Trump's legal troubles created a small but non-zero probability of him being unable to run.

The technical challenge was structuring markets so that unusual scenarios could be handled without creating chaos or unfair outcomes for traders who had positioned early.

Early Betting Patterns: What the First Bets Revealed

The initial trading patterns in the 2024 presidential market revealed fascinating dynamics about how prediction markets work and who participates in them.

The Opening Prices

When the market opened in November 2023, initial prices showed:

- Joe Biden: 52%
- Donald Trump: 38%
- Other candidates: 10%

These odds reflected several factors. Biden was the incumbent president, which historically conferred advantages. Trump faced multiple legal indictments that created uncertainty about his viability. And there was always some probability of unexpected candidates emerging or extraordinary events changing the landscape.

But these opening prices immediately attracted controversy. Biden's approval ratings were underwater, below 45% in most polls. Economic sentiment was negative despite strong employment numbers. Historical patterns suggested the incumbent party was vulnerable.

Why, then, was Biden the favorite?

The "Incumbent Premium" Debate

Prediction markets and betting odds have historically given incumbents higher probabilities than seem justified by polling or fundamentals. This pattern, called the "incumbent premium" had been documented in previous cycles.

Some argued this reflected genuine information: incumbents had advantages (name recognition, fundraising, party machinery) that polls underestimated. Others believed it was behavioral bias: bettors and traders had a status quo bias that led them to overweight the current president's chances.

For Polymarket specifically, there was another factor: the "smart money" narrative. Early traders on prediction markets tended to be sophisticated, analytical users who believed they had informational advantages. These traders might have believed that Biden's structural advantages outweighed his polling disadvantages.

Or they might have simply been wrong, exhibiting the same overconfidence that affects all traders.

The First Major Price Movements

Through late 2023 and early 2024, prices fluctuated based on polls, primary results, and news events:

- When Trump won the Iowa caucus decisively in January 2024, his odds jumped from 38% to 44%
- When Biden showed confusion in several public appearances, his odds dropped to 48%
- When Trump's legal cases proceeded to trial, his odds became more volatile
- When economic data showed persistent inflation, Biden's odds declined further

Each movement was accompanied by trading volume spikes as participants updated their positions based on new information. The market was doing exactly what prediction markets are supposed to do: aggregating distributed information and continuously updating probabilities as reality evolved.

The Billion-Dollar Milestone: When It Became Real

On May 15, 2024, total trading volume in the presidential election market crossed $1 billion. This milestone made international news.

The New York Times ran an article: "Prediction Market Surpasses $1 Billion in Presidential Betting." Bloomberg covered it as a finance story: "Polymarket Becomes Largest Political Prediction Market Ever." Even mainstream outlets that typically ignored prediction markets took notice.

The billion-dollar number was symbolic but significant. It represented:

- **Liquidity**: With that much capital deployed, market prices became harder to manipulate and more likely to reflect genuine consensus
- **Attention**: Mainstream awareness of prediction markets reached new highs
- **Stakes**: Participants had real money invested, creating strong incentives for accuracy
- **Validation**: The market was important enough that serious money was treating it seriously

For Shayne and the Polymarket team, the milestone was vindicating but also unnerving. They had built infrastructure for a high-stakes event, and now the stakes were higher than anyone had imagined. If something went wrong, if markets were manipulated, if resolution was controversial, if technical systems failed the consequences would be severe.

Who Was Betting?

The question of who exactly was placing these billion-dollar bets was murky. Polymarket didn't collect extensive user identity data, and blockchain transactions were pseudonymous. But some patterns were clear:

- **American political operatives** were definitely participating, despite geographic restrictions. The sophistication of trading around insider political developments suggested people with direct campaign involvement.

- **International traders** formed a substantial portion of the user base, particularly Europeans interested in U.S. politics and traders in regions without time zone disadvantages.
- **Cryptocurrency whales** who had made fortunes in crypto were deploying capital into prediction markets as another form of speculation and information advantage.
- **Hedge funds and institutions** were participating, either directly or through proxies, treating political prediction markets as alternative investments uncorrelated with traditional assets.
- **Retail traders** from around the world who saw political betting as more interesting than sports betting and believed they could profit from superior analysis.

The geographic distribution remained intentionally opaque. Polymarket reported that users came from dozens of countries, with strong representation in Europe, Asia, and Latin America. The company carefully avoided making claims about U.S. user participation, pointing to its geoblocking technology while acknowledging that determined users could circumvent restrictions.

The Summer Dynamics: Biden, Trump, and Uncertainty

The summer of 2024 brought unprecedented volatility to the presidential market.

The Biden Crisis: June-July 2024

On June 27, 2024, Joe Biden and Donald Trump met for their first presidential debate. Biden's performance was widely perceived as disastrous. He appeared confused, lost his train of thought multiple times, and struggled to articulate coherent responses.

Polymarket's reaction was immediate. Within hours of the debate ending, Biden's odds had crashed from 48% to 35%. Trading volume surged to record levels as participants rushed to update positions. The market was screaming: this changed everything.

Traditional political analysts were slower to react. Many initially downplayed the debate's significance, arguing that debates rarely moved elections. But Polymarket's prices told a different story, traders believed Biden's viability as a candidate had been seriously damaged.

Over the following days, as polling data confirmed the market's instant read, political commentators began acknowledging the severity of Biden's debate performance. Some credited Polymarket with seeing the truth faster than pundits who were invested in their prior narratives.

The Pressure to Withdraw

Through July, Biden's odds continued to deteriorate. Democratic party insiders began publicly calling for him to withdraw from the race. Polymarket created a new market: "Will Joe Biden be the Democratic nominee?"

This market became more actively traded than the main presidential election market for a brief period. Prices fluctuated wildly based on insider reports, statements from Democratic leaders, and Biden's own public appearances. At various points, the market gave Biden anywhere from 40% to 75% chance of remaining the nominee, massive uncertainty reflecting the genuine chaos within the Democratic party.

Traders who positioned themselves correctly during this period, betting that Biden would eventually withdraw made substantial profits when he announced on July 21, 2024, that he would not seek reelection and endorsed Kamala Harris as his replacement.

The Harris Surge

Kamala Harris's entry into the race created a new set of prediction market dynamics. New markets opened: "Will Kamala Harris be the Democratic nominee?" (answered quickly when she secured party support), "Harris vs. Trump winner?", and various Electoral College scenarios with Harris as the candidate.

Initial Harris odds were surprisingly strong. Despite concerns about her past performance as vice president and her unsuccessful 2020 presidential campaign, prediction markets opened with Harris at 44% to win the general election versus Trump's 52%.

This confounded some observers. How could Harris be nearly even with Trump when Biden, with all the advantages of incumbency had been trailing significantly? Various explanations emerged:

- Relief that Democrats had a candidate who could campaign effectively
- Underestimation of how much Biden's age had been dragging down Democratic chances
- Hope that a fresh candidate could change the race's dynamics
- Genuine uncertainty about how Harris would perform in the campaign

The market spent the next several months testing these propositions against reality.

Polymarket vs. Traditional Polls: The Divergence

As the race between Harris and Trump developed through August and September, a significant gap emerged between prediction market odds and traditional polling averages.

The Polling Consensus

Major polling aggregators like FiveThirtyEight and RealClearPolitics showed a tight race, with Harris holding a small lead of 1-3 percentage points nationally. Battleground state polls were within margin of error across the board. The consensus forecast gave Harris approximately 52-56% chance of winning, a modest but clear advantage.

Polymarket's Different Story

Polymarket told a different story. By September 2024, Trump's odds had climbed to 55% versus Harris's 45%. By October, Trump reached 58-60%, even as polls remained stable showing Harris with a slight lead.

This divergence created intense debate:

The Pro-Polymarket Argument: Prediction markets were incorporating information that polls missed, enthusiasm gaps, turnout models, on-the-ground campaign insights. Traders with money at stake were more accurate than pollsters using outdated methodologies. Remember 2016, when polls missed Trump's victory? Polymarket wouldn't make that mistake.

The Pro-Polling Argument: Polymarket was being skewed by whale traders or politically motivated betting. Polls had actually improved their methodologies since 2016. The prediction market odds reflected crypto-trader demographics (young, male, libertarian-leaning) rather than genuine electoral analysis. Polymarket was due for an embarrassing failure.

Media coverage increasingly focused on this divergence. Articles compared the two forecasting methods, interviewed pollsters and prediction market advocates, and debated which would prove correct.

For Polymarket, this attention was both an opportunity and a risk. If the platform's odds proved more accurate than polls, it would achieve unprecedented credibility. If polls were right and Polymarket was wrong, years of reputation-building would be damaged in a single night.

The International Dimension: A Global Market on American Politics

One of the most fascinating aspects of the 2024 presidential market was its international character. This wasn't just Americans betting on their own election, it was the world betting on American politics.

European traders were particularly active. Many Europeans followed American politics closely and believed they could profit from analysis unconstrained by American partisan bias. They also had more experience with political betting, which was legal and established in many European countries.

Asian traders, particularly in crypto hubs like Singapore and Hong Kong, treated the election market as another form of speculation in their diversified trading portfolios. Some ran sophisticated models incorporating polling data, economic indicators, and social media sentiment.

Latin American users, dealing with their own political volatility, found American prediction markets relatively straightforward and liquid compared to thin markets in their own countries.

This international participation raised interesting questions: Was it appropriate for global users to speculate on American elections? Did international betting affect perceptions of candidate viability? Should Americans be concerned that foreign actors might try to manipulate markets to influence election narratives?

These questions had no simple answers, but they highlighted how prediction markets existed in a different space than traditional forecasting, more global, more financial, less constrained by national boundaries.

The Media Integration: Prediction Markets Go Mainstream

By fall 2024, major media organizations had integrated Polymarket odds into their standard election coverage. This represented a dramatic shift in how prediction markets were perceived.

The New York Times' election dashboard showed Polymarket odds alongside polling averages and the Times' own forecast model. CNN displayed prediction market prices during election coverage. Even outlets that had previously dismissed prediction markets as glorified gambling now cited them as one source of information among many.

This mainstream integration was what Polymarket had been working toward, legitimacy as a forecasting tool, not just a curiosity for political junkies and crypto enthusiasts. But it also created pressure. With mainstream media citing Polymarket odds, the platform's accuracy would be judged by a much broader audience than ever before.

The Reflexivity Problem

One concern was reflexivity, the possibility that media coverage of prediction market odds could influence the reality those markets were trying to predict. If major news outlets constantly reported that Trump was the favorite according to Polymarket, would that narrative become self-fulfilling? Would donors and volunteers become demoralized? Would voters' perceptions of momentum shift?

This wasn't just theoretical. Political scientists had documented that perceptions of candidate viability affected fundraising, volunteer enthusiasm, and even voting behavior. If prediction markets were shaping those perceptions, they weren't just forecasting reality, they were potentially creating it.

Polymarket's position was that markets aggregated information, they didn't create it. If traders believed Trump was likely to win, that belief was based on underlying factors (polls, fundamentals, campaign dynamics), not on Polymarket odds themselves. The market was the messenger, not the message.

Critics weren't entirely convinced, but the debate was largely theoretical. By late October 2024, as election day approached, the question wasn't whether prediction markets mattered, everyone agreed they did. The question was whether they would be right.

The Final Weeks: Maximum Tension

As November approached, trading volume reached extraordinary levels. Days with $100 million in trading volume became routine. The market had achieved incredible liquidity, spreads were often just 1-2 cents between buy and sell prices, comparable to major stock markets.

The final prediction market odds going into election day would become historical data points, cited for years regardless of the outcome. If Trump won and Polymarket had him at 60%, the platform would be vindicated as seeing what polls missed. If Harris won and Polymarket had Trump ahead, explanations would be needed.

For Shayne Coplan and everyone at Polymarket, the pressure was immense. Four years of work had built toward this moment. The technology was ready. The markets were liquid. The world was watching.

On November 5, 2024, Americans would vote. And Polymarket's most consequential market would finally resolve.

The platform had one job: get it right.

Chapter 15

Election Night

November 5, 2024 6:00 PM EST

Shayne Coplan sat in Polymarket's office in Manhattan, surrounded by monitors displaying market prices, trading volume, news feeds, and server metrics. The engineering team had assembled in person for the first time in months, this was too important for anyone to watch from home.

Outside, Americans were still voting. Polls hadn't yet closed in most states. But inside Polymarket's office and on trading screens around the world, the action had already begun. Trading volume was spiking to levels that dwarfed even the most optimistic projections.

In the previous 24 hours alone, over $200 million had traded on the presidential election market. In the next twelve hours, that number would more than double. By the time all votes were counted, election night would see nearly half a billion dollars in trading volume, the single largest day in prediction market history.

The final odds before polls closed showed:

- Donald Trump: 62%
- Kamala Harris: 38%

Polymarket had made its call. Trump was the favorite, and not by a small margin. The platform had diverged significantly from polling averages, which showed a dead heat. Within hours, the world would know whether prediction markets had seen something polls missed, or whether Polymarket's biggest moment would become its biggest embarrassment.

7:00 PM: The First Results and Initial Volatility

The first polls closed at 7:00 PM Eastern in states like Georgia, Virginia, and Florida. These early results would set the tone for the evening.

Networks called Virginia for Harris quickly, no surprise, as the state had trended Democratic. But the vote margins were the story. If Harris was underperforming expectations even in states she was winning, it would signal a difficult night ahead.

7:15 PM

Early returns from Georgia showed Trump performing better than expected in rural counties. Nothing definitive yet, cities and suburbs would report later but the initial numbers were encouraging for Trump.

Polymarket's odds barely moved. Trump's probability inched up from 62% to 63%. The market had already priced in a Trump victory in Georgia; these early returns were just confirming existing expectations.

Trading volume, however, was extraordinary. Every tiny shift in the odds represented millions of dollars changing hands. Traders were frantically updating positions based on incoming data, trying to stay ahead of the market's collective interpretation.

7:45 PM

Florida returns started coming in, and Trump was overperforming. Miami-Dade County which Biden had won in 2020 was showing major swings toward Trump. The Latino vote had shifted dramatically.

Television commentators were cautious. "It's early," they repeated. "We need to see more data." "Urban areas haven't reported yet."

Polymarket had no such hesitation. Trump's odds jumped to 68%.

This was where prediction markets showed their advantage. Rather than waiting for enough data to make confident pronouncements, the market was continuously incorporating all available information and updating probabilities in real-time. Traders weren't making binary calls, they were adjusting probability distributions microsecond by microsecond.

8:00 PM: The Eastern Seaboard and Growing Certainty

At 8:00 PM, polls closed across much of the Eastern seaboard: Pennsylvania, Michigan, Wisconsin, Arizona, and much of the South.

These were the battleground states that would decide the election. If Harris could hold the "blue wall" of Pennsylvania, Michigan, and Wisconsin, she would likely win. If Trump broke through in even one of those states, his path to victory widened dramatically.

8:12 PM

Pennsylvania returns began flowing in. Early vote tallies, which included many mail-in ballots that had been pre-processed, showed Harris with a lead, as expected. Democrats had dominated early and mail voting.

But the margins were concerning for Harris. In Philadelphia and its suburbs, she was running behind Biden's 2020 numbers. Not by much a few percentage points but in a close race, a few points was everything.

Polymarket noticed instantly. Trump's odds climbed to 72%.

On television, analysts were still talking about how much ground Trump needed to make up as same-day votes came in. The conventional wisdom was that Trump would need overwhelming margins on election day to overcome Harris's early vote lead.

But Polymarket's traders, many of whom had built sophisticated models incorporating vote timing, geographic patterns, and historical comparisons, were calculating that Trump's election day performance would be more than sufficient. The early numbers were telling them Harris was doomed in Pennsylvania.

8:35 PM

North Carolina was called for Trump. This was expected but important. Harris had invested heavily in the state, hoping to expand the map. Her failure to flip North Carolina meant she had no margin for error in the Midwest battlegrounds.

Trump's odds: 76%.

9:00 PM: The Blue Wall Cracks

The hour between 9:00 and 10:00 PM would effectively decide the election, though major news networks wouldn't call it for hours.

9:08 PM

Georgia's returns were now comprehensive enough for Polymarket traders to reach a consensus. Trump was going to win the state. Rural turnout was high, suburban swings toward Democrats were modest, and Atlanta wasn't delivering the overwhelming margins Harris needed.

Trump's odds: 81%.

Major networks hadn't called Georgia yet. They would wait for more votes to be counted, for mathematical certainty. But prediction markets don't wait for certainty; they trade on probability, and the probability was clear.

9:23 PM

Pennsylvania data was becoming increasingly decisive. Trump was massively overperforming in rural areas. Small towns that had gone for

Trump in 2020 by 20 points were going for him by 30 points. The enthusiasm gap was real and measurable.

More troubling for Harris: suburban Philadelphia wasn't delivering the margins she needed. Bucks County, Montgomery County, Chester County, these were places where Democrats had made gains in recent years. Harris was winning them, but not by enough to offset Trump's rural dominance.

Sophisticated traders on Polymarket were running the math. With 40% of the expected vote in, they could project the final margin within reasonable confidence intervals. Unless something dramatic changed in the remaining votes and there was no reason to expect it, Trump would win Pennsylvania by 2-3 points.

Trump's odds: 87%.

This was the moment when Polymarket's election night became historic. The platform was declaring, with 87% confidence at 9:23 PM, that Donald Trump would be the next president of the United States. Television networks were still treating the race as undecided. Polling experts were explaining how Harris still had multiple paths to victory. But Polymarket had seen enough.

9:40 PM

Wisconsin data was reinforcing Pennsylvania's story. Trump was overperforming in rural areas, matching his performance in cities, and keeping suburban losses manageable. Wisconsin was going to be close, maybe decided by tens of thousands of votes but it was going to Trump.

Trump's odds: 91%.

At 91%, the election was essentially over in Polymarket's judgment. Harris would need a miracle, a massive underperformance by Trump in yet-to-report areas, polling errors that somehow systematically benefited her rather than him, a dramatic shift in late-counted ballots. These scenarios were possible but extremely unlikely.

10:00 PM: The Traditional Media Catches Up

By 10:00 PM, what Polymarket had been saying for over an hour was becoming conventional wisdom on television.

The New York Times' election needle, which had famously captured Trump's rising fortunes in 2016 swung decisively toward Trump. FiveThirtyEight's live forecast moved Trump to an 85% chance of winning. CNN's John King, standing at his electoral map, was explaining how Pennsylvania's remaining vote wasn't enough for Harris.

Polymarket's odds were now at 93%, having peaked at 95% a few minutes earlier. The market had gotten there first, an hour or more before traditional media reached the same conclusion.

The Social Media Reaction

Twitter (X) exploded with commentary about Polymarket's performance. Screenshots of the platform's odds throughout the evening went viral. Graphs showing Polymarket calling the election decisively while pundits were still hedging became memes.

"Polymarket knew at 9:00 PM" became a common refrain. Whether this was entirely fair, the odds had been building all evening, not a single moment of revelation didn't matter. The narrative was set: prediction markets had outperformed traditional media and polling.

Some users posted comparisons:

- 9:23 PM - Polymarket: Trump 87%, CNN: "Too early to call"
- 9:45 PM - Polymarket: Trump 91%, NYT: "Toss-up"
- 10:15 PM - Polymarket: Trump 93%, Networks: Finally acknowledging Trump's likely victory

The contrast was stark and, for prediction market advocates, vindicating.

11:00 PM - 1:00 AM: The Remaining Drama

Even as Trump's victory became clear, several sources of uncertainty remained that kept markets active.

The Popular Vote

One market that stayed volatile was "Will the winner also win the popular vote?" Trump was clearly winning the Electoral College, but the popular vote was closer. California's massive Democratic margins would take hours to fully count.

This market swung wildly as national vote totals updated. At various points, it suggested Trump might win the popular vote for the first time, a historic outcome. Eventually, it settled on Harris winning the popular vote by a small margin, though much closer than Biden's 2020 margin.

The Senate and House

Prediction markets on Congressional races remained active. Republicans were clearly winning the Senate, with victories in Ohio and Montana flipping Democratic seats. The House was closer, with California races that wouldn't be decided for days.

These downstream markets showed how prediction market ecosystems worked. Traders who had profited on the presidential race were deploying those winnings into Congressional races, creating liquidity and price discovery even in smaller markets.

Individual State Margins

Markets on exact Electoral College vote counts and state victory margins continued trading. Even knowing Trump won Pennsylvania, there was still money to be made predicting whether he'd win by 1-2 points or 2-3 points.

This granularity, the ability to trade on increasingly specific outcomes as information accumulated was something prediction markets did uniquely well.

2:00 AM: Trump's Victory Speech and Market Resolution

At approximately 2:30 AM Eastern time, Donald Trump appeared before supporters in Florida to claim victory. Kamala Harris did not concede, her campaign said she would speak the following day but the outcome was no longer in doubt.

Trump had won Pennsylvania, Georgia, Wisconsin, and likely Michigan and Arizona (though those were still being counted). He would have well over the 270 Electoral College votes needed for victory.

Polymarket's odds stood at 97%. The market wouldn't fully resolve until official results were certified in January 2025, but the outcome was clear. Donald Trump would be the 47th President of the United States.

The Winners and Losers

Traders who had positioned themselves correctly made extraordinary profits. Those who had bought Trump shares when he was at 38% (after Biden's strong polling in early 2024) and held through the volatility earned

160% returns. Those who had bet heavily on Trump in the final weeks, when he moved from 50% to 62%, still earned solid 60% returns.

The losers were those who had trusted polling averages showing a dead heat and bought Harris shares at 45-50 cents in the days before the election. They lost their entire stake as Harris shares became worthless.

The French trader who had made enormous bets on Trump positions so large they had generated media coverage appeared to have made over $20 million. His early, aggressive positioning on Trump had seemed reckless to many. Now it looked brilliant, though questions remained about whether he had genuine informational advantages or had simply made a calculated gamble that paid off.

The Morning After: Analysis and Vindication

November 6, 2024, brought a flood of analysis about both the election and Polymarket's performance.

The Accuracy Assessment

Polymarket had called the election correctly and had done so earlier than traditional media. But had the platform's specific odds been accurate?

The main market had shown Trump at 62% going into election day. He won decisively, with a clear Electoral College majority. In retrospect, 62% seemed well-calibrated, it indicated Trump was favored but not certain, which matched the reality of a race that could have gone differently with small shifts in turnout or sentiment.

Some individual state markets were less accurate. Polymarket had given Trump 55% odds in Wisconsin; he won it by less than 1%. That margin suggested the race was closer to 50-50, not 55-45. But perfect calibration across all markets was impossible, overall the accuracy was impressive.

The "Polymarket Called It" Narrative

Media coverage of Polymarket after the election was overwhelmingly positive. Headlines like:

- "Prediction Markets Beat Polls Again" (Wall Street Journal)
- "How Polymarket Saw Trump's Victory Coming" (Bloomberg)
- "The Rise of Prediction Market Forecasting" (The Economist)
- "Polymarket's Moment: When Betting Markets Outperformed Traditional Forecasting" (New York Times)

This coverage represented a fundamental shift in how prediction markets were perceived. They were no longer fringe curiosities or controversial gambling platforms. They were forecasting tools that had proven their value when it mattered most.

The Polling Industry's Reckoning

Traditional pollsters faced difficult questions. How had they shown a dead heat when Trump won decisively? The answer involved multiple factors:

- Persistent underestimation of Trump's support (the "shy Trump voter" phenomenon)
- Turnout models that overestimated Democratic enthusiasm
- Difficulty reaching certain voter demographics
- Response bias in who agreed to participate in polls

But whatever the explanations, the fact remained: polls had been wrong in a systematic direction, showing the race much closer than it was. Polymarket's markets, aggregating information from traders with money at stake, had been more accurate.

This raised fundamental questions about the future of election forecasting. Would political campaigns and media organizations continue to rely primarily on polling? Or would prediction markets become the dominant forecasting tool?

The Technical Performance: Infrastructure Under Pressure

While the world focused on Polymarket's forecasting accuracy, the technical team was celebrating a different achievement: the infrastructure had performed flawlessly.

Election night had brought:

- Over 400 million page views
- Nearly $500 million in trading volume
- Hundreds of thousands of simultaneous users
- Millions of API requests from third-party applications

Not a single significant outage occurred. Response times remained under 200 milliseconds for most requests throughout the night. The blockchain infrastructure handled the transaction load without slowdowns.

This technical success was as important as the forecasting accuracy. If Polymarket's systems had crashed during election night, if traders couldn't access markets or place orders during crucial moments the reputational damage would have been severe regardless of the platform's predictive accuracy.

The engineering team's months of preparation, load testing, and infrastructure investment had paid off. Polymarket had proven it could handle the biggest moments without failure.

The Significance: A Turning Point for Prediction Markets

Election night 2024 would be remembered as the moment prediction markets came of age. For years, advocates had argued that markets aggregated information better than polls or expert forecasts. Skeptics had dismissed them as niche tools with no advantage over traditional methods.

November 5, 2024, settled the debate. Polymarket had called the election earlier and more confidently than traditional forecasters. The platform's prices throughout the evening had provided better real-time information than television analysts. And the final outcome had validated the market's odds.

This validation would have far-reaching consequences. Political campaigns would pay closer attention to prediction markets in future cycles. Media organizations would integrate market odds more prominently into coverage. Institutional investors would view political prediction markets as legitimate sources of information.

For Shayne Coplan, election night was the culmination of four years of work. He had built a platform that mattered, that provided value, that had proven itself on the biggest stage possible. At 26 years old, he had created something that would change how America and the world understood political forecasting.

But triumph and controversy are often intertwined. Polymarket's success had made it visible, important, and powerful. Within a week, that power would attract attention from those who questioned whether prediction markets should have so much influence and whether Polymarket had operated within legal boundaries to achieve its success.

The raid was coming. But on the morning of November 6, 2024, with Trump's victory confirmed and Polymarket's accuracy vindicated, Shayne Coplan allowed himself a moment of satisfaction.

They had gotten it right when it mattered most.

Everything that came after, the investigations, the controversies, the questions about whether success had been worth the cost would wait for another day.

Chapter 16

Legitimacy and Vindication

The week after the 2024 election was unlike anything Polymarket had experienced. The platform that had operated largely in the shadows of cryptocurrency and betting market subcultures suddenly found itself at the center of mainstream political and media discourse.

Shayne Coplan's inbox overflowed with interview requests from publications that had never before covered prediction markets. Cable news bookers wanted him on air. Think tanks invited him to speak about the future of forecasting. Venture capitalists who had passed on earlier funding rounds were suddenly interested in investing. Even academics who had dismissed prediction markets as theoretically interesting but practically limited were reaching out to discuss collaboration.

The vindication was intoxicating. For years, Polymarket had been fighting for legitimacy against skeptics who viewed it as glorified gambling, regulators who saw it as a compliance problem, and traditional forecasters who dismissed it as a curiosity with no edge over established methods. November 5, 2024, had silenced many of those critics. Polymarket had been right when polls were wrong, fast when media was slow, and confident when experts were hedging.

But legitimacy is a complicated thing. It opens doors, but it also invites scrutiny. Success makes you important enough to matter and important enough to regulate, investigate, and potentially prosecute.

The Media Coronation

The first wave of post-election coverage treated Polymarket like a breakthrough innovation that had suddenly proven itself.

The New York Times, November 7, 2024, ran a front-page story: "How Prediction Markets Called the Election Before the Networks." The article was remarkably positive for a publication that had historically been skeptical of betting markets in politics. It detailed Polymarket's election night performance, interviewed traders who had profited from correct predictions, and quoted political scientists acknowledging that prediction markets had outperformed traditional polling.

The Times article did include caveats, noting regulatory concerns, questions about who was trading on the platform, and warnings against overstating any single forecasting success. But the overall tone was one of impressed acknowledgment. Polymarket had done something noteworthy, and the newspaper of record was treating it as legitimate news.

The Wall Street Journal took a more business-focused angle: "The Billion-Dollar Bet That Paid Off: Inside Polymarket's Election Triumph." The Journal emphasized the platform's technical sophistication, the professional traders who used it, and the institutional interest in prediction market data. For a financial publication, Polymarket wasn't a gambling curiosity, it was a new asset class and information market worth taking seriously.

Bloomberg published multiple pieces analyzing the trading patterns, the market efficiency, and the implications for financial markets. One article explored whether prediction markets might eventually be used for corporate earnings forecasts, merger probabilities, or Federal Reserve policy decisions. If markets could predict elections accurately, what else could they predict?

Even outlets that had never covered prediction markets felt compelled to address Polymarket's success. **CNN** featured a segment examining why the platform had been more accurate than the network's own analysts. **The Economist** devoted its cover story to "The Rise of Prediction Markets," using Polymarket as the central case study. **Politico** ran a piece titled "The Platform That Beat the Polls," interviewing campaign operatives who admitted they had been checking Polymarket odds despite the platform's quasi-legal status for American users.

The breadth of coverage was unprecedented. Polymarket wasn't being covered as a niche technology story or a gambling controversy, it was being treated as an important development in how societies process information and predict the future.

The Academic Validation

While media attention was gratifying, academic recognition carried a different kind of weight. Scholars had been studying prediction markets for decades, debating their efficiency, accuracy, and social value. Polymarket's election night performance gave them concrete data to analyze.

The Retrospective Studies

Within days of the election, several research teams began comprehensive analyses of Polymarket's accuracy. These weren't casual op-eds but serious quantitative studies that would eventually be published in peer-reviewed journals.

One team at the University of Chicago compared Polymarket's odds throughout election night against traditional forecasting models, betting markets in other countries, and real-time polling. Their preliminary findings showed that Polymarket had not only called the election correctly but had done so with well-calibrated probabilities. Events that the market priced at 70% likely had occurred approximately 70% of the time when looking across multiple races and scenarios.

Another study from MIT examined the speed of information incorporation. How quickly did Polymarket update its odds when new data (vote counts, exit polls, county results) became available? The research found that Polymarket typically adjusted within 30-60 seconds of new information becoming public, faster than television analysis, faster than polling expert updates, and certainly faster than traditional academic forecasting models could be recalculated.

A team at Stanford studied the volume-weighted order flow, examining whether price movements were driven by informed traders with genuine information or by momentum-following noise traders. Their analysis suggested that large, persistent price movements corresponded with actual electoral reality, indicating that informed traders dominated the market during crucial moments.

These studies mattered because they addressed the fundamental question skeptics had always raised: were prediction markets actually efficient, or were they just another form of speculation dressed up in economics jargon? The 2024 election data suggested the former, markets really did aggregate dispersed information effectively.

The Forecasting Method Debate

The election also reignited debates about optimal forecasting methods. Traditional polling had missed the election's outcome, showing a dead heat when Trump won decisively. Polling aggregation sites like FiveThirtyEight and RealClearPolitics had been similarly wrong.

But some academic forecasters, those who had built models incorporating economic fundamentals, historical patterns, and structural factors had actually predicted Trump's victory. The question became: was Polymarket better than all alternatives, or just better than polls?

This debate played out in academic journals, conference presentations, and public symposia. The emerging consensus was nuanced: prediction markets weren't magic, but they had advantages over polling in certain contexts:

- **Continuous updating:** Markets incorporated new information constantly, while polls were intermittent snapshots
- **Skin in the game:** Traders risked real money, creating stronger incentives for accuracy than poll respondents
- **Aggregation mechanism:** Markets synthesized diverse information sources rather than relying on single methodologies
- **Revealed preferences:** Trading behavior revealed genuine beliefs better than survey responses

But markets also had limitations: they could be manipulated, might reflect trader demographics rather than electoral reality, and required liquidity to function effectively. The conclusion wasn't that prediction markets should replace all other forecasting methods, it was that they should be taken seriously as one valuable tool among several.

Political Campaigns Take Notice

Perhaps the most consequential outcome of Polymarket's election night success was that political professionals began treating prediction markets as essential intelligence.

The 2028 Campaign Calculus

Even before Trump's inauguration, operatives planning for the 2028 presidential race were discussing how prediction markets would factor into their strategies. Several implications were clear:

Early Warning System: Prediction markets provided continuous feedback about campaign health. If a candidate's odds were declining despite stable polls, it might indicate problems not yet reflected in public data, fundraising difficulties, volunteer enthusiasm dropping, opposition research landing with elites who traded on prediction markets.

Messaging Testing: While campaigns couldn't officially use prediction markets to test messages (that might constitute market manipulation), they could observe how market odds responded to different campaign narratives, debate performances, or policy announcements. A candidate's odds rose after a major speech suggested the message had landed effectively.

Resource Allocation: Prediction markets on individual states could guide where campaigns allocated resources. If market odds suggested a state was truly competitive when polls showed it leaning one direction, campaigns might adjust their media buys, volunteer deployment, or candidate travel schedules.

Opposition Research Timing: Sophisticated campaigns could use market movements to detect when damaging information was circulating among informed traders before it became public. A candidate's odds suddenly dropping without obvious public cause might indicate that traders knew something journalists would report soon.

Debate Preparation: Real-time prediction market odds during debates provided instant feedback about performance. Campaigns could see which moments moved odds favorably or unfavorably, informing future messaging and strategy.

None of this was publicly acknowledged, campaigns were wary of seeming to treat elections as betting markets. But privately, operatives were clear: ignoring prediction markets in 2028 would be campaign malpractice.

The Regulatory Question

The political attention to prediction markets also raised uncomfortable questions. If campaigns were using market data for strategic decisions, and if those campaigns had inside information about candidate health, strategy, or opposition research, could campaign insiders profit from trading on that information?

This was essentially insider trading applied to political prediction markets. The same ethical and legal concerns that prevented corporate executives from trading on material non-public information might apply to political operatives trading on non-public campaign information.

Some legal scholars argued that existing insider trading laws didn't apply to prediction markets on political events, these weren't securities, and political information wasn't covered by securities fraud statutes. Others contended that using prediction markets to profit from campaign inside information was ethically problematic even if not technically illegal.

The question remained unresolved, but it highlighted how Polymarket's success had created regulatory gray areas that lawmakers and regulators would eventually need to address.

Institutional Adoption: The Financial World Pays Attention

Beyond politics, Polymarket's vindication attracted interest from financial institutions looking for alternative data sources and new forecasting tools.

Hedge Funds and Asset Managers

Several quantitative hedge funds began exploring how to incorporate prediction market data into their trading models. Political outcomes affected financial markets significantly, elections determined tax policy, regulatory approaches, trade relationships, and government spending priorities. Better political forecasting could translate into better financial forecasting.

Some funds considered direct participation in prediction markets as an investment strategy. If markets were occasionally mispriced, informed traders could profit from correcting those mispricings. The returns might be uncorrelated with traditional assets, providing valuable diversification.

Other institutions focused on using prediction market data as signals for traditional asset trading. If prediction markets suggested a particular election outcome was becoming more likely, how should equity portfolios, currency positions, or commodity exposures adjust in anticipation?

Risk Management Applications

Beyond speculation, some financial institutions explored using prediction markets for risk management. Banks could hedge regulatory risk by taking positions on prediction markets about policy changes. Multinational corporations could use political prediction markets to hedge geopolitical risk.

This wasn't theoretical, some firms began implementing these strategies. A multinational corporation with significant operations in multiple countries could use prediction markets on foreign elections to hedge against adverse political outcomes that might affect their business.

The Data Product Opportunity

Several financial data vendors began offering Polymarket data as a premium product. Bloomberg terminals could display prediction market odds alongside stock prices and economic indicators. Specialized political risk data services integrated prediction market prices into their assessments.

This commercialization represented another form of legitimacy. When professional data vendors treat your information as valuable enough to package and sell to institutional clients, you've moved from niche curiosity to established infrastructure.

The Counternarratives: Skeptics and Critics

Not everyone was convinced by Polymarket's election night performance. Several critiques emerged that complicated the simple "prediction markets work" narrative.

The Single Election Problem

Statisticians pointed out that accurately predicting one election doesn't prove general forecasting superiority. Elections are unique events; you can't run the 2024 election multiple times to test whether Polymarket's 62% Trump odds were truly well-calibrated.

Maybe Polymarket had simply gotten lucky. Maybe the platform's odds had been too confident in Trump, but Trump had happened to win anyway. One data point doesn't establish a pattern.

This critique was technically valid but unsatisfying. Yes, rigorous calibration testing required many predictions to evaluate. But Polymarket had made thousands of predictions across multiple elections and markets. The overall track record, examined comprehensively, was strong. The 2024 presidential race was just the highest-profile example.

The Whale Influence Concern

Critics noted that large traders, whales, had substantial influence on market prices. The French trader who had placed enormous bets on Trump had moved market odds through sheer position size. If wealthy individuals could shift probabilities through large trades, were markets really aggregating wisdom of crowds, or just reflecting opinions of the rich?

This concern was legitimate but nuanced. Whale influence only persisted if other traders couldn't or wouldn't take the other side. If a whale artificially inflated Trump's odds above their true probability, informed traders should have sold Trump shares, profiting from the mispricing and correcting prices in the process.

The fact that Trump's elevated odds proved accurate suggested that whales weren't distorting markets, they were either informed traders with genuine edge or lucky speculators whose bets happened to align with reality.

The Manipulation Allegations

Some commentators argued that Polymarket markets could be deliberately manipulated to create false narratives about candidate viability. A well-funded actor might buy Trump shares not to profit from prediction accuracy but to create the impression of momentum, influencing media coverage and voter perceptions.

This concern was theoretical but difficult to prove or disprove. Market manipulation is notoriously hard to detect, especially in pseudonymous cryptocurrency markets. If manipulation had occurred, the manipulators had either been unsuccessful (since Trump won, manipulation to inflate his odds would have been accurate rather than misleading) or had succeeded in ways that were indistinguishable from informed trading.

The Gambling Normalization Worry

A different category of criticism focused not on prediction accuracy but on social effects. Some commentators worried that Polymarket's success would normalize gambling on elections, treating democratic processes as entertainment and speculation rather than civic participation.

This critique raised philosophical questions about the appropriate relationship between democracy and markets. Should elections be bet on? Did financial stakes in outcomes create perverse incentives? Might prediction markets attract problem gamblers and create social harm?

These concerns couldn't be dismissed simply by pointing to forecasting accuracy. Even if prediction markets worked well technically, they might have negative social consequences that outweighed their informational benefits.

The Valuation Spike: Polymarket as Investment Target

The week after the election, venture capital interest in Polymarket surged. The company had been quietly raising a Series B funding round before the election. Afterward, the terms changed dramatically.

Pre-election, Polymarket had been valued at approximately $1.5 billion based on preliminary term sheet discussions. Post-election, VCs were discussing valuations of $2.5-3 billion or higher. Some investors who had passed on earlier rounds tried to re-enter at higher valuations.

The investment thesis was straightforward: Polymarket had proven its value proposition on the biggest stage possible. The platform was now positioned as essential infrastructure for political forecasting, with potential expansion into other prediction categories, business, finance, technology, entertainment, sports beyond what it already covered.

Moreover, the company's user growth and trading volume were accelerating post-election. November 2024 saw monthly trading volume exceed $1 billion for the first time. New user signups were at all-time highs. Media partnerships were expanding. The momentum was undeniable.

For Shayne Coplan, the valuation surge was validating but complicated. Higher valuations meant more resources to invest in the platform, but they also meant more pressure, more governance structure, and more scrutiny. The scrappy startup phase was ending. Polymarket was becoming a real company with real expectations.

Shayne's Moment: The Youngest Self-Made Billionaire

With Polymarket's valuation exceeding $2.5 billion and Shayne owning a substantial equity stake, he crossed into billionaire territory at age 26. This made him one of the youngest self-made billionaires in the world, comparable to founders like Mark Zuckerberg and Evan Spiegel at similar ages.

The billionaire designation brought its own form of attention. Forbes reached out for profile interviews. Business publications wrote "How He Did It" features. Crypto Twitter celebrated one of their own reaching elite status.

Shayne remained ambivalent about the attention. In interviews, he deflected from personal wealth to focus on Polymarket's mission. "This isn't about me becoming a billionaire," he said in one interview. "It's about building infrastructure that helps people understand reality better. The valuation is just a reflection of how much value prediction markets can create."

But the wealth was real and consequential. It gave Shayne financial security, influence in technology and political circles, and the resources to pursue Polymarket's vision at whatever scale made sense. It also made him a target for regulators concerned about his platform's influence, for critics worried about cryptocurrency enrichment, and eventually for federal investigators interested in how exactly Polymarket had become so successful.

The Brief Window: Success Without Consequences

The period from November 6 to November 13, 2024, one week exactly represented the peak of Polymarket's triumph unburdened by controversy.

During this week, Shayne Coplan experienced what every successful entrepreneur dreams of: recognition that years of work had produced something important. The media praised him. Investors competed to fund him. Users celebrated the platform. Even former skeptics acknowledged that prediction markets had proven their worth.

He appeared on podcasts and interviews, articulate and thoughtful, explaining how prediction markets worked and why they mattered. He was invited to exclusive dinners with political figures, technology leaders, and media executives. He received congratulations from people he had admired from afar when starting Polymarket years earlier.

It was a moment of pure vindication, uncomplicated by the controversies that would soon follow. Shayne had built something that worked, that mattered, that had changed how people understood political reality. He was 26 years old and had achieved more than most entrepreneurs accomplish in lifetimes.

He allowed himself to believe, briefly, that the regulatory challenges were behind him. The CFTC settlement was in the past. Polymarket was operating internationally with appropriate geographic restrictions. The platform had proven its social value. Surely success at this level would bring acceptance rather than additional scrutiny.

It was a reasonable belief, if naïve. Success doesn't end regulatory interest, it intensifies it. A small prediction market platform operating in gray areas could be overlooked. A platform that influenced election coverage and media narratives, that had made accurate predictions when establishment forecasters had failed, that had enriched its founders beyond measure, that platform would attract attention.

On the evening of November 12, 2024, Shayne Coplan went to sleep believing he had won. He had built something important, navigated regulatory challenges, and proven the value of prediction markets at the highest level.

The next morning, November 13, FBI agents arrived at his door.

The vindication was over. The investigation was beginning.

PART VI: THE FBI AND NEW CONTROVERSIES

Chapter 17

The Raid (November 13, 2024)

The knock came at 6:14 AM.

Shayne Coplan was still asleep in his Soho apartment when the sound jolted him awake. Not the casual knock of a delivery person or neighbor, this was authoritative, insistent, unmistakable in its official nature.

He pulled on clothes and walked to the door, disoriented and confused. Through the peephole, he saw several people in the hallway. Some wore FBI windbreakers. Others were in plain clothes but had the unmistakable bearing of federal law enforcement.

When he opened the door, they were already holding up badges and identification.

"Shayne Coplan?"

"Yes."

"FBI. We have a warrant to search these premises and seize electronic devices."

The agent extended a document, the search warrant, signed by a federal magistrate judge. Shayne's eyes scanned the legal language, trying to make sense of what was happening. Terms jumped out: "investigation into possible violations," "electronic devices and records," "Polymarket LLC operations."

"I don't understand," Shayne said. "What is this about?"

"We're conducting an investigation. We need to seize your phones, computers, and any other electronic devices. We'll also be conducting a search of the apartment."

The agents moved past him into the apartment without waiting for permission, the warrant gave them authority. Within minutes, Shayne's home was filled with federal investigators systematically going through his belongings.

The Search: Losing Control

Watching federal agents search your home is a peculiar form of violation. They're professional and methodical, not ransacking the place, but the intrusion is total. Privacy evaporates. Control disappears. You stand in your own apartment as a spectator while strangers inventory your life.

The agents focused on electronics. They bagged Shayne's iPhone, his MacBook Pro, his iPad, and an older laptop he used occasionally. They searched for external hard drives, USB sticks, or other storage devices. They photographed documents they found relevant to Polymarket's operations.

One agent asked questions while others searched:

"How many devices do you regularly use?"

"Do you have any computers or phones in other locations?"

"Have you destroyed or disposed of any electronic devices in the past six months?"

Shayne answered carefully, aware that lying to federal agents was itself a crime. He explained what devices he used, where they were, what they contained. He tried to understand what exactly was being investigated, but the agents were guarded.

"We can't discuss the details of an ongoing investigation," was the repeated answer.

The search lasted approximately ninety minutes. By 7:45 AM, the agents had collected what they needed: multiple phones, computers, tablets, and various documents. They provided Shayne with an inventory of seized items and a copy of the search warrant.

As they prepared to leave, the lead agent gave Shayne a business card.

"You should retain legal counsel. We'll be in touch if we need to speak with you further."

Then they were gone, leaving Shayne alone in his apartment, surrounded by the disruption of the search, trying to process what had just happened.

The First Calls: Assembling the Team

The first call Shayne made was to Polymarket's existing legal counsel, the attorneys who had handled the CFTC settlement and provided ongoing compliance advice. He reached one of the partners on his personal cell phone and explained what had happened.

The lawyer's response was immediate and unambiguous: "Don't speak to anyone about this. Don't post on social media. Don't discuss it with anyone at the company except me and the executive team. We need to bring in criminal defense attorneys immediately, this is beyond our scope."

The second call went to Polymarket's board. Shayne woke up investors and advisors with the news. The reaction was stunned silence followed by urgent questions. What exactly was being investigated? Had Shayne been arrested? Were other people being targeted?

The answers were mostly unknown. Shayne hadn't been arrested or charged with anything. The warrant mentioned an investigation but didn't specify the suspected crimes. Federal agents had taken his devices but hadn't indicated what they were looking for on them.

By mid-morning, Polymarket's legal team had expanded dramatically. The company retained a prominent white-collar criminal defense firm whose partners had extensive experience with federal investigations. These weren't the regulatory compliance attorneys who handled CFTC matters, these were former federal prosecutors who knew how DOJ investigations worked and how to navigate them.

The lead criminal defense attorney's advice was straightforward:

"We need to assume this is serious. The FBI doesn't execute search warrants on tech company founders over minor matters. They believe they have evidence of potential criminal violations. Our job is to understand what they're investigating, determine whether those allegations have merit, and develop an appropriate response strategy."

Theories and Speculation: What Was This About?

Without clear information about the investigation's focus, Shayne and his team were left to speculate about what federal investigators might be pursuing.

Theory One: CFTC Settlement Violations

The most obvious possibility was that investigators believed Polymarket had violated the terms of its 2022 CFTC settlement. That settlement had required the company to block U.S. users from accessing the platform. If the FBI had evidence that Polymarket had knowingly allowed or even facilitated U.S. user access, that could constitute criminal violations.

This theory made sense in some ways. Trading volume patterns suggested substantial U.S. user activity despite geo-blocking. If investigators had obtained user data, IP addresses, transaction patterns, communications they might have evidence that the company wasn't adequately enforcing restrictions.

But criminal prosecution for settlement violations seemed like an escalation. Typically, CFTC enforcement involved civil penalties, not criminal charges. Why would the DOJ get involved unless there was something more serious?

Theory Two: Market Manipulation

Another possibility was an investigation into market manipulation. If investigators believed that individuals or entities had artificially moved prediction market prices to influence public perception of election outcomes, that might constitute fraud or market manipulation.

The French trader who had placed enormous bets on Trump had attracted significant attention. If that trader had coordination with political campaigns or foreign entities, or if his trades were designed to manipulate narratives rather than profit from accurate predictions, that could be criminal.

But if manipulation was the focus, why raid Shayne's apartment specifically? Unless investigators believed Polymarket was complicit in or aware of manipulation schemes, the company's founder wouldn't be the primary target.

Theory Three: Illegal Gambling Operations

A third theory focused on gambling laws. Perhaps federal prosecutors had decided that Polymarket was operating an illegal gambling operation in violation of federal law. The Wire Act, the Unlawful Internet Gambling Enforcement Act, and various other statutes prohibited certain forms of online gambling.

Polymarket had always maintained it offered prediction markets, not gambling. But that distinction might not hold up under federal scrutiny. If prosecutors viewed the platform as essentially a sports betting or casino gambling operation dressed up in prediction market language, criminal charges could follow.

This theory was concerning because gambling prosecutions could be aggressive. Several online poker executives had faced criminal charges and even arrests when traveling to the United States, despite their operations being based overseas.

Theory Four: Foreign Influence or Election Interference

The most troubling theory was that investigators were examining whether Polymarket had been used for foreign election interference. If foreign nationals or governments had used the platform to influence American election narratives by manipulating market odds, that could trigger national security investigations.

The timing of the raid, one week after the election made this theory plausible. If investigators had been monitoring Polymarket's role in the election and had identified potential foreign influence operations, they might have moved quickly after the election concluded to preserve evidence.

This theory was frightening because it implied federal prosecutors might view Polymarket not as a forecasting tool but as a vector for election interference, a far more serious allegation with potential national security implications.

The Public Statement: Controlling the Narrative

By midday November 13, news of the FBI raid had leaked. Multiple reporters contacted Polymarket asking for comment. Social media was already buzzing with speculation.

Shayne and his legal team debated how to respond. Some options:

Say Nothing: Many lawyers recommend silence during investigations. Anything you say publicly can be used against you. The safest approach is often no comment whatsoever.

Minimal Statement: Acknowledge the raid without details, express confidence in the company's compliance, commit to cooperating with investigators.

Aggressive Pushback: Characterize the raid as government overreach, political retaliation for accurate election forecasting, an attack on innovation and free speech.

Detailed Defense: Explain Polymarket's compliance efforts, challenge the investigation's basis, make the case publicly that the company did nothing wrong.

After extensive discussion, they settled on a measured statement that acknowledged the situation without appearing defensive or combative:

> "We are aware that law enforcement has conducted an investigation involving Polymarket. We have not been informed of the specific basis for this investigation. Polymarket has always operated in good faith with regard to regulatory requirements and has cooperated fully with all previous regulatory inquiries. We are confident that our compliance efforts have been appropriate and look forward to resolving any questions investigators may have."

The statement was carefully worded to avoid admitting wrongdoing while not appearing hostile to investigators. It struck a tone of cooperative confidence rather than defiance or panic.

Shayne wanted to say more, to defend the company more vigorously, to characterize the raid as unwarranted but his lawyers were insistent. "The time for defending yourself is in court or negotiations with prosecutors, not in press releases," they said. "Anything aggressive you say publicly can be used as evidence of consciousness of guilt or obstruction."

The User Reaction: Community Response

Polymarket's user community reacted to news of the raid with a mixture of outrage, concern, and conspiracy theorizing.

On Twitter/X, many users characterized the raid as political retaliation. Polymarket had accurately predicted Trump's victory when establishment polls had shown a closer race. Some users suggested that Democratic operatives or deep state actors were punishing the platform for undermining their preferred narrative.

"They can't stand that Polymarket was right and they were wrong" was a common sentiment. "This is what happens when you challenge the establishment."

Others focused on regulatory overreach. "The government is terrified of prediction markets because they reveal the truth that politicians want to hide. This raid is about control, not law enforcement."

Cryptocurrency communities, which had always been sympathetic to Polymarket's permissionless approach, rallied around the platform. Many saw parallels to previous crypto enforcement actions that they viewed as government attacks on innovation. "First they came for the prediction markets..." became a common meme.

But not all reactions were supportive. Some users worried that the raid indicated genuine legal problems. If federal investigators had evidence of serious violations, knowingly facilitating illegal gambling, market manipulation, settlement violations the platform and its users could all face consequences.

A subset of users immediately began withdrawing funds from Polymarket, concerned that the platform might be shut down or that their assets could be frozen. This created some liquidity pressure on certain markets, though overall platform operations continued normally.

The Internal Response: Crisis Management

Inside Polymarket, the raid triggered immediate crisis protocols.

The executive team convened an emergency meeting to assess operational and legal risks. Key questions:

Operational Continuity: Could the platform continue operating during an investigation? Were there risks of additional law enforcement action that might disrupt service?

Employee Communication: What should employees be told? How could the company maintain morale and focus during the investigation?

User Communication: Beyond the public statement, what should users be told about platform safety and continuity?

Board and Investor Management: How should the company keep board members and investors informed? Were there disclosure obligations?

Legal Strategy: What steps were needed to cooperate with investigators while protecting the company's interests?

The technology team worked to ensure platform stability despite the turmoil. If users lost confidence and withdrew en masse, liquidity could evaporate and markets could break down. Maintaining normal operations during the crisis was essential.

The legal team began the laborious process of understanding exactly what investigators were pursuing. They reached out to the U.S. Attorney's

Office that had authorized the search warrant, seeking dialogue about the investigation's scope. Initial responses were minimal, prosecutors weren't ready to share details yet but the communication channels were opened.

Human resources worked to calm employee anxiety. Many team members were worried about their own legal exposure, about the company's future, about whether Polymarket could survive the investigation. Leadership emphasized that no employees were targets and that the company had resources to mount a vigorous defense.

The Media Narrative: From Triumph to Controversy

The media narrative around Polymarket shifted dramatically in a single day.

Just 24 hours earlier, headlines had celebrated the platform's forecasting success. Now, the story was entirely different:

"FBI Raids Polymarket Founder's Home in Federal Investigation" (New York Times)

"Prediction Market Platform Faces Criminal Investigation Days After Election" (Wall Street Journal)

"Polymarket's Triumph Short-Lived as Federal Agents Seize Founder's Devices" (Bloomberg)

Articles that had praised Polymarket's accuracy now included paragraphs about regulatory controversies, the CFTC settlement, and questions about U.S. user access. The shift in tone was whiplash-inducing.

Some coverage was measured and factual, reporting what was known about the raid without speculation. Other articles suggested various theories about the investigation's focus. A few commentators characterized the raid as evidence they had been right to be skeptical of prediction markets all along.

Political media added their own spin. Outlets sympathetic to Trump suggested the raid was politically motivated, the Biden administration retaliating against a platform that had accurately predicted Trump's victory. Publications critical of Trump speculated about foreign influence on the platform or manipulation by Trump allies.

The truth was nobody knew what the investigation was actually about, but that didn't stop extensive speculation and narrative construction.

Shayne's Long Night

That evening, alone in his apartment for the first time since the raid, Shayne tried to process what had happened.

One week ago, he had been on top of the world. Polymarket had vindicated prediction markets, proven skeptics wrong, and achieved mainstream legitimacy. He had become a billionaire at 26. The future had seemed limitless.

Now, federal investigators had seized his devices, were examining his communications, and were investigating him for crimes he didn't yet understand. Everything he had built was under threat. The legitimacy he had achieved was evaporating.

He replayed the morning's events obsessively. What had he said to the FBI agents? Had he answered their questions appropriately? What was on his seized devices that prosecutors would examine? Were there emails or messages that could be taken out of context and used against him?

The lawyers had assured him that early-stage investigations often didn't result in charges. Many federal investigations ended without prosecution.

The government might be looking at Polymarket as part of a broader inquiry that didn't focus on the company or its founder specifically.

But they had also been clear: this was serious. The FBI doesn't raid tech company founders' homes over trivial matters. Federal prosecutors wouldn't devote resources to investigating Polymarket unless they believed significant violations had occurred.

Shayne thought about the geo-blocking question, the ambiguous middle ground where Polymarket had implemented restrictions but knew they were circumventable. Had the company done enough? Had he personally done enough? The lawyers he had consulted in 2022 had said the measures were reasonable. But reasonable to lawyers and sufficient to prosecutors might be very different standards.

He thought about the growth that had followed the CFTC settlement, trading volume increasing, U.S. political markets remaining active, the unspoken reality that VPN usage was widespread. Had that growth been worth the risk? Should he have implemented more aggressive restrictions even if they hurt the product?

These questions had no good answers. The decisions had been made. The investigation was happening. All Shayne could do now was cooperate, let lawyers handle the legal strategy, and hope that whatever prosecutors were investigating would ultimately prove unwarranted.

But hope felt fragile against the machinery of federal law enforcement.

The Week After: Uncertainty and Waiting

The days following the raid settled into an uncomfortable rhythm of uncertainty.

Polymarket continued operating normally. Markets functioned, users traded, and the platform maintained stability. But everyone involved knew that normalcy was superficial. At any moment, investigators could take additional action, more raids, subpoenas for company documents, interviews of employees, perhaps even charges.

The legal team worked to understand the investigation's scope. They filed motions seeking return of seized property. They negotiated with prosecutors about potential cooperation agreements. They reviewed internal documents and communications, preparing for whatever investigators might find or request.

Shayne tried to maintain focus on running the company while living under the cloud of investigation. He attended meetings, made product decisions, and communicated with the team. But the raid had fundamentally changed his experience of success. The vindication of election night felt distant. The investigation dominated his attention.

Media coverage continued but evolved from breaking news to analysis and speculation. Some articles explored prediction market regulation comprehensively. Others examined specific theories about what prosecutors might be investigating. A few pieces were explicitly sympathetic to Polymarket, characterizing the raid as government overreach.

But sympathy in opinion pieces didn't matter if prosecutors decided to bring charges.

The question hanging over everything was simple but unanswerable: What came next? Would the investigation expand or contract? Would prosecutors seek cooperation or pursue charges? Would Polymarket survive the scrutiny or become another cautionary tale of startup hubris and regulatory miscalculation?

Shayne Coplan had built Polymarket to help people understand uncertainty, to put probabilities on future events and make the unknown knowable. Now he was living in radical uncertainty himself, with his future dependent on decisions made by prosecutors he couldn't influence and an investigation he couldn't control.

The irony wasn't lost on him. If Polymarket had a market on whether its founder would face criminal charges, he wondered what the odds would be. And whether he'd have the courage to check them.

Chapter 18

Theories and Allegations

The FBI doesn't raid apartments at six in the morning without reason. In the forty-eight hours following the seizure of Shayne Coplan's electronic devices, the internet exploded with speculation. What exactly had prompted federal agents to descend on the twenty-six-year-old billionaire's Soho residence just one week after Polymarket had arguably its greatest triumph? The official silence from both the FBI and the U.S. Attorney's office created a vacuum that conspiracy theories, political accusations, and legitimate legal concerns rushed to fill.

The timing alone invited scrutiny. November 13, 2024, marked exactly seven days since Donald Trump's decisive victory in the presidential election, an outcome that Polymarket had consistently predicted while traditional polls suggested a toss-up. The platform had processed over $3.6 billion in trading volume on the presidential race alone, dwarfing every other prediction market in history. Shayne had spent the previous week doing victory laps in the media, positioning Polymarket as the new gold standard for electoral forecasting. Now his phones and laptops sat in federal evidence bags.

The Official Investigation: What We Know

The immediate public statement from Polymarket's legal team was carefully calibrated. The company confirmed the raid, characterized it as related to the 2022 CFTC settlement, and expressed confidence that they had fully complied with all terms of that agreement. "Polymarket has implemented robust geofencing technology to prevent U.S.-based users from accessing the platform," the statement read. "We are confident that our compliance measures meet or exceed industry standards."

But that careful language raised more questions than it answered. If Polymarket's geo-blocking was so robust, why would the FBI raid Shayne's home two and a half years after the settlement? Federal investigators don't expend significant resources on open-and-shut compliance matters.

Something had triggered renewed interest, and understanding what that something might be required examining several distinct theories, each with its own evidence, proponents, and implications.

Theory One: The U.S. User Problem

The most straightforward explanation centered on the core requirement of the January 2022 CFTC settlement: Polymarket had agreed to block all U.S.-based users from accessing the platform. In exchange for a $1.4 million fine, a pittance compared to the company's eventual valuation, Shayne had promised to implement technical measures preventing American traders from participating in prediction markets that the CFTC deemed illegal event-based binary options.

From day one, skeptics questioned whether this restriction could be effectively enforced. Unlike traditional financial platforms that require extensive Know Your Customer documentation, cryptocurrency-based markets like Polymarket operated with relative anonymity. Users needed only a crypto wallet and enough USDC, a dollar-pegged stablecoin to start trading. The platform collected no Social Security numbers, no proof of residence, no bank account information that would definitively establish a user's physical location.

Polymarket's primary enforcement mechanism relied on IP address geolocation. When a user attempted to access the platform, the system checked their IP address against databases of known U.S. addresses and blocked any matches. But as anyone remotely familiar with internet privacy knows, IP addresses reveal only so much. Virtual Private Networks, or VPNs, allow users to mask their true location by routing their connection through servers in other countries. A trader in Manhattan could appear to be accessing the site from London, Toronto, or Singapore with just a few clicks.

The question wasn't whether Americans could access Polymarket—they clearly could. Screenshots of U.S.-based traders discussing their positions circulated freely on Twitter and Discord throughout 2023 and 2024. The real question was whether Polymarket had done enough to satisfy its legal obligations. The CFTC settlement hadn't required perfect enforcement, an impossible standard in the age of VPNs. It had required good-faith implementation of "reasonable measures" to prevent U.S. user access.

But what constitutes reasonable? Polymarket could have implemented more aggressive measures. Some platforms require phone number verification with SMS codes that are jurisdiction-specific. Others demand government-issued identification documents. The most stringent services employ sophisticated device fingerprinting technology that can identify users even when they mask their IP addresses, analyzing browser configurations, installed fonts, screen resolutions, and dozens of other data points to create unique profiles.

Polymarket had implemented none of these additional measures. The company's position, articulated in various forums by team members, was that imposing such requirements would fundamentally alter the platform's nature. Prediction markets derive their value from broad participation and the wisdom of crowds. Creating friction through extensive verification processes would reduce liquidity, discourage casual traders, and ultimately make markets less efficient and less accurate. In the delicate balance between compliance and functionality, Polymarket had chosen a particular equilibrium point.

Federal investigators may have concluded that balance tilted too far toward accessibility and not far enough toward genuine enforcement. If the FBI had identified substantial trading volume originating from U.S.-based users, perhaps through blockchain analysis, cooperation from VPN providers, or other investigative techniques it would constitute a clear violation of the settlement terms. Not a minor technical breach, but a fundamental failure to comply with the central requirement of the agreement.

The speculation intensified when analysts began examining Polymarket's user patterns. One widely-shared analysis posted to Twitter by a pseudonymous data scientist claimed that trading patterns on U.S. political markets showed suspicious correlations with American time zones. The analysis noted that volume consistently spiked during U.S. East Coast business hours and dropped precipitously during American overnight hours, patterns less pronounced in markets about European politics or Asian events. While not definitive proof, plenty of non-U.S. traders follow American politics closely and might trade during U.S. hours the patterns raised eyebrows.

Theory Two: Market Manipulation and Wash Trading

A second, more complex theory suggested that the FBI investigation focused less on user location and more on the integrity of Polymarket's markets themselves. Throughout 2024, questions had swirled about whether large traders were manipulating prices to create false narratives about election probabilities.

The concerns centered particularly on the so-called "French whale," a mysterious trader who had placed enormous bets on Trump's victory. Over several months, accounts apparently controlled by this individual or entity had wagered more than $30 million on Trump winning the presidency, along with substantial bets on Republicans winning the Senate and various other pro-Trump positions. The bets were large enough to move markets, pushing Trump's probability upward through sheer volume.

When the French newspaper Le Monde reported that the whale was a wealthy French trader using Polymarket data and mathematical models, not political intuition, to make calculated bets, it partially defused concerns about coordinated manipulation. But questions remained. Had these massive positions been legitimate attempts to profit from perceived market inefficiencies, or was something more nefarious at play?

One possibility: political operatives connected to the Trump campaign had used Polymarket to create the appearance of electoral strength, generating news coverage about "prediction markets favoring Trump" that could influence undecided voters or depress Democratic turnout. The theory held that by moving Polymarket prices, sophisticated actors could manufacture stories about momentum and inevitability. Every time Polymarket showed Trump with higher odds than polls suggested, conservative media amplified the message: the smart money knew Trump would win.

If federal investigators found evidence connecting major Polymarket positions to political campaigns, whether through financial flows, communications, or other links it could constitute potential violations of campaign finance law or fraud statutes. The FBI might be examining whether Polymarket had become, perhaps inadvertently, a tool for election interference through market manipulation.

Related concerns focused on wash trading, the practice of buying and selling assets to create artificial activity and misleading volume statistics. In traditional securities markets, wash trading is explicitly illegal. In the largely unregulated world of crypto prediction markets, the rules were murkier. Had traders been simultaneously taking offsetting positions to inflate volume numbers and generate publicity? If so, did Polymarket have systems to detect and prevent such activity? And had company executives, including Shayne, known about it?

The company had consistently maintained that its market design made large-scale manipulation difficult and economically irrational. Automated market makers meant that moving prices required putting real capital at risk. Unlike traditional stock markets where wash trading might be executed at neutral prices, moving a prediction market required actually buying shares at progressively worse prices as the market-making algorithm adjusted. Manipulation was theoretically possible but expensive, and successful manipulators would need to either convince others to follow their lead (not manipulation per se) or lose substantial money when markets resolved against their positions.

But theory and practice don't always align. Federal investigators might have uncovered evidence that Polymarket's safeguards were less robust than advertised, or that sophisticated actors had found ways to game the system that the company had failed to detect or address.

Theory Three: Political Retaliation

The most explosive theory, and the one that generated the most heated debate, was that the FBI raid represented political retaliation by the Biden administration against a platform that had embarrassed Democrats by correctly predicting Trump's victory.

Proponents of this theory pointed to the timing as too coincidental to ignore. The raid occurred exactly one week after the election, during the narrow window when the Biden administration still held power but Trump's victory was assured. If the goal was to intimidate Shayne or send a message to the crypto industry, this timing made strategic sense. Wait too long and Trump's inauguration would bring new leadership to the Justice Department less inclined to pursue the case. Act immediately, and critics could dismiss it as routine enforcement unrelated to political considerations.

The political retaliation theory gained traction in certain circles, particularly among crypto enthusiasts and Trump supporters who saw the raid as confirmation of their worldview about government overreach and

Democratic hostility to innovation. Shayne became, in this narrative, a martyr for free markets and decentralized truth-telling, punished for creating a platform that exposed the unreliability of mainstream polling and media narratives.

Several prominent figures amplified this interpretation. Elon Musk tweeted that the raid was "obviously political" and represented "the regime going after truth-tellers." Conservative media personalities described Shayne as a victim of the "deep state" targeting political enemies. Some crypto Twitter accounts circulated the hashtag #FreePolymarket, treating the investigation as a civil liberties issue rather than a regulatory matter.

The counter-argument held that this theory vastly overstated the coherence and vengefulness of government enforcement actions. FBI investigations typically take months or years to develop. Warrants require probable cause and judicial approval. The idea that the Biden White House had ordered the FBI to raid Shayne's apartment because Polymarket made Democrats look bad required believing in a level of direct political control over law enforcement that most legal experts considered implausible, if not impossible.

Moreover, the SDNY, the U.S. Attorney's office for the Southern District of New York, which would handle any prosecution had a reputation for independence from political pressure. While no federal office operates in a completely apolitical vacuum, SDNY prosecutors had built careers on pursuing both Democratic and Republican wrongdoing without apparent partisan bias.

Still, the political theory persisted because it tapped into broader narratives about crypto regulation and government hostility to decentralized systems. Whether or not the Biden administration had directly ordered action against Polymarket, crypto advocates argued that the regulatory state harbored ideological opposition to prediction markets and decentralized finance generally. The raid might not have been ordered by the White House, but it reflected a culture within regulatory agencies antagonistic to innovation that threatened traditional power structures.

Theory Four: Follow the Money

A fourth theory, discussed more quietly in financial and legal circles, suggested that the investigation might have less to do with Polymarket's operations and more to do with money laundering concerns or potential sanctions violations.

Cryptocurrency's pseudo-anonymous nature has long attracted scrutiny from law enforcement and financial regulators concerned about its use in illicit activities. Polymarket's use of blockchain technology and stablecoin-denominated trading made it theoretically possible for bad actors to move money across borders while evading traditional banking oversight. Had federal investigators identified suspicious patterns suggesting that organized crime, sanctioned entities, or terrorist organizations were using Polymarket to launder funds or circumvent financial restrictions?

This theory explained several puzzling aspects of the raid. If the investigation primarily concerned CFTC settlement compliance, investigators might have started with subpoenas and document requests rather than jumping straight to a raid. Raids typically happen when authorities worry about evidence destruction or when they need to secure information without alerting the subject first. Money laundering or sanctions investigations often warrant such aggressive tactics because of the serious national security implications and the sophistication of the actors involved.

Polymarket processed billions of dollars in trading volume, much of it from international sources. Did the company have adequate anti-money-laundering procedures? Were they properly screening users against sanctions lists? Had they implemented systems to detect suspicious transaction patterns? These were open questions. The company's focus on maintaining user privacy and reducing friction in the trading experience might have come at the cost of robust financial crime prevention measures.

The theory also explained why the FBI, rather than CFTC investigators, had executed the raid. Money laundering and sanctions violations fall under federal criminal law, within the FBI's core jurisdiction. While the CFTC has civil enforcement authority over its settlement agreements, criminal investigations require different agencies and different legal standards.

Theory Five: The Insider Trading Angle

A less discussed but potentially significant theory centered on insider trading concerns. Prediction markets, by their nature, aggregate information. But what if some of that information was non-public and material? What if traders with inside knowledge of election campaigns, corporate decisions, or other events were using Polymarket to profit from confidential information?

Traditional insider trading law applies to securities markets, not prediction markets, creating regulatory gray areas. But if federal investigators had identified instances of individuals trading on Polymarket based on stolen information, hacked emails, or confidential campaign data, it could constitute computer fraud or other federal crimes. And if Polymarket had failed to implement systems to detect and report such activity, the company might face liability as an accessory or for failing to maintain adequate controls.

This theory would explain why the FBI wanted Shayne's personal devices. If they were investigating potential insider trading rings using Polymarket, they would want to examine whether company executives had knowledge of or involvement in such schemes. Text messages, emails, and internal communications on Shayne's phone and laptop might contain evidence of awareness that certain large trades were based on illicit information access.

The 2024 election had been marked by numerous leaks, hacks, and information security breaches. If someone with access to internal campaign polling, debate preparation materials, or other confidential information had used that knowledge to make bets on Polymarket, and if the platform had facilitated rather than prevented such activity, both the traders and potentially the company could face legal exposure.

The Silence and Its Meaning

As theories proliferated, what remained striking was what nobody was saying. The FBI maintained complete public silence, standard practice for ongoing investigations. The U.S. Attorney's office declined to comment. Polymarket's legal team said only that the company was cooperating fully with authorities. Shayne himself made no public statements after the initial confirmation of the raid, following what was almost certainly careful legal advice to avoid saying anything that might complicate his situation.

This silence allowed speculation to flourish unchecked. Every theory found adherents, and the absence of official information meant none could be definitively ruled out. The truth might be simpler than any of the elaborate theories suggested, perhaps investigators had received a credible tip about specific violations and were doing routine due diligence. Or the truth might be more complex, involving multiple concurrent concerns that spanned jurisdictions and legal categories.

What seemed clear was that Shayne's moment of triumph had become simultaneously a moment of maximum vulnerability. Having proven Polymarket's value to the world, having built a billion-dollar company and achieved celebrity in tech and financial circles, he now faced the reality that success at the intersection of crypto, finance, and regulation invited scrutiny from multiple powerful institutions with the resources to investigate thoroughly and prosecute aggressively.

In the offices of venture capital firms that had backed Polymarket, the raid prompted urgent conversations about downside risks and potential exit scenarios. Among Polymarket's competitors, particularly Kalshi, which had taken a more conventional regulatory approach, the FBI's interest validated their more cautious strategy. In crypto communities, the raid became another data point in the ongoing debate about whether to seek regulatory approval or push boundaries and accept enforcement risks.

For Shayne Coplan, sitting in some attorney's office reviewing what would be seized from his devices and what conversations might come back to haunt him, the theories swirling through the internet were more than academic. One of them, or some combination of them, represented the federal government's actual concerns. Understanding which theory was correct would determine whether he faced minor penalties, major fines, criminal charges, or exoneration.

The next phase of the story would depend on facts still hidden in sealed warrant applications, grand jury proceedings, and FBI interview transcripts. Until those facts emerged, if they ever did the theories would continue to multiply, each reflecting not just interpretations of Polymarket's actions but fundamental disagreements about innovation, regulation, political power, and the price of building something new in America's increasingly complicated legal landscape.

The only certainty was that the billion-dollar bet Shayne Coplan had made on prediction markets had become deeply personal. He was now living inside his own uncertainty, waiting to discover what the future held, with no market to consult for odds.

Chapter 19

The Broader Regulatory Battle

The FBI raid on Shayne Coplan's apartment was not an isolated incident but rather a vivid chapter in a much larger story about how America regulates emerging technologies, financial innovation, and the increasingly blurred line between prediction and gambling. To understand what happened to Polymarket requires understanding the broader regulatory battlefield on which prediction markets, cryptocurrency platforms, and decentralized finance protocols have been fighting for legitimacy since the blockchain revolution began.

The battle over prediction markets in America stretches back decades before Shayne Coplan was born, rooted in fundamental questions about what these markets actually are. Are they information aggregation mechanisms that help society make better decisions? Are they unregulated securities exchanges that threaten investor protection? Are they simply gambling dressed up in economic theory? The answer determines which regulatory agency has jurisdiction, what rules apply, and whether platforms like Polymarket can legally operate at all.

The Historical Context: From Academic Theory to Regulatory Reality

Prediction markets entered serious academic discourse in the 1980s and 1990s through the work of economists who recognized that aggregating dispersed information through market mechanisms could produce remarkably accurate forecasts. The Iowa Electronic Markets, launched by the University of Iowa in 1988, became the proof of concept. By allowing participants to trade contracts based on election outcomes, the IEM demonstrated that market prices often predicted results more accurately than traditional polls.

But academic respectability did not translate into regulatory clarity. The IEM operated under a no-action letter from the CFTC, essentially a promise not to prosecute that was narrow, specific, and limited to non-profit educational research. When entrepreneurs tried to commercialize the concept, they encountered a regulatory framework designed for commodity futures and stock options, not information markets.

The core problem was definitional. The Commodity Exchange Act gives the CFTC jurisdiction over futures contracts and options on commodities, which includes not just physical goods like wheat and oil but also financial instruments and, critically, "event contracts", derivatives whose value depends on whether a particular event occurs. Under a straightforward reading of the law, prediction markets offering contracts on election outcomes, Supreme Court decisions, or whether a celebrity couple would divorce all fell within CFTC jurisdiction as event-based binary options.

This interpretation had profound implications. If prediction markets were CFTC-regulated derivatives, platforms would need to register as designated contract markets or swap execution facilities, implement extensive reporting requirements, maintain substantial capital reserves, and comply with position limits and other rules designed for professional commodity trading. These requirements, reasonable for Chicago Mercantile Exchange or established futures brokerages, were practically impossible for startups trying to create consumer-friendly prediction platforms.

The Early Platforms and Their Fates

The regulatory challenges weren't theoretical. Multiple prediction market platforms launched in the 2000s and 2010s, and nearly all eventually collided with regulatory authorities.

Intrade, an Irish-based platform that became immensely popular for U.S. political prediction markets, processed hundreds of millions of dollars in trades before the CFTC shut down its U.S. operations in 2012. The commission alleged that Intrade offered commodity options transactions in violation of the ban on off-exchange options trading. Despite operating overseas, Intrade's acceptance of U.S. customers brought it under CFTC jurisdiction. The platform eventually closed entirely in 2013, a cautionary tale about regulatory reach and enforcement.

PredictIt, launched by Victoria University of Wellington in New Zealand, took a different approach. It secured a no-action letter similar to the Iowa Electronic Markets', limiting accounts to $850 and positioning itself as an academic research project. This allowed it to operate legally in the U.S., but the constraints were severe. Low betting limits meant professional traders largely ignored it, limiting liquidity and market efficiency. The platform became popular among political junkies but never achieved the scale or accuracy that advocates believed prediction markets could deliver.

Then in 2022, the CFTC suddenly moved to revoke PredictIt's no-action letter, giving the platform until February 2023 to wind down operations. The decision stunned the prediction market community. PredictIt had operated transparently for eight years under CFTC supervision, publishing academic research and maintaining strict account limits. What had changed? The CFTC offered no detailed explanation, citing only that the platform had grown beyond its original educational scope. Cynics noted the timing coincided with increased regulatory scrutiny of crypto markets and election betting following the 2020 presidential race.

Augur represented yet another approach: complete decentralization. Built on the Ethereum blockchain and launched in 2018, Augur had no company to prosecute, no servers to seize, no identifiable operators to target. The platform existed as smart contracts on a public blockchain, theoretically unstoppable by regulators. In practice, Augur struggled with usability, liquidity, and market quality. Decentralization solved regulatory problems but created user experience problems that limited adoption.

This was the landscape Shayne Coplan entered when he founded Polymarket: a graveyard of failed platforms, overly constrained academic experiments, and decentralized systems that proved too complicated for mainstream users. Each approach had failed in different ways, but all shared a common obstacle: American regulatory hostility to prediction markets.

The Cryptocurrency Complication

Polymarket's use of blockchain technology and cryptocurrency added layers of complexity to an already fraught regulatory situation. By 2020, when Shayne launched the platform, crypto regulation had become one of the most contested areas of financial policy.

The Securities and Exchange Commission, under Chairman Gary Gensler, had taken an aggressive stance that most cryptocurrencies were unregistered securities subject to SEC jurisdiction. The CFTC, meanwhile, had declared Bitcoin and Ethereum to be commodities within its regulatory purview. Meanwhile, the Treasury Department's Financial Crimes Enforcement Network imposed anti-money-laundering requirements on crypto exchanges. State regulators added their own money transmitter licensing requirements. The result was overlapping, contradictory, and often unclear regulatory obligations.

Polymarket's architecture placed it squarely in this contested space. The platform used USDC, a dollar-pegged stablecoin, for all transactions. Users deposited cryptocurrency, not dollars. Trading occurred on the Polygon blockchain, a layer-2 Ethereum scaling solution. Smart contracts, not traditional clearinghouses, handled settlement. From a technical perspective, Polymarket looked like a decentralized finance application, part of the crypto ecosystem that advocates argued represented a new financial paradigm requiring new regulatory approaches.

From a regulator's perspective, however, these technical details might have seemed like obfuscation. Regardless of the underlying technology, Polymarket allowed people to bet money on future events and either profit or lose based on outcomes. Calling it "trading event contracts on a blockchain" didn't change the fundamental economics. If the CFTC had jurisdiction over traditional event-based binary options, why wouldn't it have jurisdiction over blockchain-based ones?

This question went to the heart of a larger debate about crypto regulation: Should new technologies require new regulatory frameworks, or should existing rules apply regardless of the technical implementation? Crypto advocates argued that blockchain's decentralized, transparent, and programmable nature made it fundamentally different from traditional finance, requiring bespoke regulation that recognized its unique properties. Regulators often responded that scams, manipulation, and investor harm looked the same whether they happened on a blockchain or through traditional means, and that existing consumer protection law should apply.

Kalshi's Strategic Gambit

While Polymarket fought with regulators, a competitor took a radically different approach. Kalshi, founded in 2018 by two MIT graduates, decided to work within the system rather than around it. The company spent years and millions of dollars pursuing full CFTC registration as a designated contract market, the first prediction market platform to attempt this since the Iowa Electronic Markets received its special dispensation decades earlier.

The Kalshi founders, Tarek Mansour and Luana Lopes Lara, recognized that regulatory approval would be expensive and time-consuming but calculated that it offered long-term competitive advantages. A fully regulated platform could operate openly in the United States, partner with mainstream financial institutions, and avoid the existential risk of enforcement action. They hired expensive Washington lawyers, engaged in extensive negotiations with CFTC staff, and designed their platform to meet every regulatory requirement.

In November 2021, the CFTC granted Kalshi's application, making it the first regulated prediction market exchange in U.S. history. It was a watershed moment. Kalshi could offer Americans prediction markets on everything from economic indicators to award show outcomes to weather patterns, all legally transparently, and with the CFTC's blessing.

But there was a catch. The CFTC approval came with restrictions on "gaming" markets, essentially events where the outcome could be influenced by individual actors or where the market might be seen as too close to gambling. Most significantly, this initially excluded political election markets, the category that generated the most interest and liquidity on platforms like Polymarket and PredictIt.

Kalshi immediately began pushing the boundaries of these restrictions. In 2022, the company applied to the CFTC for approval to list congressional control contracts, markets on which party would control the House and Senate. The application triggered intense debate within the agency and sharp opposition from commissioners who argued that political prediction markets crossed ethical lines and could undermine democratic processes.

The CFTC rejected Kalshi's congressional control of markets in September 2023, reasoning that such contracts raised novel policy questions about the interaction between commodity futures regulation and election integrity. Kalshi immediately sued, challenging the rejection in federal court. The case became a referendum on political prediction markets themselves, with implications extending far beyond one company's product offering.

In September 2024, Kalshi won. A federal judge ruled that the CFTC had overstepped its authority in rejecting the contracts and that nothing in commodity law gave the agency power to ban event contracts based on political or ethical concerns unrelated to market integrity. The decision was a stunning victory for prediction markets and a rebuke to regulators who had long treated election betting as categorically problematic.

Kalshi immediately began offering congressional control contracts to U.S. customers, processing millions of dollars in trades during the final weeks before the 2024 election. The platform's legal status gave it media credibility and attracted institutional interest that gray-market platforms like Polymarket couldn't match, despite Polymarket's larger volume and international user base.

The International Divide

The regulatory hostility prediction markets faced in the United States contrasted sharply with approaches elsewhere. The United Kingdom, which had legalized and regulated betting on political events for decades, saw prediction markets as a natural extension of existing gambling regulation. Betfair, Ladbrokes, and other British bookmakers had been offering odds on elections, referendums, and political developments for years without controversy.

The UK approach treated prediction markets as gambling rather than as securities or commodity derivatives. This meant they fell under the Gambling Commission's jurisdiction, with requirements around consumer protection, advertising standards, and responsible gambling measures. But the framework was clear, established, and workable. British prediction market operators knew what rules applied and could build businesses with confidence.

Continental Europe varied by jurisdiction, but many countries took similar approaches to the UK, regulating political betting through gambling frameworks rather than securities law. France, Germany, and other nations imposed varying restrictions, but the regulatory question was settled: these were bets, they could be legal if properly regulated, and the appropriate regulator was whoever handled gambling, not financial markets.

This international regulatory arbitrage created obvious opportunities. Polymarket, blocked from U.S. markets after its CFTC settlement, could operate freely in many other jurisdictions. The platform became particularly popular in Europe, Asia, and Latin America, where users faced no legal barriers to participation. The irony was stark: Americans who wanted to trade on American election outcomes had to use VPNs and technically violate U.S. law, while people in dozens of other countries could trade those same markets freely and legally.

The geographic restrictions created market distortions. Polymarket's prices on U.S. political events were being set primarily by non-American traders, potentially less informed about U.S. political dynamics than Americans themselves. Whether this improved or degraded market accuracy was debatable, but it certainly undermined the theoretical case for prediction markets as information aggregation mechanisms. How could you efficiently aggregate American political knowledge while excluding most Americans from participation?

Congressional Interest and Proposed Legislation

The 2024 election brought prediction markets into mainstream political consciousness in unprecedented ways. Polymarket's success in forecasting Trump's victory generated extensive media coverage and prompted serious discussions about whether prediction markets deserved regulatory recognition as valuable information sources.

Several members of Congress began exploring legislation to clarify prediction market status. Representative Bryan Steil, a Wisconsin Republican, proposed the Commodity Futures Trading Commission Market Transparency and Modernization Act, which would have explicitly permitted political prediction markets under CFTC oversight. The bill aimed to overturn what Steil called "arbitrary regulatory barriers" that prevented Americans from accessing information tools available to people in other democracies.

Senator Cynthia Lummis of Wyoming, a vocal crypto advocate, introduced companion legislation in the Senate. Lummis argued that prediction markets represented exactly the kind of innovation that American regulatory policy should encourage rather than suppress. She pointed to academic research showing that prediction markets outperformed polls and that the information they generated had social value that justified their existence beyond mere entertainment or gambling.

But the legislative efforts faced significant opposition. Progressive Democrats, including Senator Elizabeth Warren, argued that legitimizing betting on elections would commodify democracy and create perverse incentives for actors to influence outcomes. Warren noted that wealthy individuals or foreign entities could theoretically manipulate prediction markets to create false narratives about electoral strength, potentially influencing voter behavior or campaign donations.

Good government groups raised concerns about conflicts of interest. Should members of Congress be allowed to trade prediction markets on their own reelection? Should campaign staffers bet on races they were working on? What about journalists covering elections they were trading? Traditional gambling law had developed extensive conflict-of-interest provisions precisely because betting created incentives to influence outcomes. Prediction markets would need similar guardrails.

The Federal Election Commission weighed in with concerns about campaign finance implications. If political prediction markets became significant and legal, would large trades constitute in-kind contributions to campaigns? If someone bet heavily on a candidate and that candidate won, enriching the bettor, was that functionally different from donating money? The commission requested explicit statutory guidance before endorsing any prediction market legalization.

None of the proposed legislation advanced beyond committee hearings before the 2024 election. The issue remained controversial, partisan, and complicated, exactly the kind of policy question Congress preferred to avoid absent overwhelming pressure to act. Kalshi's court victory provided a temporary resolution in one narrow context, but broader legal status for prediction markets remained uncertain.

The Crypto Regulatory Siege

Polymarket's regulatory troubles cannot be separated from the broader regulatory assault on cryptocurrency that accelerated in 2022 and 2023. The SEC, under Gary Gensler's chairmanship, brought enforcement actions against dozens of crypto platforms, alleging they had operated as unregistered securities exchanges or broker-dealers. Major platforms including Coinbase, Kraken, and Binance faced investigations or lawsuits claiming their business models violated securities law.

The enforcement approach followed a pattern: rather than creating clear rules prospectively, the SEC brought cases retroactively, arguing that existing securities law always applied to crypto and that platforms should have known they needed to register. This generated fury in the crypto industry, where executives argued they had repeatedly asked for regulatory clarity and received none, only to face enforcement actions later.

The CFTC, generally viewed as more crypto-friendly than the SEC, nonetheless brought its own enforcement actions against platforms it deemed to have violated commodity trading law. The regulatory environment became increasingly hostile, with platforms shutting down, leaving the U.S. market, or dramatically curtailing services to avoid legal risk.

Polymarket existed at the intersection of prediction markets and crypto, making it doubly vulnerable. The platform faced both the historical regulatory skepticism toward prediction markets and the contemporary regulatory hostility toward cryptocurrency. This combination created extraordinary legal risk that no amount of careful structuring could entirely eliminate.

The crypto winter of 2022, when cryptocurrency prices collapsed and multiple major platforms failed amid fraud allegations, intensified regulatory scrutiny. Platforms like FTX, which had seemed legitimate and well-funded, turned out to be fraudulent enterprises that had stolen billions in customer funds. The revelations validated regulatory skepticism and provided political cover for aggressive enforcement.

In this environment, any crypto platform that pushed regulatory boundaries faced elevated risk. Even platforms that believed they operated legally couldn't be certain regulators would agree, couldn't be confident that courts would side with them over agencies, and couldn't be sure that political winds wouldn't shift in ways that made today's aggressive interpretation tomorrow's settled law.

The Philosophical Divide

Underlying the regulatory battles over prediction markets were fundamentally different worldviews about markets, information, and the government's role in protecting citizens from risk.

Prediction market advocates, drawing on libertarian and market-fundamentalist traditions, believed that voluntary exchange of information through market mechanisms was inherently valuable and that government restrictions represented unjustified paternalism. If people wanted to bet on elections, that was their right. If the aggregated bets produced useful information about likely outcomes, that was a positive externality. The government's role should be limited to preventing fraud and manipulation, not prohibiting the markets themselves.

This view held that existing regulations reflected outdated assumptions about technology and information flows. The laws governing commodity futures were written for agricultural hedging and financial risk management, not information markets. Applying those rules to prediction platforms was a category error that stifled innovation without protecting anyone from meaningful harm. The solution was new regulatory frameworks designed specifically for prediction markets, recognizing their unique properties and social benefits.

Regulators and their defenders saw things differently. They argued that prediction markets, whatever their theoretical elegance, were in practice just another form of gambling. Dressing up bets in market terminology and blockchain technology didn't change the fundamental activity: people risking money on uncertain future events. Gambling had been heavily regulated throughout American history precisely because it created social harms including addiction, fraud, and organized crime involvement. Regulatory caution was appropriate, not obstructionist.

Moreover, regulators questioned whether prediction markets actually generated socially valuable information or just created illusions of knowledge. Markets could be manipulated. They reflected the views of whoever happened to be trading, not any objective truth. Giving them credibility might lead people to rely on them inappropriately, mistaking prices for predictions and speculation for certainty. The regulatory responsibility to protect the public from misleading information justified skepticism toward platforms that claimed to reveal truth through trading.

These philosophical differences couldn't be resolved through technical legal analysis or empirical studies. They reflected deeper disagreements about markets, government, risk, and freedom, the same fundamental divides that shaped debates about cryptocurrency, financial regulation, and much else in contemporary American political economy.

The Post-Raid Landscape

The FBI raid on Shayne Coplan's apartment in November 2024 crystallized these tensions and marked a potential turning point. If federal prosecutors ultimately charged Polymarket or its founder with serious violations, it would send a clear signal that aggressive regulatory avoidance carried real consequences. Other platforms would take note and either seek regulatory approval like Kalshi or exit the U.S. market entirely.

Alternatively, if the investigation concluded without charges, or with only minor penalties, it might embolden other platforms to test regulatory boundaries. The crypto industry had long operated on the principle that it was easier to ask forgiveness than permission. If Polymarket survived its regulatory confrontation intact, that philosophy would seem vindicated.

For Shayne Coplan, these broader regulatory battles provided context but no comfort. His company had become the test case, his personal freedom potentially the price of resolving longstanding regulatory ambiguities. The billion-dollar valuation and media celebration following the election now seemed premature, achieved before the fundamental question of Polymarket's legal status had been finally resolved.

The regulatory battle over prediction markets would continue long after Shayne's personal ordeal ended, one way or another. But his story had become inseparable from that broader struggle, a human face on abstract questions about innovation, regulation, and whether American law would embrace or exclude one of the most interesting developments in information markets that the digital age had produced.

PART VII: THE BILLIONAIRE

Chapter 20

Valuation and Wealth

The headlines appeared within days of the 2024 election results: "Polymarket Founder Becomes Youngest Self-Made Billionaire." The stories varied in their details and certainty, but the narrative was irresistible. Shayne Coplan, just twenty-six years old, had built a platform that processed billions in trading volume, revolutionized political forecasting, and made him personally wealthy beyond most people's wildest dreams. In an era fascinated by young tech entrepreneurs and crypto fortunes, Shayne seemed to represent the ultimate success story. Mark Zuckerberg for the prediction market age.

But the reality behind those headlines was considerably more complex than the simplified mythology. Becoming a billionaire, particularly in the world of venture-backed startups and cryptocurrency platforms, doesn't mean having a billion dollars in your bank account. It means owning equity in a company that someone, somewhere, believes is worth billions. Whether that belief is justified, whether the valuation will hold, and whether the founder can ever actually convert paper wealth into liquid assets are entirely different questions.

Understanding how Shayne Coplan became a billionaire and what that designation actually meant requires understanding the peculiar mechanics of startup valuations, the specific trajectory of Polymarket's fundraising, and the unique challenges of valuing a crypto platform operating in regulatory gray areas. The story of his wealth is inseparable from the story of his company, and both are far more precarious than the word "billionaire" might suggest.

The Fundraising Journey

Polymarket's path to unicorn status and beyond followed a familiar pattern for successful startups, though compressed into an unusually short timeframe. The company's first meaningful capital raise occurred in 2020, shortly after launch. The initial seed round, led by Polychain Capital and other crypto-focused funds, valued the company at roughly $20 million post-money. Shayne and any co-founders owned the majority of equity at this stage, having given up perhaps twenty to thirty percent to investors in exchange for the capital needed to build the platform and team.

At a $20 million valuation, even owning seventy percent of the company would make Shayne worth only $14 million on paper, substantial for someone in his early twenties, but nowhere near billionaire territory. This initial valuation reflected Polymarket's status as an unproven experiment. The platform had launched, but trading volume was modest, regulatory status uncertain, and whether prediction markets could achieve mainstream adoption remained an open question.

The next eighteen months transformed everything. COVID-19 created unprecedented demand for reliable forecasting on everything from vaccine timelines to infection rates to policy responses. Polymarket became a go-to source for real-time pandemic predictions, generating media attention and user growth that exceeded even optimistic projections. The platform processed millions in daily trading volume across dozens of markets. More importantly, several high-profile predictions proved remarkably accurate, building credibility with traders and observers alike.

This growth attracted the attention of major venture capital firms that typically avoided crypto platforms. In early 2021, Polymarket raised a Series A round led by prominent investors that valued the company at approximately $200 million. The step-up from $20 million to $200 million in less than a year reflected both Polymarket's execution and the broader market euphoria around cryptocurrency and decentralized finance. Every crypto platform seemed to be raising capital at valuations that would have been unthinkable for traditional fintech companies.

The Series A diluted existing shareholders, including Shayne, but his stake in a $200 million company was worth far more than his larger stake in a

$20 million company. Assuming he still owned fifty to sixty percent after the new investors came in, his paper wealth had grown to $100-120 million. He was now by most definitions worth nine figures, extraordinarily wealthy for someone still in his mid-twenties.

But Polymarket's valuation trajectory was just beginning its exponential climb. Throughout 2021 and 2022, as the platform expanded internationally following its CFTC settlement, trading volume continued to grow. The 2022 midterm elections drove enormous traffic and established Polymarket as the leading prediction market for political events. By late 2022, industry observers estimated the company's valuation had climbed to $500-700 million based on private secondary market transactions where early employees and investors sold small portions of their shares.

The real valuation explosion came in 2023 and 2024. As the 2024 presidential election approached and Polymarket's competitive advantages became clear, the company raised what insiders called a "pre-emptive Series B", a large funding round at a substantial valuation intended to prevent competitors from gaining ground and to give the company resources to capitalize on the election opportunity.

This round, led by Peter Thiel's Founders Fund along with several other prominent venture firms and crypto funds, valued Polymarket at $1.2 billion. The unicorn milestone had been crossed. More importantly for Shayne personally, the valuation implied that his equity stake, still estimated at forty to fifty percent after multiple dilution events, was worth $480-600 million. He wasn't yet a billionaire, but he was within striking distance.

The final leap came in the months following the 2024 election. Polymarket had processed $3.6 billion in election-related trading volume, had been vindicated in its predictions, and had achieved mainstream media recognition as a legitimate forecasting tool. The platform's monthly active users had grown tenfold. Trading volume across all markets had reached levels that made Polymarket larger than many established cryptocurrency exchanges.

In December 2024, just weeks after the FBI raid, reports emerged that Polymarket was in discussions for a new funding round that would value the company at $2-3 billion. Some reports suggested the valuation might be even higher, as much as $4 billion if the regulatory uncertainty could be resolved favorably. At a $2.5 billion midpoint valuation and assuming Shayne still owned forty percent of the company, his stake would be worth $1 billion. He had officially crossed into ten-figure wealth territory.

The Mechanics of Paper Wealth

The headlines calling Shayne a billionaire were technically accurate but practically misleading. His wealth existed almost entirely on paper, in the form of equity ownership in a private company. Unlike Mark Zuckerberg, who could sell Facebook shares on the public market any day he chose, or Elon Musk, who could borrow against his Tesla holdings, Shayne's wealth was largely illiquid and theoretical.

Private company equity comes with significant restrictions. Shareholders typically cannot sell their shares without company approval. Even when approved, finding buyers for large equity stakes in private companies is difficult. There's no liquid market, no established price discovery mechanism, and most potential buyers conduct extensive diligence before committing capital. The process can take months and often results in prices well below the company's official valuation as buyers demand discounts for illiquidity risk.

Moreover, Shayne's shares almost certainly came with additional restrictions. Founders typically sign agreements preventing them from selling substantial portions of their equity for years after fundraising rounds. These lockup provisions ensure founders remain committed to building the company rather than cashing out. Venture capitalists invest based on the assumption that founders will stay intensely focused on creating value, not counting their paper profits.

The practical reality was that despite being nominally worth a billion dollars, Shayne probably had relatively modest liquid wealth. Some secondary sales of founder shares during fundraising rounds would have given him some cash, perhaps $10-50 million based on typical startup patterns. This money would be more than enough for a comfortable lifestyle, but it represented a small fraction of his paper net worth.

This distinction between paper wealth and liquid assets is crucial for understanding Shayne's situation following the FBI raid. If federal prosecutors brought criminal charges that resulted in conviction, or if regulatory actions forced Polymarket to shut down or drastically curtail operations, his billion-dollar valuation could evaporate almost instantly. The wealth was contingent on the company's continued success, and success was contingent on navigating regulatory challenges successfully.

Valuation Methodology and Skepticism

How does a private company with uncertain regulatory status and blocked from its home market get valued at billions of dollars? The question vexed skeptics and even gave pause to some supporters who worried that Polymarket's valuation reflected crypto-era excess rather than fundamental business value.

Traditional company valuation relies on some combination of revenue, profitability, growth rates, and comparable company analysis. Public companies trade at multiples of their earnings, and private companies are valued by reference to those public market multiples with appropriate adjustments. A profitable software company growing twenty percent annually might trade at ten times revenues or thirty times earnings. Apply similar multiples to the private company's metrics, and you derive a valuation.

Polymarket's valuation didn't follow these traditional frameworks neatly. The platform's business model relied on taking a small percentage of trading volume as fees, a commission structure similar to cryptocurrency exchanges or stock brokerages. During peak periods like the 2024 election, Polymarket might process $50-100 million in daily volume. At a one to two percent fee rate, that translated to $500,000 to $2 million in daily revenue, or $180-730 million annualized during peak periods.

But volume was highly variable. Election seasons drove enormous activity, but between major political events, volume could drop seventy to eighty percent. Annualizing peak revenue would be misleading. More realistic estimates suggested Polymarket might generate $100-200 million in annual revenue across an average year including both peak and trough periods.

At a $2.5 billion valuation, investors were paying twelve to twenty-five times revenues, high, but not unprecedented for fast-growing technology platforms. Cryptocurrency exchanges like Coinbase and Kraken had traded at similar or higher multiples during bull markets. The valuation reflected expectations of continued growth, expansion into new markets, and potential relaxation of U.S. market restrictions that could dramatically expand the addressable market.

Critics argued the valuation made little sense. Polymarket generated revenue primarily from a single product category, political prediction markets that experienced demand only episodically. The platform faced existential regulatory risks, as the FBI raid had made clear. Competition from Kalshi and others threatened to erode market share. Perhaps most fundamentally, the entire prediction market category might never grow beyond a niche interest, limiting Polymarket's ultimate addressable market.

These critics pointed to the history of startup valuations during speculative bubbles. During the dot-com boom, companies with minimal revenue raised capital at absurd valuations based on optimistic projections of internet commerce growth. Most collapsed when reality failed to match the hype. During the 2017 cryptocurrency bubble, projects raised millions via initial coin offerings based on little more than whitepapers and promises. Nearly all proved worthless.

Polymarket's billion-dollar valuation, skeptics suggested, reflected similar irrational exuberance. Venture capitalists awash in capital and desperate for crypto exposure had bid up valuations based on temporary election-season volume that wouldn't persist. When the next major fundraising round occurred, the company would face a down round, a valuation below the previous level as investors recognized that earlier prices had been unjustified.

Comparisons to Other Young Billionaires

If the billion-dollar valuation held, Shayne would join a select group of entrepreneurs who had achieved ten-figure net worth before age thirty. The comparison to other young tech billionaires was inevitable, even as the differences were as important as the similarities.

Mark Zuckerberg famously became a billionaire at twenty-three when Facebook's user growth and revenue convinced investors the company was worth multiple billions. By age twenty-six, when Shayne achieved the same milestone, Zuckerberg's wealth had grown to tens of billions as Facebook went public and became one of the world's most valuable companies. But Zuckerberg had built a platform with nearly a billion users and clear paths to monetization through advertising. Polymarket's user base numbered in the hundreds of thousands, and its business model depended on continued interest in prediction markets.

Evan Spiegel, Snapchat's founder, became a billionaire at twenty-four when the app's explosive growth among young users attracted venture capital at huge valuations. Like Shayne, Spiegel faced skepticism about whether the valuation made sense and whether the platform could sustain growth. Unlike Shayne, Spiegel operated in a clearly legal space without existential regulatory threats.

Sam Bankman-Fried, the FTX founder, had become a billionaire by age twenty-eight based on his cryptocurrency exchange's growth during the 2020-2021 bull market. At FTX's peak, Sam's net worth was estimated at $26 billion, making him one of the wealthiest people under thirty in the world. The comparison to Shayne was particularly apt given both men's crypto focus, both platforms' regulatory challenges, and both founders' cultivation of oddly similar public personas as eccentric geniuses building the future of finance.

Of course, Sam Bankman-Fried's story ended with a spectacular collapse. FTX turned out to be fraudulent, customer funds had been stolen, and Sam was now in federal prison serving a twenty-five-year sentence. His billions had evaporated overnight when the fraud was exposed. The cautionary tale hung over every young crypto billionaire, including Shayne. Paper wealth in the crypto industry was particularly contingent and fragile.

Other comparisons included Vitalik Buterin, Ethereum's founder, whose holdings of the cryptocurrency he created had made him a billionaire by his mid-twenties. Brian Armstrong, Coinbase's founder, had achieved billionaire status in his thirties as his cryptocurrency exchange grew. Each represented different paths to crypto wealth, but all shared the common thread of building platforms that facilitated new forms of digital transactions and markets.

Shayne occupied an interesting position in this cohort. He was younger than most, having achieved the milestone at twenty-six. His platform was smaller and more specialized than Facebook or Snapchat but had achieved remarkable visibility and credibility. Unlike Sam Bankman-Fried, there were no allegations of fraud or misappropriation, Shayne's legal troubles stemmed from regulatory disputes, not criminal conduct. Among young tech billionaires, he represented a particularly pure case of regulatory arbitrage creating wealth: building something innovative in a legal gray area and hoping authorities would eventually embrace rather than destroy it.

What the Wealth Meant and Didn't Mean

For Shayne personally, the billionaire designation carried contradictory implications. On one hand, it represented validation. He had conceived of Polymarket, convinced investors to fund it, built a team to execute the vision, and navigated extraordinary challenges to create something valuable. The valuation meant that sophisticated investors believed in the company's future and were willing to back that belief with enormous sums of capital. This was success by the most conventional metrics of startup culture.

The wealth also provided security, at least in theory. Even if Shayne could access only a small fraction of his paper net worth, that fraction represented financial freedom. He would never need to worry about money in the ordinary sense. He could take risks, pursue projects based on interest rather than compensation, and operate with the confidence that comes from economic security.

But the billionaire label also brought burdens. It made Shayne a target for criticism, scrutiny, and envy. Every decision became colored by his wealth. When he made public statements about regulation or markets, critics could dismiss him as a self-interested billionaire protecting his fortune rather than a principled advocate for innovation. The FBI raid might have generated sympathy if he'd been a struggling entrepreneur fighting regulatory overreach. As a billionaire, the narrative became more complicated, a wealthy crypto magnate who'd perhaps gotten too big too fast and now faced consequences.

The wealth created expectations. Investors who had funded Polymarket at billion-dollar valuations expected returns commensurate with that investment. They would push for growth, expansion, and eventually a liquidity event, an IPO or acquisition that would allow them to convert their paper gains into real profits. Shayne's personal preference might have been to build steadily and sustainably, but investors worth billions commanded attention and influence. The path forward would reflect their interests as much as his vision.

Perhaps most significantly, the wealth was hostage to forces largely outside Shayne's control. Federal prosecutors could destroy it with criminal charges. The CFTC could eliminate it through aggressive enforcement. Congressional legislation could undermine the regulatory arbitrage that made Polymarket possible. A prolonged crypto bear market could drain trading volume. Competitors could erode market share. The billion-dollar valuation rested on assumptions about the future that might prove false.

This uncertainty distinguished Shayne's wealth from that of founders who had taken their companies public or sold to acquirers for cash. Until Polymarket achieved a similar liquidity event, the billions remained contingent and reversible. Shayne was Schrödinger's billionaire, simultaneously enormously wealthy and potentially one bad regulatory decision away from seeing that wealth evaporate.

The Valuation After the Raid

The FBI raid in November 2024 created immediate uncertainty about Polymarket's valuation. Would the December funding round that had been under discussion proceed at the rumored $2.5 billion valuation? Would nervous investors pull back, demanding lower prices to compensate for increased regulatory risk? Or would the raid perversely increase interest, attracting investors who believed the publicity and controversy would ultimately benefit the platform?

In the weeks following the raid, conflicting signals emerged. Some reports suggested that certain investors had put discussions on hold pending clarity about the investigation. Others claimed that several prominent crypto funds saw the raid as a buying opportunity, a chance to invest at favorable terms before regulatory issues resolved positively and the valuation climbed higher.

The uncertainty extended to Shayne's personal net worth. Financial media that had reported his billionaire status now added caveats and question marks. "Embattled Polymarket Founder's Fortune in Question" read one headline. "Can Shayne Coplan Keep His Billions?" asked another. The wealth that had seemed so solid just weeks earlier now appeared fragile and conditional.

For Shayne, this volatility reinforced a truth that all startup founders eventually learn: paper wealth is not real wealth until it's liquid. You can't buy a house with equity certificates. You can't fund other ventures with restricted shares. You can't achieve actual financial security with theoretical billions. The number that appeared next to his name on rich lists was aspirational, not descriptive, a representation of what his stake might be worth if everything went right, if the company kept growing, if regulations became favorable, if investors maintained enthusiasm, if a liquidity event eventually occurred on favorable terms.

The billionaire designation had become both his greatest achievement and his most visible vulnerability. It marked him as extraordinarily successful and simultaneously painted a target on his back. It represented dreams realized and dreams endangered. It meant everything and, in practical terms, almost nothing. Until Shayne could convert paper to cash, something that seemed increasingly distant as legal complexities mounted his billions would remain in a peculiar state of quantum superposition: real enough to make headlines, but too intangible to spend.

As he waited to learn whether federal prosecutors would bring charges, whether investors would complete the next funding round, whether Polymarket would survive its regulatory challenges intact, Shayne's wealth hung in the balance, a billion-dollar bet whose outcome remained uncertain.

Chapter 21

The Price of Success

Success, the conventional wisdom holds, solves problems. Money creates options. Fame opens doors. Achievement brings satisfaction and security. For most of human history, these truths have held reasonably well. But extreme success at an extremely young age in an extremely scrutinized industry creates problems of an entirely different order, problems that money cannot solve and that most people never have to confront.

At twenty-six, Shayne Coplan had achieved what most entrepreneurs spend lifetimes pursuing. He had built a platform that processed billions in transactions, attracted hundreds of millions in venture capital, and made him nominally a billionaire. Polymarket had become a household name among politically engaged Americans and a legitimate force in forecasting and information markets. By conventional measures, Shayne had won.

But victory came with costs that were only beginning to manifest as the FBI investigation proceeded through late 2024 and into 2025. The price of building Polymarket of pushing regulatory boundaries, of scaling rapidly, of operating at the intersection of crypto, politics, and gambling was exacted in personal sacrifices that rarely appeared in the triumphant media profiles. Understanding what Shayne gave up to achieve what he built requires looking beyond the valuation headlines to the human reality of life under investigation, constant scrutiny, and the peculiar isolation that comes with being simultaneously celebrated and targeted.

The Erosion of Privacy

The most immediate cost of Shayne's success was the complete collapse of anything resembling a private life. The FBI raid itself was the most dramatic invasion of privacy, federal agents in his apartment, searching through his possessions, seizing his electronic devices but it was merely the culmination of a longer process of privacy erosion that had accelerated with Polymarket's growth.

Every young tech founder experiences some loss of privacy as their company gains prominence. Journalists want profiles. Investors want access. Users want to know who's building the platforms they use. But for founders in controversial spaces, crypto, prediction markets, anything touching politics the scrutiny intensifies dramatically. Every public appearance is recorded and analyzed. Every social media post is screenshot and dissected. Every personal connection is examined for conflicts of interest or hidden agendas.

For Shayne, this meant living with the constant awareness that nothing was truly private. His phone, even before the FBI seized it, was potentially compromised. Sophisticated actors, whether government agencies, corporate competitors, or malicious hackers had both the motivation and capability to monitor his communications. The rational response was to assume that every text message, every email, every phone call might eventually be read by hostile parties.

This awareness changed how he communicated and ultimately how he thought. Conversations became careful. Spontaneity disappeared. The kind of casual brainstorming that fuels innovation, throwing out half-formed ideas, exploring weird tangents, saying the wrong thing and correcting it became dangerous. Every statement might later be taken out of context, misinterpreted, or used as evidence of wrongdoing.

The surveillance extended beyond digital communications. After Polymarket's prominence in the 2024 election, Shayne couldn't appear in public without someone recognizing him, taking photos, posting his location on social media. The loss of anonymity that comes with any kind of fame was amplified by the controversial nature of his platform. Some people who recognized him wanted selfies and congratulations. Others wanted to confront him about prediction markets, crypto, or politics. Moving through the world became an exercise in constant awareness and management.

Dating became complicated to the point of near impossibility. Any romantic interest faced immediate scrutiny. Was she interested in Shayne or in his wealth? Would the relationship become public, inviting commentary and criticism? Would a partner be able to handle the pressure of dating someone under federal investigation? The power imbalance created by his wealth and notoriety made authentic connection difficult. How could he know if someone loved him or loved the idea of him, the successful founder, the billionaire, the celebrity?

Friends from before Polymarket reported changes in Shayne's demeanor and availability. He was harder to reach, more guarded in conversation, less likely to engage in the unfiltered discussions that had characterized their earlier relationships. Some understood these changes as necessary adaptations to his circumstances. Others felt shut out, mourning the loss of the person they'd known before success transformed him into someone simultaneously more powerful and more constrained.

The Weight of Responsibility

Polymarket's growth meant Shayne bore responsibility not just for his own success but for dozens of employees, millions of users, and the investors who had entrusted him with hundreds of millions of dollars. This weight manifested in concrete ways that shaped every decision and colored every day.

The employees were people who had left secure positions at established companies to bet their careers on Shayne's vision. They had families, mortgages, student loans. They depended on Polymarket continuing to operate and grow. When the FBI raided Shayne's apartment, these employees woke up to news alerts wondering if they still had jobs, whether their equity would become worthless, whether their bet on Polymarket had been a catastrophic career mistake.

Shayne felt this responsibility acutely. In team meetings following the raid, he tried to project confidence and reassurance, but the strain showed. How do you tell your team everything will be fine when federal agents have seized your devices and you don't know what they'll find or what charges might result? How do you ask people to stay committed to a company facing existential regulatory threats? The responsibility for their wellbeing sat heavily on shoulders that, for all his achievements, were still just twenty-six years old.

The users presented a different kind of responsibility. Millions of people had funds deposited on Polymarket, trading on markets they trusted the platform to resolve fairly and accurately. If regulatory action forced the platform to shut down abruptly, what would happen to those funds? Could users withdraw their money? Would they face losses? The technical architecture of blockchain-based platforms offered some protection, smart contracts could theoretically continue operating even if the company dissolved but regulatory seizure or legal injunctions could freeze funds regardless of technical safeguards.

Shayne received messages from users expressing both support and concern. Some were traders who had won substantial sums on the 2024 election and credited Polymarket with providing information that traditional sources had missed. Others were casual users who enjoyed the platform but worried about its legal status. Still others were critics accusing him of facilitating gambling, enabling election manipulation, or violating laws. Each message represented a human being whose life Polymarket had touched, for better or worse, and for whose experience Shayne bore ultimate responsibility.

The investors added yet another layer. Venture capitalists who had funded Polymarket at billion-dollar valuations expected returns. They had portfolio companies to manage, limited partners to answer to, and reputations to maintain. If Polymarket collapsed under regulatory pressure, they would lose their investment, but more importantly, their judgment would be questioned. Why had they backed a company with such obvious legal risks? Shayne felt the pressure to vindicate their faith in him, to prove that their bet had been smart rather than reckless.

Life Under Investigation

The FBI investigation created a peculiar form of stress that permeated every aspect of Shayne's life. Unlike acute crises that build to a climax and resolve, federal investigations can grind on for months or years, creating sustained uncertainty that becomes its own form of psychological torture.

Every phone call from his lawyers brought a spike of anxiety. Was there news? Had prosecutors filed charges? Had the investigation expanded or narrowed? The not-knowing was in some ways worse than bad news would have been. Bad news at least provided clarity and direction. Uncertainty meant living in a state of permanent anticipation, unable to plan, unable to relax, unable to think about anything else for long.

The financial costs of the investigation were substantial. White-collar defense attorneys at major law firms charge $1,500 to $2,000 per hour, and complex federal investigations can generate hundreds or thousands of billable hours. Shayne's legal bills likely ran into the millions, money that despite his paper wealth, represented real cash he had to access through whatever means available. The irony was not lost on him: his success had created wealth he couldn't easily access while simultaneously generating legal problems that required immediate liquidity.

Beyond legal fees, the investigation affected Polymarket's operations and fundraising. Potential investors grew skittish. Some who had been in advanced discussions for the Series B round put negotiations on hold pending resolution of the criminal inquiry. Others demanded additional protections or reduced valuations to compensate for the risk. The company's ability to hire top talent suffered as well. Would a senior engineer leave Google to join a startup whose founder might be criminally charged?

The psychological toll was perhaps the heaviest cost. Shayne had built Polymarket believing he was creating something valuable, a platform that aggregated information, improved forecasting, and contributed to public discourse. The investigation forced him to question those assumptions. Had he been naive about the legal risks? Had his ambition blinded him to warning signs? Was he actually a visionary entrepreneur or just someone who had gotten lucky pushing boundaries until authorities finally pushed back?

Friends reported that Shayne developed a hunted quality, eyes constantly scanning rooms, hyperaware of who might be watching or recording, startled by unexpected questions. He slept poorly. He lost weight. He found it hard to focus on anything except the investigation and its potential outcomes. The mental space that should have been occupied by strategy, innovation, and leadership was instead consumed by legal scenarios, evidentiary concerns, and worst-case planning.

The Isolation of Extreme Success

Wealth and achievement create peculiar forms of isolation that most people never experience. Shayne discovered that becoming a billionaire, even a paper billionaire, fundamentally altered his relationships with nearly everyone in his life.

Old friends related to him differently. Some became deferential, treating him as somehow special or separate. Others grew resentful, seeing his success as a rebuke to their more modest achievements or as evidence that the system was rigged to benefit people like Shayne who took risks they couldn't afford. Either way, the easy equality that had characterized earlier friendships was gone, replaced by something more complicated and less comfortable.

New relationships were suspect from the start. When someone expressed interest in friendship or business partnership, was it genuine or mercenary? Did they value Shayne for himself or for what he could do for them? The inability to trust new connections deepened his isolation. He found himself falling back on a shrinking circle of people he'd known before Polymarket, but even those relationships were strained by the vast gulf between his circumstances and theirs.

Within the tech and crypto communities, Shayne occupied an uncomfortable middle ground. He wasn't established enough to be accepted as an elder statesman but was too prominent to be just another founder. Other entrepreneurs treated him as a competitor or a curiosity. Established tech leaders largely ignored prediction markets as too niche or too risky to warrant serious attention. The crypto community celebrated him when Polymarket succeeded but maintained distance as the investigation proceeded, nobody wanted to be too closely associated with someone who might become an example of regulatory overreach.

The isolation extended to decision-making. As founder and largest shareholder, Shayne bore ultimate responsibility for major strategic choices, but he couldn't freely discuss his thinking with most people. Board members had their own agendas and interests. Employees would be biased by their stake in the company. Investors would push for outcomes that maximized their returns. Even his lawyers, while zealous advocates, were focused on legal risk rather than business strategy or personal wellbeing.

This meant Shayne often sat alone with impossible choices. Should Polymarket fight the investigation aggressively or cooperate fully and hope for leniency? Should the company raise more capital despite unfavorable terms or preserve existing shareholders' equity? Should he personally take a higher profile to shape the narrative or maintain silence on lawyers' advice? Each decision carried enormous consequences, and each had to be made with incomplete information and without anyone fully understanding the full range of pressures he faced.

The Sacrifice of Youth

Perhaps the most poignant cost of Shayne's success was the loss of his twenties to Polymarket. Most people in their mid-twenties are experimenting, exploring, making mistakes without catastrophic consequences. They travel, party, date casually, change career paths, discover who they are and what they want. Shayne had instead spent those years building a company, managing employees, negotiating with investors, and now defending himself against federal investigation.

He hadn't traveled for pleasure in years. Every trip was business-related, every destination chosen for strategic reasons. He hadn't taken a genuine vacation, time completely disconnected from work since founding Polymarket. The platform required constant attention, and his equity stake meant he had hundreds of millions of reasons to stay focused.

He had missed weddings of friends who lived across the country because he couldn't spare the time. He had skipped reunions and celebrations. He had said no to spontaneous adventures because the company demanded reliability and presence. These small sacrifices accumulated into a larger loss: the loss of the unstructured, unplanned experiences that form the texture of a normal young adulthood.

The intensity of startup life meant Shayne had specialized extremely early. While peers were developing broad capabilities and exploring different fields, he had become an expert in prediction markets, blockchain technology, and regulatory arbitrage. This specialization created career risks. If Polymarket failed, what would he do? His resume was impressive but narrow. He had proven he could build one thing spectacularly well. Could he do it again? Would anyone give him the chance, or would he forever be known as the founder whose regulatory gamble failed?

There was no obvious off-ramp. At twenty-six, with a billion-dollar company and an ongoing federal investigation, Shayne couldn't simply walk away and do something else. He was locked in, committed for better or worse to seeing the Polymarket story through to whatever conclusion awaited. The optionality that most people his age enjoyed, the freedom to pivot, to start over, to try something completely different had been traded for the possibility of spectacular success and the reality of intense pressure.

Relationships and Romance

The practical challenges of Shayne's situation were compounded by the difficulty of maintaining romantic relationships under such circumstances. Several people close to him suggested that the succession of short-lived relationships that marked his mid-twenties reflected not his preferences but the impossibility of normal dating given his profile and pressures.

The power dynamics were inevitable and insurmountable. Any romantic partner would be dating someone worth a billion dollars on paper, someone whose life was under federal investigation, someone who couldn't fully confide in them about the details of either. How could such a relationship be equal? How could it be normal?

The demands on Shayne's time and attention made sustained intimacy nearly impossible. Polymarket required constant engagement. The investigation demanded hours of preparation, legal meetings, and strategic discussions. What was left for a partner? A few distracted hours here and there, dinners interrupted by urgent calls, vacations canceled for depositions or emergency board meetings?

Moreover, any serious relationship would inevitably become public, inviting scrutiny and commentary. A partner would have to accept becoming part of the Polymarket story, their own identity subsumed into the narrative of the embattled young billionaire and his companion. Few people would willingly accept such a role, and those who would might be motivated by precisely the wrong reasons, the fame, the wealth, the association rather than genuine connection to Shayne as a person.

Friends noted that Shayne seemed lonely in ways that his success couldn't address. He was surrounded by employees, investors, lawyers, and hangers-on but had few people with whom he could be unguarded and vulnerable. The mask he wore in public, confident, visionary, unworried by the investigation couldn't come off even in private without creating risks. Vulnerability could be exploited. Doubt could be weaponized. Even with people he trusted, full honesty was dangerous.

The Counterfactual Question

As the investigation dragged on and the personal costs accumulated, people who knew Shayne wondered if he ever asked himself the counterfactual question: What if he had chosen differently? What if he had built Polymarket more conservatively, seeking regulatory approval like Kalshi before launching? What if he had accepted the constraints of the CFTC framework and built a smaller but legal platform? What if he had chosen a different industry entirely, something with clearer rules and lower stakes?

Such thinking was probably inevitable in dark moments, though Shayne never publicly expressed regret. The choice he had made, to build aggressively, to push boundaries, to operate in gray areas had created Polymarket's success and his wealth. A more cautious approach might have avoided legal troubles but also might have produced a smaller, less impactful company. The counterfactual Shayne who played it safe might sleep better but would also be less wealthy, less famous, and less accomplished.

This was cold comfort during sleepless nights when the investigation's potential outcomes haunted him. Criminal charges could mean prison time, not just financial loss. Even if prosecutors settled for civil penalties, his reputation would be tarnished, his achievement forever asterisked by the acknowledgment of legal violations. The aggressive strategy that had built Polymarket might ultimately destroy both the company and its founder.

Yet walking away wasn't an option. The equity structure, investor expectations, employee dependence, and his own commitment all locked him into seeing things through. He had made his bet, pushed his chips to the center of the table, and now had to wait for the cards to fall. There was no folding, no hedge, no way to reduce his exposure without abandoning everything he'd built.

The Inner Circle's Perspective

Those closest to Shayne, family members, founding team members, early friends watched his transformation with mixed emotions. They were proud of his achievements but worried about the costs. They celebrated his success but grieved for the person he'd been before the pressure, the scrutiny, and the investigation had reshaped him.

His parents, who had supported his entrepreneurial ambitions, now faced their own form of torment. Their son was simultaneously a billionaire and under federal investigation. They couldn't help him, this was beyond parental comfort or advice and could only watch as he navigated pressures they couldn't fully understand. Every news article about Polymarket and the FBI was both a point of pride in his achievement and a source of anxiety about his future.

Early Polymarket employees who had joined when the company was just an idea saw the trajectory differently than later hires. They remembered Shayne as excited and idealistic, driven by genuine belief in prediction markets' potential rather than by wealth or fame. They had watched the regulatory pressures, the growth demands, and the constant scrutiny gradually wear down that idealism, replacing it with something harder and more calculating. Some mourned the change while understanding its necessity. Others felt it vindicated their decision to leave before the stakes became so high.

The founding team members still with the company carried their own burdens. They had made the same bet Shayne had, accepted the same risks, and now faced similar consequences. Their wealth was tied to his, their careers dependent on Polymarket's survival. They couldn't abandon him without abandoning their own interests, creating a shared foxhole mentality that was both camaraderie and trap.

The Unspoken Question

Perhaps the most painful aspect of Shayne's situation was the question nobody asked directly but everyone wondered: Was it worth it? Had the achievement of building Polymarket, of reaching billionaire status, of revolutionizing prediction markets justified the personal costs? The lost privacy, the strained relationships, the constant stress, the federal investigation, the sacrifice of a normal young adulthood, had it been a fair trade?

The question was impossible to answer while the story was still unfolding. If Polymarket survived, if the investigation concluded without serious consequences, if the company eventually went public or sold for billions in actual cash, then the sacrifice might seem worthwhile in retrospect. Victory would retrospectively justify the costs.

But if federal prosecutors brought charges, if Polymarket was shut down, if the billion-dollar valuation evaporated, if Shayne ended up in prison or financially ruined despite his paper wealth, then the whole enterprise would appear as tragic overreach, ambition exceeding wisdom, youth and hubris leading to preventable catastrophe.

For now, suspended between possible triumph and possible disaster, Shayne lived with the accumulating costs of success without knowing whether the ultimate price would be one worth paying. The billions existed on paper. The sacrifices were entirely real. And the final accounting, whether his bet on Polymarket would ultimately be remembered as visionary courage or reckless arrogance remained unknown, dependent on decisions being made in federal offices by people who didn't know him and didn't care about the human costs of whatever judgment they ultimately rendered.

Chapter 22

Philosophy and Vision

To understand why Shayne Coplan built Polymarket, why he made the choices he made, and why he was willing to accept the personal and legal risks that eventually materialized, requires understanding the worldview that animated his work. Shayne was not simply an entrepreneur pursuing profits or fame. He was, in his own conception and in the eyes of supporters, engaged in something more consequential: the construction of new mechanisms for discovering truth and distributing information in ways that could fundamentally improve how society makes decisions.

This vision emerged from a particular intellectual tradition, libertarian in its politics, Austrian and Chicago School in its economics, crypto-native in its technology preferences that saw markets not merely as allocation mechanisms but as epistemological tools. Markets, in this view, were humanity's most powerful technology for aggregating dispersed information and revealing truths that could not be discovered through central planning, expert panels, or democratic deliberation. Prediction markets represented the purest expression of this idea: creating financial incentives for people to reveal what they actually believed about the future, stripped of bias, virtue signaling, and wishful thinking.

Shayne articulated these ideas in interviews, blog posts, and public appearances throughout Polymarket's rise. His philosophy evolved and sharpened as the platform matured, but the core convictions remained remarkably consistent. To his admirers, these views marked him as a serious thinker building something genuinely important. To his critics, they revealed either naive idealism or convenient self-justification for a business model that was ultimately just gambling with extra steps.

Markets as Truth Machines

The foundational premise of Shayne's worldview was that markets reveal truth more effectively than any alternative mechanism. This wasn't a claim about market efficiency in the narrow sense that asset prices instantly reflect all available information though that theory informed his thinking. It was a broader claim about markets as computational systems that processed distributed knowledge no single person or organization could possess.

The intellectual lineage ran through Friedrich Hayek's famous essay "The Use of Knowledge in Society," which argued that the price system's genius lay in its ability to coordinate millions of individual decisions without requiring anyone to understand the whole system. When the price of copper rises, manufacturers reduce their copper usage without needing to know whether the price increase reflects a mine collapse in Chile, a surge in demand for electric vehicles, or speculative trading. The price aggregates all relevant information into a single signal that guides behavior.

Prediction markets extended this logic from commodity prices to future events. Instead of asking experts to forecast election outcomes or pandemic trajectories, prediction markets let anyone with an opinion and capital back that opinion with real money. The resulting prices represented the market's aggregated judgment about probability, not perfect, but incorporating far more information than any individual forecaster could consider.

Shayne frequently cited examples of prediction markets outperforming experts. The Iowa Electronic Markets had beaten polls in presidential elections for decades. Intrade had correctly predicted Supreme Court rulings that surprised legal scholars. Internal prediction markets at companies like Google and Ford had forecasted product launch outcomes more accurately than executive projections. These successes weren't accidents, Shayne argued, but demonstrations of a fundamental principle: when you force people to put money behind their beliefs, you get closer to truth than when you simply ask for opinions.

This view had radical implications. If markets were superior truth-discovery mechanisms, then society should create markets for everything important: climate change outcomes, technological breakthroughs, geopolitical developments, public health trends. The world would make better decisions if decision-makers could consult market probabilities rather than relying on potentially biased experts, incomplete polls, or their own flawed intuitions.

Traditional institutions, universities, think tanks, media organizations, government agencies claimed authority to interpret reality and forecast futures. Shayne saw these institutions as inherently limited by their incentive structures, ideological commitments, and centralized decision-making. A university professor forecasting election outcomes faced no penalty for being wrong. A newspaper columnist making bold predictions suffered no consequences when events proved them mistaken. But a trader risking real capital on prediction markets lost money if they were wrong, creating powerful incentives for accuracy.

The Epistemic Case for Decentralization

Shayne's enthusiasm for prediction markets was inseparable from his broader commitment to decentralization, a value that pervaded crypto culture and informed Polymarket's technical architecture. Centralized systems, whether governments, corporations, or traditional financial institutions concentrated power in ways that created both efficiency problems and corruption risks. Decentralized systems distributed power, making them more resilient, harder to manipulate, and ultimately more trustworthy.

Polymarket's use of blockchain technology wasn't merely a technical choice but a philosophical statement. By building on public blockchains like Polygon, the platform ensured that trades were transparent, verifiable, and resistant to retroactive manipulation. No single entity could alter market outcomes or erase inconvenient results. The blockchain provided what Shayne called "credible neutrality", a system whose rules were encoded in software rather than subject to human discretion.

This commitment to decentralization extended to Shayne's views about information and censorship. He was deeply skeptical of centralized gatekeepers deciding what information was true or false, what speech was acceptable or harmful, what opinions deserved amplification or suppression. The 2020s had seen increasing efforts by governments and platforms to moderate content, fact-check claims, and limit the spread of misinformation. Shayne worried these efforts, however well-intentioned, created their own problems.

Who decided what counted as misinformation? How could fact-checkers themselves be held accountable? What happened when the consensus view later proved wrong, as with early claims about COVID-19 transmission, vaccine efficacy, or the origins of the virus? Centralized information control meant that official errors became entrenched as truth, with dissenting voices silenced before their views could be evaluated on merits.

Prediction markets offered an alternative. Rather than declaring certain views true or false, markets let people bet on outcomes and discover over time which views proved accurate. If someone believed that the mainstream media was wrong about election probabilities, they could express that belief through trades, and the market would eventually adjudicate whether they were right. No central authority needed to decide ex ante who deserved credibility.

This approach had obvious appeal in an era of declining trust in institutions. If you didn't trust polls, you could consult Polymarket. If you thought mainstream media was biased, market prices offered an alternative information source. If expert predictions seemed politically motivated, traders risking their own money provided a counterbalance.

Decentralization promised not just efficiency but legitimacy, information you could trust because it emerged from thousands of individual decisions rather than institutional decree.

Libertarian Roots and Crypto Ethos

Shayne's philosophy reflected the libertarian political culture that dominated much of the cryptocurrency world. Though he rarely discussed partisan politics explicitly, his views aligned with a broader movement skeptical of government intervention, enthusiastic about markets, and committed to individual liberty and responsibility.

The libertarian case for prediction markets was straightforward: if adults wanted to risk their money betting on future events, the government had no legitimate basis for preventing them. The state's role should be limited to preventing fraud and enforcing contracts, not dictating what kinds of voluntary exchanges were permissible. Laws prohibiting prediction markets reflected paternalism, the assumption that regulators knew better than individuals what was good for them.

This libertarian framework extended to views about financial regulation more broadly. The elaborate apparatus of securities law, commodity regulation, and banking oversight existed ostensibly to protect consumers and maintain market integrity. But libertarians argued these rules primarily protected incumbent institutions from competition, raised barriers to entry that prevented innovation, and restricted individual freedom without commensurate benefits.

Shayne saw Polymarket as participating in a larger crypto movement to create alternative financial infrastructure outside traditional regulatory frameworks. Bitcoin had demonstrated that people could transact value without banks. Ethereum had shown that smart contracts could enforce agreements without courts. DeFi protocols were building lending, trading, and investment tools without brokerages or exchanges. Polymarket was extending this logic to information markets, proving that forecasting didn't require licensed exchanges or government-approved mechanisms.

The crypto ethos emphasized building rather than asking permission. Instead of spending years negotiating with regulators to create approved prediction markets, Shayne had simply built one and let people decide whether it was valuable. This "permissionless innovation" approach had created much of the internet's value, crypto advocates argued, and would continue driving progress if governments didn't crush it through overregulation.

Critics saw this attitude as reckless disregard for laws designed to protect the public. Supporters saw it as necessary defiance of regulatory capture and governmental overreach. Shayne occupied the complicated middle ground of someone who genuinely believed he was creating value while also recognizing that his approach entailed legal risks. The question was whether the social benefits justified taking those risks, a judgment call that depended heavily on one's priorities about market regulation and institutional authority.

Views on Democracy and Governance

Perhaps Shayne's most controversial views concerned prediction markets' relationship to democracy itself. Critics had long argued that allowing betting on elections would corrupt the democratic process, creating incentives to manipulate outcomes or generating misleading narratives about electoral strength. Shayne rejected these concerns and went further, suggesting that prediction markets could actually improve democratic governance.

The core problem with democracy, in Shayne's analysis, was information. Voters made decisions based on incomplete data, biased media coverage, and their own limited attention. Politicians could lie or exaggerate without immediate consequences. Interest groups could manufacture fake grassroots support. The whole system operated with pervasive information asymmetries that prevented good decision-making.

Prediction markets could address these problems by making information legible and actionable. If voters could see market probabilities for various policy outcomes, they might make better choices. If politicians knew markets were betting on whether their promises would be fulfilled, they might be more careful about commitments. If policy proposals had associated prediction markets about their effects, debate might become more empirical and less ideological.

Some of Shayne's public statements hinted at even more radical possibilities. What if government funding decisions consulted prediction markets about which programs would succeed? What if regulatory agencies used market probabilities to prioritize enforcement resources? What if Congress incorporated prediction market forecasts into legislative analysis? These applications would transform prediction markets from entertainment or information sources into actual governance mechanisms.

Critics found this vision either naive or dangerous. Naive because it assumed market prices represented truth rather than the collective biases of whoever happened to be trading. Dangerous because it would subordinate democratic deliberation to market outcomes, giving disproportionate influence to wealthy traders who could move prices through large bets. The whole point of democracy was that each person got one vote regardless of wealth. Prediction markets gave more influence to those with more capital to risk.

Shayne's response was that markets didn't replace democracy but informed it. Voters would still make ultimate decisions; markets would just provide better information for those decisions. And while wealthy traders could attempt to manipulate prices, they would lose money if their manipulation conflicted with reality. The market's self-correcting nature meant that misleading prices couldn't persist, someone would bet against them and profit from the correction.

Whether this response was persuasive depended on whether you believed markets were fundamentally wise or fundamentally corruptible. Shayne was firmly in the former camp, convinced that betting markets revealed truth precisely because traders faced financial consequences for being wrong. His critics worried that this faith in markets overlooked how power and wealth could distort market prices just as they distorted other information systems.

The Information Revolution and Society's Future

Shayne positioned Polymarket within a broader narrative about humanity's evolving relationship with information and truth. The 20th century had been dominated by centralized information systems, mass media, academic institutions, government agencies that claimed authority to determine what was true. The 21st century, Shayne believed, would belong to decentralized information systems that derived legitimacy from mechanism design rather than institutional authority.

This transition was already underway. Wikipedia had demonstrated that crowd-sourced knowledge could rival expert-written encyclopedias. Twitter and social media had shown that distributed networks could break news faster than traditional journalism. Cryptocurrency had proven that decentralized consensus could maintain financial records without centralized institutions. Prediction markets were the next frontier using crowds and incentives to forecast futures more accurately than experts.

The implications were profound. If markets could forecast elections more accurately than polls, perhaps they could also predict technological breakthroughs, identify promising research directions, forecast climate impacts, anticipate geopolitical developments, and warn about emerging risks. Society's ability to anticipate and prepare for the future would improve dramatically if prediction markets became widely available and trusted.

But realizing this vision required overcoming not just regulatory obstacles but cultural skepticism about markets' epistemic authority. Many people remained uncomfortable with the idea that trading could reveal truth, that profit motives could align with accurate forecasting, that gambling-like activities could serve serious social purposes. Changing these attitudes would take time, successful predictions, and growing familiarity with how prediction markets worked.

Shayne saw himself as an educator as much as an entrepreneur. Every successful Polymarket prediction, whether the 2024 election, COVID-19 milestones, or technological developments helped shift public perception. Every media appearance where he explained prediction market theory planted seeds that might eventually flower into acceptance. The work of normalizing prediction markets as legitimate information sources was as important as the technical work of building and operating the platform.

The Long View and Historical Context

When discussing Polymarket's significance, Shayne often adopted a historical perspective that placed current regulatory battles in a broader context. New technologies always faced resistance from established interests and legal systems designed for previous eras. Railroads had been opposed by canal owners. Automobiles had faced restrictions from horse carriage industries. The internet had initially seemed lawless and dangerous before society adapted its institutions.

Prediction markets were experiencing similar growing pains. Laws written for commodity futures and options didn't fit information markets well, but that reflected the laws' inadequacy rather than prediction markets' illegitimacy. Eventually, Shayne believed, regulatory frameworks would evolve to accommodate prediction markets just as they had accommodated previous innovations. The question was whether American regulation would adapt quickly enough to let American companies lead, or whether innovation would migrate to more permissive jurisdictions.

This historical framing positioned Shayne as someone on the right side of inevitability. Prediction markets would eventually be accepted, he argued, because they worked too well to be ignored. The 2024 election had been a proof point, markets had beaten polls, demonstrated value, and achieved mainstream attention. Future successes would compound this credibility until even skeptics had to acknowledge that prediction markets deserved a place in the informational ecosystem.

Of course, this confident historical narrative could be self-serving. Every entrepreneur believes they're riding the wave of history rather than tilting at windmills. Shayne's conviction that prediction markets were inevitable might prove correct, or it might be the same overconfidence that had led countless other founders to crash against regulatory and social resistance. Only time would tell whether Polymarket represented the future or was merely an interesting experiment that couldn't survive contact with American law.

What Drove Him Forward

Beneath the philosophical arguments and grand visions, what actually motivated Shayne Coplan to build Polymarket and accept its risks? Was he genuinely driven by commitment to markets as truth machines, or were the philosophical justifications convenient rationalization for pursuing wealth and status?

Those who knew him best suggested the motivations were mixed and evolved over time. In the early days, Shayne seemed genuinely excited by the intellectual challenge and the opportunity to instantiate ideas he'd encountered in economics and computer science. Building a prediction market platform was interesting problem-solving, market design, smart contract architecture, user experience and liquidity bootstrapping. The early team remembered late nights debating mechanism design, not discussing potential valuations.

As Polymarket grew and success became apparent, motivations likely shifted. The prospect of building a unicorn company, becoming wealthy, achieving recognition, these became real possibilities rather than abstractions. It would be extraordinary if such prospects didn't influence decision-making. The choice to grow aggressively rather than seek cautious regulatory approval probably reflected ambition as much as philosophical commitment to permissionless innovation.

But through the FBI investigation and its aftermath, when the costs of those earlier choices became painfully apparent, Shayne's continued defense of prediction markets and Polymarket's value suggested the philosophical commitments weren't merely instrumental. Someone purely motivated by wealth might have settled quickly, accepted penalties, and moved to less risky ventures. Shayne's insistence on fighting for Polymarket's legitimacy and prediction markets' importance suggested he genuinely believed in the vision he'd been articulating.

Perhaps the truest answer was that philosophy and self-interest had become genuinely inseparable. Shayne believed in prediction markets partly because he'd built one, and he'd built one partly because he believed in them. The worldview and the business model reinforced each other in ways that made it impossible to disentangle conviction from rationalization. This wasn't unusual, most successful entrepreneurs became true believers in their own missions precisely because sustaining the effort and risk required genuine faith, not merely calculated self-interest.

The Vision's Limits and Blind Spots

Even sympathetic observers recognized that Shayne's vision contained limitations and overlooked certain problems. The faith in markets as truth-revealing mechanisms assumed rational actors, relatively efficient information flow, and absence of systematic manipulation. Real markets often violated these assumptions. They could be manipulated by coordinated actors. They reflected the biases of whoever happened to be trading. They sometimes created self-fulfilling prophecies where market prices influenced outcomes rather than simply predicting them.

The libertarian framework struggled with questions about market access and inequality. If prediction markets became important information sources, wealth inequality would translate into epistemic inequality, rich traders would have disproportionate influence on apparent consensus probabilities. This raised justice concerns that pure market theory had difficulty addressing. Should information systems that society relied upon for important decisions be permissibly influenced more by wealthy participants?

The crypto-native enthusiasm for decentralization and permissionless innovation sometimes seemed to undervalue the legitimate purposes of regulation. Not all regulatory frameworks existed merely to protect incumbents. Some addressed real problems, fraud prevention, consumer protection, market integrity and systemic stability. The attitude that one could simply build around regulations because they were unjust or outdated risked recreating problems those regulations had been designed to solve.

And the grand vision of prediction markets improving social decision-making remained largely speculative. Yes, markets had beaten polls in some elections. But would they actually improve policy-making if integrated into governance? Would politicians and voters actually use market information well, or might they cherry-pick probabilities that confirmed existing preferences? Would markets on policy outcomes be manipulable by those implementing the policies? These questions remained open, their answers unknown.

Shayne acknowledged some of these concerns in more reflective moments, though he generally maintained that markets' imperfections were still preferable to alternatives' greater flaws. The vision wasn't that prediction markets were perfect truth machines, but that they were better than existing mechanisms. That comparative claim was harder to reject than absolute claims about market wisdom.

Legacy and Impact on the Movement

Regardless of Polymarket's ultimate fate, Shayne had already influenced how a generation of technologists, investors, and policy thinkers viewed prediction markets. He had taken concepts that existed primarily in academic papers and niche platforms and demonstrated their viability at scale. He had shown that blockchain-based prediction markets could process billions in volume, that millions of people would participate, and that resulting predictions could be remarkably accurate.

This proof of concept would outlive any particular company or founder. Even if Polymarket disappeared tomorrow, the ideas and architecture Shayne had developed would inform future efforts. The playbook for building prediction markets, technical architecture, market design, community building and media strategy had been written and would be available to successors.

Within crypto communities, Shayne had become a symbol of both the promise and peril of permissionless innovation. His success demonstrated what could be built by ignoring regulatory constraints and moving fast. His legal troubles demonstrated the risks of that approach. Future founders would study both dimensions, making their own calculated decisions about how much regulatory risk to accept in pursuit of their visions.

The philosophical arguments Shayne had articulated and popularized would continue shaping debate about markets, information, and governance long after the FBI investigation concluded. Whether one agreed with his views or not, he had forced serious engagement with questions about how society should aggregate information, whether markets deserved epistemic authority, and what role decentralized systems should play in democratic governance.

In this sense, Shayne had already achieved a form of success independent of wealth or legal outcomes. He had moved conversations, influenced thinking, and demonstrated possibilities. The ideas were now in the world, available for others to build upon, refine, or reject. Whatever judgment history ultimately rendered on Shayne Coplan personally, the vision he'd articulated and instantiated had become part of the ongoing conversation about technology, markets, and truth in the 21st century.

PART VIII: POLYMARKET'S IMPACT

Chapter 23

Changing How We See the Future

On the morning of November 6, 2024, as Americans woke to the news that Donald Trump had won the presidential election decisively, a curious phenomenon occurred across newsrooms, political offices, and living rooms nationwide. Alongside the usual post-election analysis, parsing exit polls, dissecting campaign strategies, interviewing voters a new conversation emerged: Why had Polymarket been right when almost everyone else was wrong?

This wasn't merely a technical question about forecasting methodology. It represented a fundamental shift in how sophisticated observers thought about predicting the future. For decades, elections had been forecast through a well-established system: polling firms called likely voters, aggregators like FiveThirtyEight applied statistical models to poll data, and media organizations reported the resulting probabilities with varying degrees of confidence. This system had its critics and known limitations, but it represented the consensus approach to election forecasting.

Polymarket had offered an alternative that most mainstream observers initially dismissed as either irrelevant or actively misleading. A crypto-based betting platform where anonymous traders wagered on outcomes? How could that possibly compete with scientific polling conducted by professionals? Yet when the votes were counted, Polymarket's probabilities had aligned remarkably well with the actual results, while traditional polls had suggested a much closer race than materialized.

The implications extended far beyond a single election. Polymarket's success represented a proof of concept for prediction markets as legitimate forecasting tools and began reshaping how various institutions, journalism, political campaigns, businesses and academia approached the fundamental challenge of anticipating future events.

The Media's Reluctant Conversion

Nothing illustrated prediction markets' growing legitimacy more clearly than their integration into mainstream media coverage. Major news organizations that had largely ignored or dismissed Polymarket before the 2024 election began treating it as a serious data source worthy of regular citation and analysis.

The New York Times, which had run skeptical pieces about prediction markets in prior years, published detailed explainers about how Polymarket worked and why its prices might contain valuable information. The Wall Street Journal created a dedicated feature tracking prediction market odds alongside traditional polls in its election coverage. CNN incorporated Polymarket probabilities into its election night broadcasts, with John King referencing market movements at his famous magic wall alongside vote counts and exit polls.

This shift reflected pragmatic calculation as much as intellectual conversion. Media organizations exist in competitive markets themselves, and audiences clearly found prediction market data interesting and valuable. Ignoring Polymarket meant ceding audience attention to outlets that covered it. Moreover, after the platform's successful election prediction, continuing to dismiss it would have made news organizations appear out of touch or ideologically biased against markets.

But the integration went deeper than mere competitive necessity. Journalists themselves began using prediction markets as reporting tools. Political reporters checked Polymarket prices to gauge how various news developments affected electoral expectations. Financial journalists consulted crypto prediction markets to understand market sentiment about Fed decisions or economic indicators. Technology reporters looked at prediction markets for product launches and corporate events.

This created a feedback loop. As journalists cited prediction markets in their coverage, audiences became more familiar with them. As audiences consulted prediction markets directly, they became less dependent on traditional media to interpret political and economic developments. Some media executives worried that prediction markets might eventually disintermediate journalism itself, why read political analysis when you could simply check market probabilities?

The most sophisticated media organizations recognized that prediction markets were complements rather than substitutes for journalism. Markets aggregated information but didn't generate it. Someone needed to investigate, report, and contextualize events. Prediction markets processed that information into probabilistic forecasts, but the underlying reporting remained essential. The challenge was figuring out how journalism and prediction markets could productively coexist, each performing the function it did best.

Some publications experimented with creating their own prediction markets or partnerships with platforms like Polymarket. The Economist explored hosting markets on its website. Bloomberg considered integrating prediction market data more deeply into its financial terminals. These experiments remained tentative, constrained by legal uncertainties and questions about whether news organizations should be facilitating what some still considered gambling. But the direction of travel was clear: prediction markets were becoming part of the informational infrastructure that media organizations both relied upon and reported about.

Political Campaigns as Market Participants

Perhaps the most profound impact of Polymarket's emergence was how political campaigns themselves began thinking about and engaging with prediction markets. By the 2024 cycle, every major presidential campaign employed staff members whose job included monitoring prediction market probabilities and understanding what they revealed about the race's dynamics.

Initially, campaigns treated prediction markets with suspicion. Politicians and strategists worried that market odds showing their candidate trailing would create self-fulfilling prophecies, donors would stop giving, volunteers would lose motivation, and voters would decide supporting a losing candidate was pointless. Some campaigns explicitly instructed staff and surrogates to dismiss prediction market data as unreliable or manipulated, emphasizing internal polls that showed more favorable pictures.

But sophisticated campaign operatives recognized that prediction markets offered genuine strategic intelligence. Unlike public polls, which might be weeks old and subject to response bias, prediction markets updated constantly as new information emerged. Unlike private campaign polling, which might be optimistic to maintain morale, prediction markets reflected real money backing real beliefs. A campaign that ignored prediction market signals while opponents heeded them would be strategically disadvantaged.

This led to increasingly sophisticated engagement. Campaigns hired quantitative analysts to model the relationship between prediction market movements and underlying electoral fundamentals. They conducted experiments to understand whether events that moved market probabilities actually translated into changed voter behavior. They developed strategies for responding when markets moved against them, sometimes challenging the market's judgment, sometimes adjusting tactics to address the concerns market movements revealed.

Some campaigns went further, actively participating in prediction markets themselves. Not to manipulate prices, that would be both expensive and potentially illegal but to hedge political risks or signal confidence. A campaign facing difficult fundraising might point to market odds showing a close race as evidence that investment was worthwhile. A campaign enjoying market momentum might amplify those signals to attract bandwagon supporters.

The ethics of campaign participation in prediction markets became hotly debated. Should candidates be allowed to bet on their own races? Should campaign staff? What about major donors? The potential conflicts of interest were obvious, a candidate losing an election but winning a large bet faced perverse incentives. Most campaigns established policies prohibiting direct trading by candidates and senior staff, though enforcement was difficult given prediction markets' pseudo-anonymous nature.

More significant than direct participation was how prediction markets influenced campaign strategy and resource allocation. Modern campaigns make hundreds of decisions about where to campaign, how to spend advertising dollars, which demographics to target, and what messages to emphasize. Traditionally, these decisions relied on polls, focus groups, and strategists' intuitions. Prediction markets offered an additional data source that campaigns began incorporating into decision frameworks.

If prediction markets showed particular swing states becoming more competitive than polls suggested, campaigns might redirect resources accordingly. If markets indicated that certain demographic groups were moving away from a candidate, campaigns could adjust messaging. If markets reacted strongly to particular events or controversies, campaigns learned what voters actually cared about rather than what pundits claimed mattered.

This strategic use of prediction markets represented a form of organizational learning. Campaigns that incorporated market signals into planning processes gained advantages over campaigns that relied solely on traditional methods. Over electoral cycles, this competitive pressure would push the entire industry toward greater prediction market integration, regardless of individual strategists' philosophical views about markets' epistemic authority.

Business and Investment Applications

Beyond politics, Polymarket's success accelerated prediction markets' adoption in business and investment contexts. Corporations had experimented with internal prediction markets for years, letting employees trade on questions like product launch success, sales targets, or competitor behavior but these remained niche management tools. Polymarket's visibility and demonstrated accuracy prompted broader interest in prediction markets' business applications.

Investment firms began treating prediction markets as alternative data sources similar to satellite imagery, credit card transactions, or social media sentiment. Hedge funds hired analysts to monitor prediction markets for signals about political risk, regulatory changes, or macroeconomic developments that might affect portfolio positions. Proprietary trading firms developed algorithms that incorporated prediction market data alongside traditional indicators.

The logic was compelling. If prediction markets aggregated dispersed information about future events, and those events affected asset prices, then prediction market data should help forecast market movements. A hedge fund that recognized electoral developments before competitors could trade profitably on that information. An investment bank that better understood regulatory probabilities could advise clients more effectively.

Some of the largest quantitative hedge funds experimented with trading on prediction markets directly, both to profit from any inefficiencies and to access market-generated forecasts for their primary investment strategies. These sophisticated participants brought more capital and analytical firepower to prediction markets, potentially improving price efficiency but also raising questions about whether retail traders could compete against institutional resources.

Corporations used prediction markets differently. Rather than seeking trading profits, businesses wanted better forecasts about their competitive environment. A pharmaceutical company might consult prediction markets about FDA approval timelines, regulatory changes, or competitor clinical trial outcomes. A technology company might look at markets predicting product launch success, technology adoption rates, or industry consolidation. An energy company might use markets forecasting climate policy, commodity prices, or geopolitical developments affecting supply chains.

Some companies went beyond passive observation to create sponsored prediction markets. They would fund liquidity or offer prizes to encourage trading on questions relevant to their business, essentially paying for market-generated forecasts. This approach raised methodological questions, did financial incentives from interested parties bias market prices? but offered companies direct access to crowd-sourced predictions on questions that mattered to their strategies.

The consulting industry took notice. Major firms like McKinsey, BCG, and Bain began incorporating prediction market analysis into their offerings. They helped clients understand how to interpret market data, identify strategic implications, and occasionally design internal prediction markets for organizational decision-making. A new subspecialty emerged: consultants who specialized in prediction market strategy and implementation.

Academic Validation and Research

Polymarket's 2024 election success provided academic researchers studying prediction markets with compelling new data. Scholars had long argued theoretically that prediction markets should outperform other forecasting methods, but empirical evidence had been limited to small-scale experiments or platforms with minimal liquidity. Polymarket offered something unprecedented: billions in trading volume on politically significant questions with clear resolution criteria and detailed public data.

Research papers analyzing Polymarket's accuracy proliferated. Political scientists compared market probabilities to poll-based forecasts and evaluated which performed better. Economists examined market microstructure questions, how quickly prices incorporated new information, whether large traders influenced prices disproportionately, how liquidity affected forecast quality. Computer scientists analyzed trading patterns using blockchain data, identifying the network structure of market participants and information flow.

The findings were nuanced. Polymarket had indeed outperformed polls in the 2024 presidential race, but analysis revealed this reflected a combination of factors. Markets incorporated information about polling bias that poll aggregators had underweighted. Market participants included some traders with access to superior information or analytical models. And critically, markets updated continuously as new information emerged while polls became stale between releases.

But researchers also identified limitations. Prediction markets sometimes exhibited herding behavior, with large movements driven by momentum rather than new fundamental information. Markets on niche topics with low trading volume showed wide bid-ask spreads and potentially unreliable prices. Questions without clear resolution criteria generated disputes that undermined market functioning. And persistent concerns about manipulation remained, while large-scale price distortion was expensive, smaller markets might be vulnerable to concerted efforts by motivated actors.

Academic validation proceeded unevenly across disciplines. Economics and political science, where prediction market theory had originated, generally embraced the empirical findings while debating methodological details. Sociology and psychology remained more skeptical, emphasizing how markets might reflect and reinforce existing biases rather than correcting them. Legal scholars focused on regulatory questions, debating whether prediction markets should be treated as information tools deserving protection or as gambling requiring restriction.

Business schools began teaching prediction markets as part of forecasting and decision-making curricula. Students learned both theoretical foundations and practical applications, with Polymarket serving as a prominent case study. Whether this academic integration would lead to broader societal acceptance or would remain confined to specialized research communities remained unclear, but the intellectual legitimacy prediction markets gained through serious scholarly attention represented a significant milestone.

Government and Policy Applications

The most speculative but potentially transformative impact of prediction markets involved government and policy applications. If markets could forecast elections, might they also predict policy outcomes, program effectiveness, or geopolitical developments? Could governments use prediction markets to make better decisions, allocate resources more efficiently, or identify emerging risks earlier?

Some government agencies had experimented with prediction markets internally. The intelligence community had tested classified prediction markets where analysts traded on questions about terrorism, proliferation, and foreign government behavior. The Defense Department had explored markets predicting military technology development and operational outcomes. These programs remained small and controversial, but Polymarket's success prompted renewed interest.

Proponents argued that prediction markets could address systematic problems in government decision-making. Agencies faced perverse incentives where admitting uncertainty or forecasting program failure harmed careers and budgets. Bureaucratic consensus often produced bland, hedged predictions that provided little actionable guidance. Political appointees sometimes demanded optimistic projections regardless of evidence. Prediction markets could cut through these pathologies by creating forums where analysts could express genuine beliefs anonymously without career risk.

Imagine a prediction market on whether a proposed government program would meet its stated objectives. If market probabilities were low, it might suggest reconsidering the program design or budget allocation. If markets forecasted that a regulatory approach would fail to achieve intended outcomes, policymakers might explore alternatives before committing resources. If markets predicted geopolitical crises, intelligence and diplomatic resources could be preemptively directed to address emerging threats.

Critics raised fundamental objections. Should unelected traders influence democratic decision-making? Would markets on policy outcomes be manipulable by those implementing the policies, creating perverse incentives? Would political appointees simply ignore market signals that conflicted with their preferences? And practically, would sufficient informed traders participate in government policy markets to generate meaningful prices?

Despite these concerns, some policy advocates pushed for pilot programs. Proposals included creating prediction markets on economic indicators to supplement traditional forecasting, markets on climate policy outcomes to inform international negotiations, and markets on public health interventions to guide resource allocation during crises. The COVID-19 pandemic had revealed how poor governmental forecasting could be; prediction markets might have provided earlier warning about disease spread, treatment efficacy, or vaccine development timelines.

Legislative interest remained tentative. Some members of Congress saw prediction markets as innovative tools deserving exploration. Others viewed them as dangerous encroachments on democratic processes or inappropriate gambling on serious policy questions. Without clear political consensus, government adoption of prediction markets would likely remain limited to narrow experimental applications rather than systematic integration into decision-making processes.

The Transformation of Forecasting Culture

Beyond specific institutional applications, Polymarket's emergence contributed to broader cultural shifts in how people thought about forecasting and uncertainty. For generations, predictions had been expressed in vague qualitative terms, experts declaring outcomes "likely" or "unlikely" without specifying precise probabilities. Polymarket normalized quantitative probabilistic thinking, encouraging people to think in terms of specific percentage likelihoods rather than binary yes/no predictions.

This shift had subtle but significant effects. When political pundits appeared on television after the 2024 election, they faced harder questions about their pre-election predictions. Had they said Trump had a 20% chance of winning or 45%? The distinction mattered. Saying something was "unlikely" but giving it a 30% chance of occurring was different from giving it a 5% chance. Polymarket's precise probabilities created a standard against which vague punditry could be evaluated.

Financial markets had long operated with probabilistic thinking, traders constantly assessed odds and managed risk portfolios. But for other domains, politics, culture and technology such explicit quantification had been less common. Polymarket's visibility spread probabilistic reasoning beyond finance into broader public discourse. People began expressing views as "I'd put 70% odds on that happening" rather than "I think that will probably happen."

This cultural shift complemented broader movements toward quantification and data-driven thinking. Just as FiveThirtyEight had normalized discussing elections through polling averages and statistical models, Polymarket normalized discussing them through market probabilities. The next generation of politically engaged citizens would grow up expecting multiple quantitative frameworks for thinking about uncertain futures rather than relying solely on expert pronouncements or personal intuitions.

The transformation wasn't universally welcomed. Critics worried about false precision, expressing forecasts as specific probabilities suggested confidence that might not be warranted. They noted that some questions fundamentally resisted quantification, involving values and judgments rather than predictable events. They feared that excessive focus on probabilistic forecasts might crowd out other valuable forms of analysis and deliberation.

But defenders argued that explicit probabilities revealed uncertainty rather than concealing it. Saying an event had 60% odds made clear that it might not occur, unlike confident predictions that created false certainty. Quantification forced clarity about what forecasters actually believed rather than letting them hide behind ambiguous language. And probabilistic thinking enabled better decision-making by encouraging people to consider multiple scenarios and their relative likelihoods.

The Network Effects of Adoption

As prediction markets gained acceptance across multiple domains, media, politics, business, academia, and potentially government network effects began amplifying their value and influence. The more institutions consulted prediction markets, the more informed traders became interested in participating. The more sophisticated participants traded, the more efficient and accurate prices became. The more accurate markets proved, the more institutions relied on them.

This virtuous cycle suggested prediction markets might be approaching an inflection point where they became permanently embedded in society's informational infrastructure. Just as stock markets became essential despite early skepticism, prediction markets might evolve from controversial experiments into taken-for-granted tools that people consulted without much thought about underlying mechanisms.

Polymarket sat at the center of this emerging ecosystem. Its early-mover advantage, liquidity, brand recognition, and proven accuracy gave it structural advantages that would be difficult for competitors to overcome. Network effects in prediction markets were particularly strong, traders gravitated to platforms with the deepest liquidity and most participants because that was where prices were most reliable and trading was easiest.

This raised questions about market structure and competition. Would prediction markets become natural monopolies dominated by single platforms? Would regulatory fragmentation across jurisdictions prevent global markets from forming? Would traditional financial institutions eventually enter the space and leverage their resources to displace crypto-native startups? The answers would shape whether Polymarket specifically or prediction markets generally achieved the transformative potential their advocates envisioned.

Limits of the Revolution

Despite growing adoption and demonstrated success, prediction markets faced real constraints on their impact. Many important questions didn't lend themselves to market-based forecasting. Markets required clear resolution criteria, defined events with observable outcomes. But much of human concern involved inherently ambiguous questions about meaning, value, and quality that couldn't be reduced to binary yes/no propositions.

Markets worked best for questions where informed traders had strong incentives to acquire information and trade on it. Obscure topics that few people cared about generated thin markets with unreliable prices. Questions whose outcomes wouldn't be known for years attracted little trading volume because capital was locked up too long. Very short-term questions sometimes resolved before markets could process information effectively.

The manipulation problem, while perhaps overstated, remained genuine. Sufficiently motivated actors with sufficient capital could move markets, at least temporarily. For questions where perception mattered as much as reality, political momentum, brand reputation, market confidence manipulated prediction market prices might become self-fulfilling regardless of underlying fundamentals. Distinguishing legitimate information from attempted manipulation would remain an ongoing challenge.

And fundamentally, markets reflected the information and biases of whoever participated. If systematic blind spots existed, entire classes of information that no traders possessed markets would miss those blind spots. If participants shared common misconceptions, markets would aggregate and reinforce errors rather than correcting them. The wisdom of crowds worked only when crowds contained diverse perspectives and information sources.

These limitations meant prediction markets would complement rather than replace other forecasting methods. Traditional polling, expert analysis, statistical modeling, and human judgment would all remain valuable. The revolution Polymarket had catalyzed wasn't the replacement of existing tools but the addition of a powerful new option that institutions could use alongside traditional approaches, creating richer and more robust understanding of possible futures than any single method could provide alone.

Chapter 24

Criticisms and Concerns

The champagne had barely been poured when the critics sharpened their knives.

In the aftermath of Polymarket's stunning accuracy during the 2024 election, Shayne Coplan found himself in an unfamiliar position: simultaneously vindicated and vilified. While mainstream media outlets that had dismissed prediction markets now scrambled to understand them, a chorus of skeptics, academics, regulators, and concerned observers raised fundamental questions about what Polymarket had become and what it meant for society.

The criticisms weren't new. They had accumulated like sediment over the platform's four-year existence, each controversy adding another layer of concern. But success brought scrutiny, and with billions of dollars now flowing through Polymarket's markets, the stakes of getting this wrong, of allowing a fundamentally flawed or dangerous platform to influence public discourse had never been higher.

The Manipulation Question

Dr. Sarah Hutchins, an economist at MIT who had spent two decades studying prediction markets, put it bluntly in a November 2024 paper: "We have no reliable way to distinguish between a market revealing information and a market being manipulated to create a narrative."

The concern was theoretical but grounded in observable reality. Unlike traditional financial markets with extensive surveillance, reporting requirements, and regulatory oversight, Polymarket operated in a gray zone where the identity of traders remained obscure and their motivations unknowable. When a single wallet moved $3 million into "Trump wins," was that an informed bet or an attempt to shift the narrative?

The most prominent case study arrived in October 2024, when a cluster of accounts, later traced back to similar wallet behaviors and funding sources, placed over $30 million on Donald Trump to win the presidency. The press dubbed the bettor the "French whale," and Polymarket itself claimed to have identified a single wealthy French individual making informed bets based on superior polling data.

But the episode raised uncomfortable questions. The massive bets moved the market significantly, shifting Trump's implied probability by several percentage points. Media outlets reported these movements as news: "Prediction markets surge for Trump." Political operatives cited Polymarket prices in fundraising emails and strategy memos. The feedback loop was complete, the bet itself had become information, independent of whether it reflected genuine predictive insight.

"This is the fundamental problem," argued Marcus Chen, a former CFTC economist who had become one of Polymarket's most vocal critics. "In financial markets, we accept that large trades move prices because we believe markets aggregate information efficiently. But in prediction markets about political events, a large bet doesn't just move the price, it potentially influences the outcome. Someone betting $30 million on Trump doesn't just predict Trump winning; they might contribute to Trump winning by creating a narrative of inevitability."

Polymarket's defenders countered that manipulation was financially irrational. To profitably manipulate a market, you'd need to move the price, influence the real-world outcome, and then benefit from that influence, all while risking millions of dollars. The French whale, after all, had been right, turning his $30 million into approximately $50 million in profit. Didn't that suggest genuine insight rather than manipulation?

But critics pointed out that the payoff for manipulation might not be financial. What if a foreign government wanted to demoralize opposition voters by making their candidate appear doomed? What if a political operative wanted to generate media coverage of their candidate's "momentum"? What if a wealthy ideologue simply wanted to promote their preferred narrative, viewing any financial loss as a cost of political activism?

The platform had no reliable defenses against such tactics. While Polymarket employed analysts to watch for suspicious trading patterns, the pseudonymous nature of blockchain transactions made it nearly impossible to identify coordinated behavior across multiple wallets. Unlike traditional exchanges that required know-your-customer verification, Polymarket's users hid behind cryptocurrency addresses and VPNs.

The Whale Problem

Related but distinct from manipulation concerns was the simple concentration of capital. By late 2024, data analysts studying Polymarket's order books estimated that roughly a dozen accounts controlled over 40% of the liquidity in major political markets. These "whales" didn't need to coordinate or manipulate, their sheer size gave them outsized influence over market prices.

The problem manifested most clearly in smaller markets. When Polymarket created a market on whether a specific bill would pass Congress, a single trader with $100,000 could essentially set the price. Other traders, seeing the whale's position, often followed suit, creating a cascade where one person's view became the market's consensus.

"It's not the wisdom of crowds," explained Dr. Hutchins. "It's the wisdom of whales, with some crowd noise in the background."

This concentration created a paradox. The whales, by providing liquidity, made the markets possible. Without them, spreads would widen to the point of uselessness. But their dominance meant that Polymarket prices often reflected the views of a few dozen wealthy, risk-tolerant individuals rather than genuine crowd wisdom.

The identity of these whales remained largely mysterious. Some were known professional gamblers who had migrated from sports betting. Others were crypto traders who understood blockchain mechanics and saw prediction markets as a natural extension of their expertise. A few were political operatives or hedge fund analysts looking for an information edge. But many remained completely anonymous, their motivations and information sources unknown.

This opacity troubled researchers. When a traditional poll shows a candidate leading, we can evaluate the methodology, sample size, and potential biases. When Polymarket showed a candidate leading, we saw only a price with no way to know whether it reflected the collective wisdom of thousands of small traders or the idiosyncratic views of three guys in a Discord channel with deep pockets.

Prediction Versus Influence

Perhaps the most philosophically vexing criticism centered on the distinction between predicting events and influencing them. Prediction markets worked best for events completely outside traders' control, the weather, sports outcomes, box office results. But many of Polymarket's most popular markets concerned events where public perception mattered.

The 2024 election provided the perfect case study. Throughout October, Polymarket showed Trump with higher odds than most polls suggested. Media coverage of this discrepancy became its own story. "Why Are Prediction Markets and Polls Telling Different Stories?" asked the New York Times. "Is Polymarket Seeing Something Pollsters Miss?" wondered The Economist.

The coverage itself became a factor in the election. Republican operatives seized on Polymarket's Trump-favorable odds as evidence of momentum. Democratic donors, seeing the odds, reportedly became more pessimistic about their fundraising pitches. Undecided voters, observing the prediction market odds, potentially experienced a bandwagon effect.

When Trump won, Polymarket's defenders claimed vindication, see the market was right! But critics asked: Right about what? Had the market predicted an inevitable outcome, or had it contributed to creating that outcome by shaping the narrative around the election?

The distinction mattered enormously. If prediction markets merely forecasted events, they were valuable tools for understanding the future. But if they influenced events while claiming to predict them, they became something else entirely, a new form of media manipulation disguised as neutral information aggregation.

"We've created Schrödinger's prediction market," joked one political scientist, though his underlying point was serious. "The act of observing the market changes the outcome, but we can never know how much."

The Gambling Concern

Underneath the sophisticated debates about market efficiency and information aggregation lay a simpler concern: Polymarket was gambling, and gambling destroyed lives.

By early 2025, online forums and Reddit threads contained hundreds of stories from individuals who had lost significant money on Polymarket. Some had bet their rent money on election outcomes. Others had taken out loans to place larger bets, convinced they had superior insight. A few had lost six-figure sums, wiping out savings or college funds.

"My husband became obsessed with Polymarket in 2023," wrote one anonymous poster in a gambling addiction support forum. "At first it was small amounts on whether it would rain or whether a celebrity couple would stay together. But by the election, he was spending every evening analyzing polls, refreshing the markets, moving money between positions. He lost $45,000 betting on the election. Money we had saved for our daughter's education."

Polymarket's defenders argued that this was no different from stock market losses or poker losses, any form of risk-taking could become problematic for individuals prone to addiction. The platform included warnings about risk and prohibited minors from participating. What more could they do?

But critics pointed out key differences. Stock markets ostensibly served a productive economic function, allocating capital to businesses. Sports betting, while clearly gambling, was at least transparent about what it was. Polymarket occupied an uncomfortable middle ground, presenting itself as a tool for information discovery and forecasting while functioning, for many users, as pure gambling.

The gamification elements didn't help. The platform included leaderboards showing top traders, achievement badges for certain milestones, and a social feed where users could share their positions and trash-talk others. These features, borrowed from social media and gaming, were designed to increase engagement, which they did. But they also amplified the addictive potential.

Public health researchers noted troubling parallels to sports betting apps that had exploded in the wake of legal changes in the 2020s. Those apps had combined ease of access, constant action, social features, and sophisticated psychological hooks to drive higher betting volumes. Problem gambling rates had risen significantly, particularly among young men. Polymarket, with its 24/7 markets on everything from elections to celebrity gossip, threatened to expand the addiction vectors even further.

"We're watching the gamification of civic life," warned Dr. Jennifer Martinez, a psychiatrist specializing in behavioral addictions. "People aren't just watching political news anymore, they're constantly checking their positions, feeling the dopamine hit of their candidates rising in the markets, experiencing the despair of losses. We're turning democracy into a casino."

The Ethics of Tragedy Markets

Some of Polymarket's markets ventured into morally fraught territory. The platform had hosted markets on whether specific public figures would die within certain timeframes, whether natural disasters would kill more than certain numbers of people, and whether terrorist attacks would occur in specific locations.

These "tragedy markets" sparked fierce ethical debates. Defenders argued that such markets served valuable purposes, hospitals could hedge against pandemic waves, disaster relief organizations could prepare for hurricanes, security agencies could take threats seriously when markets showed elevated risk.

But critics found the very concept repugnant. "Creating a market where people profit from human death is grotesque," argued bioethicist Professor Robert Callahan. "It doesn't matter if there's some theoretical social benefit. We don't allow people to bet on whether their neighbors will die, even though such bets might incentivize safety precautions. Some things shouldn't be reduced to markets."

The most controversial example came in August 2023, when Polymarket created a market on whether a specific kidnapped journalist would be found alive. The market drew immediate outrage from the journalist's family and from press freedom organizations. Critics argued that it turned a human tragedy into entertainment and that traders betting "no" were effectively rooting for someone's death.

Polymarket removed the market and issued an apology, but the damage to its reputation lingered. The incident revealed a fundamental tension: the platform's success depended on offering markets on whatever users found interesting, but some topics crossed ethical lines that even the most libertarian market advocates found uncomfortable.

The challenge was determining where to draw those lines. Polymarket prohibited markets on assassinations, reasoning that such markets could encourage violence. But was a market on whether a politician would die of natural causes much different? The platform allowed markets on war casualties but not on specific civilian deaths. It permitted markets on whether celebrities would divorce but not on whether they would commit suicide.

These distinctions often seemed arbitrary, more focused on avoiding public relations disasters than on consistent ethical principles. The decentralized ethos that animated Polymarket's technology, anyone should be able to create any market crashed into the reality that some markets felt fundamentally wrong.

Data Privacy and Surveillance

While Polymarket marketed itself as protecting user privacy through blockchain pseudonymity, researchers raised concerns about what the platform actually knew about its users and how that information might be used.

Every trade on Polymarket generated data, not just the public blockchain transaction, but metadata about timing, IP addresses (for users not using VPNs), browser fingerprints, and trading patterns. Combined with external data sources, this information could potentially be used to identify users and understand their beliefs, biases, and information sources.

"This is an unregulated data bonanza," warned privacy researcher Dr. Kimberly Okafor. "Polymarket knows what thousands of people believe about upcoming events, often before those beliefs become public. They know who has information before others. They can see coordination and communication patterns. This is incredibly valuable intelligence, and there are essentially no rules governing how they can use it."

The concern wasn't purely theoretical. In 2024, several news organizations had approached Polymarket requesting data on trading patterns for investigative stories. While the platform generally declined, the requests highlighted the surveillance potential. Authoritarian governments could theoretically demand such data to identify dissidents. Corporate competitors could pay for insights into business intelligence. Political campaigns could target advertisements based on users' revealed preferences.

Polymarket's privacy policy, buried in legal text that few users read, reserved the right to share anonymized data with third parties and to comply with legal requests. Given that blockchain transactions were permanently public, even "anonymized" data could potentially be de-anonymized by sophisticated analysts cross-referencing multiple data sources.

The Retail Trader Problem

Despite Polymarket's emergence as a serious forecasting tool, analysis of its user base revealed a troubling pattern of retail traders, ordinary individuals betting small amounts consistently lost money, while sophisticated whales consistently profited.

A study by researchers at Stanford analyzing six months of Polymarket data in 2024 found that accounts trading less than $1,000 per month lost money in aggregate, while accounts trading over $100,000 per month showed consistent profits. The pattern resembled poker or sports betting, where professionals systematically extracted value from amateurs.

"This isn't the wisdom of crowds," concluded the study's lead author. "This is the fleecing of crowds. Ordinary users provide liquidity and lose money while sophisticated traders with better information or analysis tools profit. The aggregation mechanism works because retail traders effectively subsidize the information gathering of professionals."

The finding raised questions about Polymarket's social utility. If the platform primarily served as a wealth transfer mechanism from naive retail traders to professional gamblers and financial analysts, did it really serve democracy or information discovery? Or was it simply a new vehicle for separating fools from their money?

Polymarket's response emphasized that users were adults making voluntary choices and that losses in prediction markets were no different from losses in any other market. But critics pointed out that the platform's marketing emphasized civic participation and forecasting accuracy, not the reality that most users would lose money to better-informed professionals.

Regulatory Arbitrage and the Offshore Shell Game

Even after its 2022 CFTC settlement, Polymarket continued to face accusations of deliberately evading US regulations while serving US customers.

Investigative journalism in late 2024 revealed that despite geo-blocking, substantial trading volume appeared to originate from US IP addresses. While Polymarket claimed these were VPN users from other countries, analysts noted suspicious patterns, trading activity that peaked during US East Coast business hours, markets focused on hyperlocal US political races that would interest few international traders, and linguistic patterns in user forums suggesting American users.

"They're playing a shell game," argued former CFTC enforcement attorney David Brenner. "They agreed not to serve US customers, but they've designed their system to make it trivially easy for US customers to access the platform. They don't require meaningful identity verification. They don't employ the robust VPN detection that gaming sites use. This isn't compliance, it's compliance theater."

The concern extended beyond US regulations. Polymarket operated without gambling licenses in most jurisdictions, arguing that prediction markets weren't gambling under their local laws. This regulatory arbitrage allowed the platform to avoid consumer protections, responsible gambling requirements, and tax collection that traditional gambling operators faced.

Critics saw this as unfair competition, Polymarket could undercut regulated operators because it didn't bear the costs of compliance. Defenders saw it as innovation, creating new products that didn't fit neatly into existing regulatory categories and forcing regulators to adapt.

The Existential Question

Underlying all specific criticisms was a deeper concern: Did prediction markets make society better or worse?

Proponents argued that Polymarket improved information flow, held forecasters accountable, and revealed truth through market mechanisms. The platform's success in the 2024 election, they claimed, demonstrated its value.

But critics wondered whether the costs outweighed the benefits. Had Polymarket produced any information that rigorous polling and analysis wouldn't have eventually revealed? Had it improved democratic discourse or simply added another layer of noise and anxiety? Had it helped people make better decisions or simply provided another avenue for gambling addiction?

The most pessimistic critics saw Polymarket as emblematic of a broader problem, the financialization of everything. Politics, disasters, personal tragedies, celebrity gossip all reduced to tradeable markets, all converted into opportunities for profit and loss. In this view, prediction markets didn't discover information so much as they hollowed out civic life, replacing deliberation and solidarity with speculation and gambling.

"We're creating a world where everything is a bet," wrote cultural critic Amanda Foster in a widely-shared essay. "Where every event is an opportunity for profit, every tragedy a chance to make money, every election a casino. This isn't innovation. It's nihilism disguised as disruption."

The Defense

Shayne Coplan read the criticisms with a mixture of frustration and defiance. In his view, critics were attacking Polymarket because it challenged comfortable assumptions and threatened established institutions. Pollsters and pundits criticized prediction markets because they revealed their own fallibility. Regulators attacked because they couldn't control the flow of information. Gambling critics opposed because they were paternalistic.

In interviews, he emphasized that Polymarket was transparent, anyone could see the prices and understand the methodology. Traditional polls were black boxes, with sample selection and weighting decisions hidden from public scrutiny. Prediction markets put money behind forecasts, creating accountability that polling lacked.

As for the ethical concerns, Shayne argued that information was information. Markets on difficult topics didn't create the tragedies, they helped people understand and prepare for them. The discomfort people felt about tragedy markets reflected squeamishness about acknowledging reality, not genuine ethical insight.

"People don't want to admit that the world operates on probabilities and incentives," he told one interviewer. "They want to pretend that good intentions and right thinking are enough. Prediction markets force us to confront reality. That's uncomfortable, but it's necessary."

The criticisms, in his view, were the price of success. Every transformative technology faced resistance from those invested in the old ways. Personal computers, the internet, cryptocurrency all had been dismissed as dangerous toys before they changed the world. Prediction markets would follow the same trajectory.

But late at night, alone with his thoughts, even Shayne sometimes wondered. Not whether prediction markets were valuable, of that he remained convinced. But whether Polymarket, in its specific implementation, had gotten everything right. Whether the pursuit of growth had led to compromises that would haunt the platform. Whether the criticisms, however overwrought, contained kernels of truth that deserved more than dismissive responses.

The questions lingered, unanswered, as Polymarket surged toward its uncertain future.

Chapter 25

The Competition

Tarek Mansour stood in front of the CFTC commissioners in September 2023, his hands steady, his presentation rehearsed to perfection. As the co-founder and CEO of Kalshi, he was making the pitch that Shayne Coplan couldn't or wouldn't make, that event contracts could operate legally, profitably, and openly in the United States.

"We're not asking for permission to operate in a gray zone," Mansour told the commissioners. "We're asking you to regulate us. To oversee us. To hold us accountable. We believe prediction markets serve a vital economic function, and we want to build them the right way."

The contrast with Polymarket's approach couldn't have been starker. Where Shayne had chosen disruption, decentralization, and regulatory arbitrage, Mansour had chosen the establishment path: lawyers, licenses, and legitimacy. The competition between these two visions, outlaw versus insider, crypto versus traditional finance, move fast versus move carefully would define the prediction market industry's future.

But Kalshi wasn't Polymarket's only competition. By 2024, the space was crowded with challengers, each offering a different answer to the question of how prediction markets should work. Some would succeed. Most would fail. All of them existed in Polymarket's shadow, trying to capture a piece of the attention and liquidity that Shayne's platform had demonstrated was possible.

Kalshi: The Regulated Alternative

Tarek Mansour and Luana Lopes Lara had founded Kalshi in 2018, before Polymarket existed, with a clear vision: bring prediction markets to America by doing everything legally. Both had MIT backgrounds, Mansour in computer science, Lopes Lara in economics and both had worked in traditional finance. They understood how markets worked, but they also understood how regulation worked.

The path they chose was arduous. Rather than launching quickly and asking forgiveness later, Kalshi spent two years and millions of dollars in legal fees obtaining a Designated Contract Market (DCM) license from the CFTC. This designation, normally reserved for major derivatives exchanges like CME Group, gave Kalshi the explicit authority to offer event contracts in the United States.

The process was exhausting. Every market design had to be approved. Risk management systems had to be built to regulatory specifications. Compliance officers had to be hired. Bank relationships had to be established. Customer funds had to be segregated according to strict rules. The overhead was enormous, everything Polymarket had avoided by operating offshore.

But by 2021, Kalshi had what Polymarket could never claim: complete legal certainty. American users could trade on Kalshi without VPNs or workarounds. Institutional investors could participate without legal risk. Media organizations could cite Kalshi prices without the asterisk that accompanied Polymarket data.

The early markets were cautious, would inflation exceed certain levels, would Congress pass specific legislation, would COVID cases hit certain thresholds. Nothing controversial, nothing that would spook regulators. Trading volume was modest, measured in thousands of dollars rather than millions.

Then came the breakthrough. In 2023, the CFTC approved Kalshi's proposal for congressional control markets, contracts on which party would control the House and Senate after the 2024 elections. These were explicitly political prediction markets, operating legally on U.S. soil for the first time since the Iowa Electronic Markets' academic exemption decades earlier.

The approval unleashed a flood of interest. Kalshi's trading volume exploded, growing from a few million dollars per month to over $100 million during the 2024 election cycle. Major news organizations began citing Kalshi alongside traditional polls. Political operatives opened accounts. Hedge funds allocated capital to political trading strategies.

"We proved it could be done," Mansour said in a November 2024 interview, days after Kalshi's congressional markets successfully predicted Republican control. "You don't need to operate in legal gray zones. You don't need crypto or blockchain. You can build a real business with real regulatory approval."

The jab at Polymarket was unmistakable. So was the underlying tension. Kalshi's success validated the prediction market concept that Polymarket had pioneered, but it also threatened to steal Polymarket's market share by offering something Shayne couldn't: legal access for U.S. users.

Yet Polymarket maintained significant advantages. Its blockchain architecture allowed for more complex markets and faster innovation. Its offshore status meant lower overhead and fewer restrictions. Most importantly, it had liquidity, the network effect that made markets efficient. Kalshi's spread between bid and ask prices remained wider than Polymarket's, making it less attractive for serious traders.

The competition was far from over, but by 2025, it had clarified into a clear dynamic: Kalshi owned legal U.S. access, while Polymarket owned global scale and crypto-native traders. The question was whether either advantage would prove decisive.

PredictIt: The Academic Survivor

Long before either Polymarket or Kalshi existed, a small prediction market called PredictIt had been operating under an unusual arrangement. Launched in 2014 by Victoria University of Wellington in partnership with Aristotle International, PredictIt operated under a CFTC no-action letter that allowed it to function as an academic research project.

The restrictions were severe: individual positions were capped at $850, market sizes were limited, and the platform had to share data with researchers. These constraints made PredictIt useless for serious traders but perfect for academic studies of prediction market behavior.

For years, PredictIt had the political prediction market space largely to itself. Its prices became media staples, cited in hundreds of news articles during each election cycle. The platform developed a loyal community of small-stakes traders who enjoyed the gamification of politics.

Then came the newcomers. By 2022, PredictIt faced competition from both Polymarket's scale and Kalshi's regulatory approval. Worse, the CFTC under pressure from Kalshi and other competitors moved to revoke PredictIt's no-action letter, arguing that the platform had exceeded its research mandate and become a commercial operation.

PredictIt sued, and legal battles dragged on through 2023 and 2024. The uncertainty chilled the platform's growth. Why would traders invest time and money learning a platform that might shut down? By the 2024 election, PredictIt's volume had been eclipsed by both major competitors.

Yet the platform persisted, sustained by legal stays and its community's loyalty. In interviews, PredictIt's leadership emphasized their academic mission and their years of research contributions. They had published dozens of papers, validated prediction market theory, and educated thousands of Americans about probabilistic thinking.

"We're not trying to be the biggest," explained John Phillips, PredictIt's COO. "We're trying to be the most intellectually rigorous. Our data has informed understanding of American politics in ways that pure commercial markets never could."

It was a noble pitch, but by 2025, it was unclear whether noble was enough. PredictIt had been the pioneer, but pioneers often get overtaken. The question was whether its academic focus could sustain it as the market matured, or whether it would become a footnote in the prediction market revolution it had helped start.

Augur: The Decentralization Dream

If Polymarket represented crypto pragmatism using blockchain for specific advantages while maintaining usability Augur represented crypto idealism, a completely decentralized prediction market with no central authority whatsoever.

Launched in 2018 after a groundbreaking ICO that raised $5 million, Augur was built on Ethereum with a bold vision: anyone could create any market on any topic, and a decentralized network of token holders would resolve disputes. No company could be shut down. No CEO could be arrested. The platform would exist as long as Ethereum existed.

The vision attracted developers, libertarians, and crypto purists. Here was the ultimate expression of decentralized finance, markets on anything, resistant to censorship, governed by code rather than committees.

But the reality proved more complicated. Augur's user interface was notoriously difficult, requiring deep technical knowledge and multiple blockchain transactions for simple actions. Gas fees on Ethereum made small bets economically irrational. The dispute resolution system, while theoretically sound, moved slowly and sometimes reached controversial conclusions.

Most problematically, Augur's openness attracted the markets that other platforms rejected. Assassination markets appeared and had to be resolved by the community. Markets on child abuse and terrorism drew law enforcement attention. The platform's anonymity made it a haven for the prediction markets that society found most objectionable.

By 2020, when Polymarket launched, Augur had proven both the promise and the pitfalls of full decentralization. The technology worked, markets could be created and resolved without central authority. But the user experience and ethical challenges made mainstream adoption nearly impossible.

Augur's developers launched Augur v2 in 2020, addressing some technical issues, but by then Polymarket had demonstrated a better path: use blockchain for its advantages (transparency, composability, global access) while maintaining enough centralization to ensure usability and ethical guardrails.

"Augur showed us what not to do," one Polymarket developer admitted privately. "Pure decentralization is beautiful in theory, but users want platforms that work easily and don't host markets on horrific topics. You need some governance."

By 2024, Augur's trading volume had dwindled to a tiny fraction of Polymarket's. The platform still operated, sustained by true believers, but its moment had passed. It remained an important proof of concept, decentralized prediction markets were technically possible but the market had spoken: users wanted pragmatic decentralization, not ideological purity.

The Sports Betting Giants Eye the Prize

The real threat to prediction markets didn't come from other prediction markets. It came from sports betting companies that had spent the 2020s conquering America.

DraftKings, FanDuel, BetMGM, and Caesars had collectively spent billions of dollars building infrastructure, obtaining licenses, and marketing to American sports fans. By 2024, they controlled a sports betting market generating over $100 billion in annual handle. They had the technology, the liquidity, the regulatory relationships, and the customer bases.

What they didn't have was explicit permission to offer political betting. But they were watching the prediction market space carefully, and some were moving to enter.

In August 2024, FanDuel filed an application with the CFTC for authorization to offer event contracts. The filing was vague on details but clear on intent: America's largest sports betting company wanted into prediction markets.

The move sent shockwaves through the industry. If FanDuel received approval, it could leverage its millions of existing customers and its massive marketing budget to dominate the space. Why would traders use Polymarket or Kalshi when they could use the same app they already had for NFL games?

"This is an extinction-level event for the current players," warned one venture capitalist who had invested in prediction markets. "FanDuel has more customers than all prediction market platforms combined. They have relationships with every media company. They have state-by-state gambling licenses. If they get federal approval for event contracts, game over."

Polymarket's leadership tried to appear unconcerned. Sports betting companies understood gambling, they argued, but prediction markets were about information aggregation. The user bases were different, serious traders versus casual bettors. The use cases were different, forecasting versus entertainment.

But privately, the concern was real. If the sports betting giants entered prediction markets with full regulatory approval and unlimited marketing budgets, how could offshore crypto platforms compete? The very success that Polymarket had achieved in 2024, proving that huge demand existed for political prediction markets had attracted predators with far more resources.

The silver lining was timing. FanDuel's application would take months or years to approve. The CFTC moved slowly, especially on controversial topics like political betting. That gave Polymarket a window to consolidate its position, build stronger network effects, and perhaps find a regulatory path of its own.

But the clock was ticking.

International Competitors and Copycats

Beyond the U.S. market, prediction market competitors emerged globally, each adapting the model to local conditions.

In Europe, Smarkets and Betfair had long offered political betting markets, though neither had fully embraced the prediction market framing or blockchain technology. Both saw Polymarket's success and began expanding their offerings, adding more diverse markets and promoting their forecasting accuracy.

In Asia, several blockchain-based prediction platforms launched, targeting the massive Chinese market through various offshore structures. These platforms operated in legal gray zones even murkier than Polymarket's, facing both crypto restrictions and gambling prohibitions. Few achieved significant scale, but they represented a growing awareness that prediction markets had value.

More concerning for Polymarket were the direct clones. The open nature of blockchain meant that Polymarket's smart contracts were visible and copiable. By 2024, at least a dozen platforms had launched with nearly identical technology, differing only in branding and marketing.

Most of these clones failed to gain traction. Network effects in prediction markets were powerful, traders went where liquidity existed, and liquidity existed where traders went. Without some meaningful differentiation, clones couldn't bootstrap the critical mass needed for functional markets.

But the clones served a purpose: they kept Polymarket on edge. Any misstep, a major hack, a controversial market that alienated users, or a regulatory crackdown could send traders fleeing to alternatives that were ready and waiting.

Manifold Markets: The Free Alternative

One competitor took a completely different approach. Manifold Markets, launched in 2022, offered prediction markets with play money. Users could create markets on anything, trade with fake currency, and track their forecasting accuracy without financial risk.

The model seemed absurd, prediction markets without real money lacked the incentive alignment that made them work. Why would traders research carefully if they couldn't win or lose real money?

Yet Manifold attracted a devoted community, particularly among rationalist and effective altruism circles. Users treated their play money balances as reputational capital, striving to be accurate to prove their forecasting skill. The platform became a laboratory for market design experiments that would be too risky with real money.

More importantly, Manifold solved the gambling problem. Because no real money changed hands, the platform operated without gambling licenses or regulatory approval. Anyone could use it, including American users, without legal concerns.

By 2024, Manifold hosted thousands of markets on everything from personal predictions ("Will I finish my novel?") to serious forecasting questions. Its prices weren't as reliable as Polymarket's, play money created different incentives but they were surprisingly accurate for many topics.

"We're not trying to compete with Polymarket on election forecasting," explained Manifold's founders. "We're trying to make prediction markets accessible to everyone and to build a culture of quantitative thinking. If someone later graduates to real-money platforms, that's fine. We're the on-ramp."

The strategy had merit. Manifold users learned how prediction markets worked without financial risk. Many eventually moved to Polymarket or Kalshi for high-stakes markets while continuing to use Manifold for casual forecasting. Rather than direct competition, the relationship was ecosystem development.

The AI Wildcard

The most unpredictable competition came from an unexpected direction: artificial intelligence.

By 2024, large language models had become remarkably good at aggregating information and making probabilistic predictions. Several startups had launched AI-powered forecasting platforms that analyzed news, polls, economic data, and social media to generate probability estimates for future events.

These platforms weren't prediction markets, they didn't aggregate human judgment through trading. But they threatened to commoditize the core value proposition: accurate forecasts. If an AI could analyze all available information and spit out reliable probabilities, why did society need prediction markets?

Polymarket's defenders argued that markets captured information that AI couldn't, private knowledge, tacit understanding, and information that hadn't yet been published. A trader might know something from personal experience that no AI could discover. Markets also adapted instantly to new information, while AI models needed retraining.

But the AI companies were improving rapidly. By late 2024, several AI forecasting platforms had achieved accuracy comparable to prediction markets on some questions. They had advantages too: no need for liquidity, no manipulation concerns, and the ability to explain their reasoning.

"The existential question is whether prediction markets are truly necessary," said Dr. Philip Tetlock, the psychologist who had studied forecasting for decades. "If AI can aggregate public information efficiently, markets may only be valuable for capturing private information. That's a narrower use case than the prediction market advocates claim."

Shayne disagreed vehemently. AI, he argued, was just sophisticated pattern matching. It couldn't replace the skin-in-the-game incentives that made markets work. It couldn't capture the dispersed knowledge that individuals held. And it certainly couldn't be trusted without human oversight.

But even as he argued against the AI threat, Polymarket was quietly building its own AI tools, models that analyzed trading patterns, detected manipulation, and helped identify profitable opportunities. The future, it seemed, would involve both markets and AI, though exactly how they would coexist remained uncertain.

Maintaining the Edge

By early 2025, Shayne faced a crowded field. Kalshi had regulatory approval. Sports betting giants had resources. Clones had identical technology. AI had comparable accuracy. How could Polymarket maintain its lead?

The answer, his team believed, lay in the network effects they'd built. Polymarket had liquidity that no competitor could match. It had brand recognition, when people thought "prediction markets," they thought Polymarket. It had a community of sophisticated traders who wouldn't easily migrate to inferior platforms.

But maintaining those advantages required constant innovation. The platform needed to stay ahead on features, user experience, and market diversity. It needed to defend against manipulation while maintaining openness. It needed to navigate regulatory challenges while preserving its global accessibility.

Most critically, it needed to avoid catastrophic failure. A major hack, a devastating scandal, or a complete regulatory shutdown could shatter the network effects overnight. In markets defined by trust and liquidity, there were no second chances.

"Every day we're competing not just against other platforms," Shayne told his team in a December 2024 meeting. "We're competing against the idea that prediction markets can't work, that they're too easily manipulated, that they're just gambling. Every mistake we make validates the skeptics. Every success we have creates more competitors."

It was an exhausting treadmill, made more so by the knowledge that competitors were learning from Polymarket's innovations while avoiding its mistakes. Kalshi could watch what markets succeeded on Polymarket and then launch regulated versions. Sports betting companies could see what user interface features worked and replicate them with bigger budgets.

In theory, being first mover and largest player should have created insurmountable advantages. In practice, it meant painting a target on your back.

As Shayne looked at the competitive landscape in early 2025, he saw threats from every direction. But he also saw opportunity. The proliferation of prediction market platforms validated the concept. The market was growing faster than any individual competitor could capture. There was room for multiple winners, perhaps even room for Polymarket to dominate.

The question was whether he could navigate the regulatory challenges, avoid catastrophic failures, and continue innovating fast enough to stay ahead. The competition wasn't going away. It was only going to intensify.

And somewhere in Silicon Valley, in a sports betting company's strategy room, or in a crypto developer's Discord server, the person who would build the next great prediction market was probably already at work, studying Polymarket's strengths and weaknesses, planning their move.

The race was far from over.

PART IX: WHAT'S NEXT

Chapter 26

The Road Ahead

The morning after the FBI raid, Shayne Coplan sat in his lawyer's office and confronted a question he'd been avoiding for years: What did he actually want Polymarket to become?

The answer had once seemed obvious, the world's premier prediction market, processing billions in volume, forecasting everything from elections to economic indicators. But that vision had been built on assumptions that November 2024 had shattered. The U.S. government wasn't going to leave Polymarket alone. Regulators weren't going to simply accept crypto prediction markets as inevitable progress. The path forward, if one existed at all, would be far more complicated than the path that had gotten him here.

"We need to think in three timeframes," his lead attorney, Margaret Chen, told him. "Short-term is survival, resolving this investigation without criminal charges or catastrophic fines. Medium-term is a sustainable business model, figuring out how to operate profitably and legally. Long-term is legacy, what you want this company to be in ten years."

Shayne nodded, exhausted but focused. For the first time since founding Polymarket, he couldn't simply charge forward and figure it out later. The decisions he made in the coming months would determine whether his creation became a transformative institution or a cautionary tale.

Short-Term: Navigating the Investigation

The immediate crisis was the FBI investigation. Agents had seized phones, computers, and hard drives containing years of communications, strategy documents, and internal debates about regulatory compliance. Whatever they found would shape the government's next moves.

Shayne's legal team had already begun damage control. They'd prepared detailed chronologies of Polymarket's regulatory interactions, documented the geo-blocking measures implemented after the 2022 CFTC settlement, and assembled technical evidence of the platform's compliance efforts. The goal was to demonstrate good faith that even if some U.S. users had accessed the platform through VPNs, Polymarket had made reasonable efforts to exclude them.

But "reasonable efforts" was a subjective standard, and prosecutors had discretion. If the government wanted to make an example of crypto prediction markets, they had the tools. Wire fraud, money laundering, operating an unlicensed money services business, the potential charges were numerous and severe.

"Best case, they decide this is a civil matter and refer it back to the CFTC for another settlement," Chen explained. "You pay a fine, maybe a bigger one than last time, implement enhanced compliance measures, and move on. Worst case, they file criminal charges and this becomes a years-long legal battle that destroys the company."

There was a middle path too, one that several people in Shayne's orbit were whispering about. Polymarket could cooperate proactively, offering to restructure the business to achieve full U.S. regulatory compliance. Essentially, become Kalshi but bigger, trading its crypto-native offshore status for legal certainty in the American market.

The idea made Shayne's stomach turn. Everything that made Polymarket special, its global accessibility, its low friction, its innovation speed would be sacrificed to appease regulators. The platform would become just another licensed exchange, buried under compliance costs and restricted in what markets it could offer.

Yet the alternative might be worse. Fighting the U.S. government rarely ended well, especially in crypto. Sam Bankman-Fried had learned that the hard way. Even winning battles could mean years of legal fees, distracted management, and reputational damage that drove users away.

The decision would come down to what prosecutors found and what they offered. For now, all Shayne could do was wait, cooperate, and hope that the evidence painted a picture of good-faith compliance rather than willful evasion.

Medium-Term: The Business Model Question

Beyond the immediate legal crisis lurked deeper questions about Polymarket's business model. The platform had raised over $70 million from venture capitalists, achieving a valuation that made Shayne a billionaire on paper. But valuations meant nothing if the business couldn't generate sustainable revenue and profit.

Prediction markets were paradoxically difficult to monetize. Polymarket took no fee on trades, a deliberate choice to maximize liquidity and growth. The platform made money through cryptocurrency arbitrage and by providing liquidity in its own markets, but these revenue streams were modest compared to the company's expenses and its ambitions.

Traditional financial exchanges charged fees on every transaction, generating billions in revenue. But Polymarket couldn't simply flip a switch and start charging fees. Traders were price-sensitive, and competitors like Kalshi were already charging lower fees than legacy futures exchanges. If Polymarket raised its prices, users might migrate to alternatives.

"We need to think about this differently," argued Sarah Kim, Polymarket's head of strategy, in a December 2024 planning session. "We're not just an exchange. We're a data platform, a forecasting tool, a news source. There are multiple ways to monetize what we've built."

The team sketched out possibilities:

Data licensing: News organizations, hedge funds, and political campaigns all wanted access to Polymarket's real-time probability data and trading patterns. The platform could offer premium data feeds and analytics tools for institutional customers. Bloomberg and Reuters paid millions for financial market data, why not prediction market data?

API access: Professional traders and algorithmic trading firms needed fast, reliable access to place orders and monitor markets. Premium API tiers with better rate limits and support could generate recurring revenue from the platform's most active users.

Market creation fees: While basic markets would remain free, Polymarket could charge organizations to create custom, high-visibility markets. A media company wanting a branded market on the Oscars or a corporation wanting to hedge specific business risks could pay for privileged placement and custom features.

B2B products: Corporations increasingly wanted to harness internal forecasting for business planning. Polymarket could offer white-label prediction market software to enterprises, letting companies run internal markets on sales forecasts, project completion dates, or product success.

Token economics: The platform could launch a governance token that gave holders voting rights on market categories, fee structures, and platform development. Done carefully, this could create new revenue streams while deepening community engagement.

Each approach had proponents and skeptics. Data licensing was proven revenue in financial markets but might alienate users who provided the data. Fees risked reducing liquidity. Token launches drew regulatory scrutiny and smelled of desperation to many crypto observers.

The fundamental tension was that Polymarket's value came from being open and accessible, but monetization required creating scarcity and charging for access. How to balance those competing demands would determine whether the company could build a sustainable business or would eventually run out of venture capital and collapse.

The U.S. Market Question

Every strategic conversation eventually circled back to the same question: Should Polymarket try to re-enter the U.S. market legally?

The arguments for were compelling. America represented perhaps 40% of the potential prediction market customer base, wealthy, educated, politically engaged users who were exactly the demographic that made prediction markets work. Excluding U.S. users meant operating with one hand tied behind your back.

Legal U.S. access would also unlock institutional investment that was currently impossible. American hedge funds, family offices, and proprietary trading firms couldn't officially participate in an offshore platform that excluded U.S. persons. Regulatory compliance would open those floodgates.

Media legitimacy would follow. News organizations cited Polymarket with disclaimers and caveats about its legal status. A fully compliant platform could become the go-to source for probabilistic forecasting, quoted without qualification in the New York Times and on CNN.

But the path to legal U.S. operation was narrow and expensive. It meant obtaining either CFTC registration as a derivatives exchange or state-by-state gambling licenses. Both approaches required massive compliance infrastructure, ongoing regulatory reporting, and restrictions on what markets could be offered.

Kalshi had proven CFTC registration was possible, but their experience showed the costs. Years of legal work, millions in expenses, and a lengthy approval process for every market category. Polymarket would need to rebuild its entire compliance program, hire dozens of regulatory specialists, and slow its innovation pace to a crawl.

State gambling licenses were even worse, a jurisdictional nightmare requiring separate approvals in dozens of states, each with different requirements and restrictions. The sports betting companies had spent hundreds of millions building that infrastructure over years. Polymarket couldn't simply replicate it quickly.

"There's a third option," suggested Marcus Chen, Polymarket's CFO. "We don't enter directly. We spin out a separate U.S. entity that licenses our technology and operates independently. That entity plays by all the rules while the main Polymarket platform continues serving international users."

The idea had appeal, have your cake and eat it too. A regulated U.S. subsidiary could capture American market share while the main platform preserved its competitive advantages internationally. The two entities would share technology and brand but maintain legal separation.

The risk was that regulators would see through the structure. If Polymarket controlled the U.S. entity, prosecutors might argue it was just a shell company designed to evade prior settlements. The separation would need to be genuine, with independent management, separate investors, and real legal walls between the entities.

As 2025 began, Shayne hadn't decided which path to take. Part of him wanted to fight for Polymarket's original vision, a global, permissionless platform that no single government could control. But the pragmatist in him recognized that excluding the American market was eventually untenable. The question was whether the price of re-entry was worth paying.

Long-Term: The Vision

Look past the legal crises and business model questions, and a more fundamental question emerged: What did Shayne want prediction markets to become?

In optimistic moments, he imagined a future where prediction markets were ubiquitous infrastructure, as common as stock markets, as trusted as opinion polls, as essential as weather forecasts. Every organization would use internal prediction markets for planning. Every election would have liquid markets revealing real probabilities. Every business decision would be informed by market-based forecasts.

This future had prediction markets integrated into democratic governance. Legislators would consult market prices when evaluating policy proposals. Voters would see probability forecasts alongside traditional polling. The epistemic value of aggregating dispersed information through markets would be recognized as a public good.

In this vision, Polymarket would be the Bloomberg Terminal of prediction markets, the professional-grade platform that serious institutions used for forecasting and risk management. The company would be valued in the tens of billions, employ thousands, and process trillions in annual volume. Shayne would be remembered not as a crypto entrepreneur but as the person who made prediction markets mainstream.

But darker visions intruded. Perhaps prediction markets would remain forever niche, a tool for gamblers and speculators, never quite achieving legitimacy. Perhaps they'd be regulated out of existence in developed markets, banned as gambling or restricted as derivatives. Perhaps the criticisms about manipulation and negative social effects would prove prescient, and prediction markets would be remembered as a failed experiment in financializing civic life.

Or perhaps the technology would succeed but Polymarket would fail. Maybe Kalshi or a sports betting giant would dominate the legal markets. Maybe a better-designed blockchain platform would emerge. Maybe AI forecasting would make human prediction markets obsolete. Success for the concept didn't guarantee success for the company.

"The honest answer," Shayne told his closest advisors in a rare moment of vulnerability, "is that I don't know what's possible anymore. Six months ago I thought we were on a clear trajectory to grow volume, prove accuracy, and eventually regulators accept us. The FBI raid changed that calculus. Now I'm not sure if we're building something permanent or just having a moment."

Expansion Plans

Whatever the long-term vision, the medium-term roadmap required concrete plans. Polymarket's product team had outlined several expansion areas for 2025-2026:

Financial markets: Beyond political prediction, there was enormous potential in economic forecasting. Markets on inflation rates, GDP growth, unemployment, interest rate decisions, and corporate earnings could attract a completely different user base of professional traders and financial institutions. The challenge was that existing financial derivatives already covered much of this territory, so Polymarket would need to offer something distinctive.

Sports betting integration: While Polymarket had avoided head-to-head competition with sports betting platforms, there was room for prediction markets on sports-adjacent questions that traditional bookmakers didn't cover well. Season outcomes, career milestones, coaching decisions, and longer-term sports questions could attract sports bettors looking for different bet types.

Science and technology: Markets on scientific discoveries, technology milestones, and research outcomes could serve academic and corporate R&D communities. When would fusion energy become commercially viable? Would a certain drug trial succeed? Which technology standards would win? These markets could provide valuable forecasting for long-horizon planning.

Local and hyperlocal markets: Most prediction markets focused on national or global questions, but there was potential in local forecasting. City council decisions, local business openings, neighborhood development, even weather and traffic predictions could engage users in their immediate environments.

Collaborative forecasting: Rather than just binary markets, Polymarket could develop tools for collective probability estimation, scenario planning, and decision analysis. This enterprise offering could position the platform as a business intelligence tool rather than just a trading venue.

Each expansion required resources, developer time, liquidity provision, marketing, and community building. With finite capital and team capacity, Polymarket would need to choose carefully which directions to pursue.

The IPO Question

In Silicon Valley board rooms and venture capital conference rooms, the IPO question loomed large. Polymarket's investors had backed the company expecting eventual liquidity, either through acquisition or public offering. With valuations in the billions, the pressure to provide an exit was building.

A traditional IPO seemed nearly impossible given the regulatory uncertainty. No underwriter would take Polymarket public while FBI investigations loomed and CFTC violations remained possible. The company would need years of clean regulatory compliance before U.S. capital markets would accept it.

But alternatives existed. A direct listing on a crypto-friendly exchange could provide liquidity without traditional IPO requirements. Several exchanges had begun offering tokenized equity that traded 24/7 with minimal regulatory friction. Polymarket could potentially list on such a platform, giving investors and employees an exit while avoiding traditional securities regulation.

Or the company could raise later-stage private funding at higher valuations, giving early investors partial liquidity through secondary sales. Several crypto unicorns had used this approach to delay IPOs while still rewarding backers and employees.

Most radically, Polymarket could launch a token that somehow represented ownership or governance rights, essentially using crypto mechanisms to create liquidity. But this path was fraught with securities law risks and had resulted in SEC enforcement actions against numerous other projects.

"We're probably five years from a realistic exit," one board member told Shayne frankly. "Maybe longer if the regulatory situation doesn't improve. Investors knew this was a long-term bet, but you need to communicate that timeline clearly and deliver enough progress to keep everyone believing."

The longer timeline had implications for talent retention too. Employees with equity compensation were more likely to leave if they didn't see a path to liquidity. Polymarket would need to offer secondary sale opportunities or cash bonuses to prevent its best people from defecting to competitors or starting their own ventures.

Building for Resilience

Perhaps the most important strategic shift was cultural—moving from growth-at-all-costs to resilience and sustainability. The FBI raid had revealed the fragility of Polymarket's position. A single government action had thrown the entire company into crisis mode.

Building resilience meant several things:

Geographic diversification: Rather than concentrating operations in any single jurisdiction, Polymarket needed to distribute its team, infrastructure, and legal entities across multiple countries. If one government cracked down, the platform could continue operating from elsewhere.

Decentralization of infrastructure: While Polymarket couldn't be as radically decentralized as Augur, it could push more functionality onto the blockchain and reduce reliance on centralized servers. Smart contract upgrades, decentralized market resolution, and peer-to-peer order matching would all make the platform more censorship-resistant.

Community ownership: Transitioning some level of control to token holders or a decentralized autonomous organization could shield the company from being shut down through individual criminal prosecution. If no single person controlled Polymarket, no single arrest could stop it.

Legal redundancy: Rather than fighting every regulatory battle, Polymarket could selectively comply in jurisdictions where it made sense while maintaining offshore operations where it didn't. Multiple legal entities, each tailored to different regulatory regimes, created options and flexibility.

Financial independence: The ultimate resilience would come from profitability. A company that generated consistent revenue and profit didn't need to raise capital, could outlast regulatory pressure, and couldn't be strangled by cutting off funding. Getting to profitability became not just a business goal but an existential imperative.

The Personal Cost

For Shayne personally, the road ahead meant confronting difficult questions about what he wanted his life to become. At 26 years old, he was a billionaire on paper, the CEO of a high-profile company, and a figure of fascination to the tech and crypto communities. But he was also under federal investigation, facing potential criminal prosecution, and shouldering responsibility for hundreds of employees and thousands of users.

The weight was crushing. Sleep came irregularly. Relationships suffered under the strain of constant crisis management. The simple pleasures that had motivated his work, the intellectual satisfaction of solving hard problems, the excitement of building something new had been replaced by legal strategy sessions and risk mitigation.

Friends suggested he step back, hire a seasoned CEO, take a chairman role, preserve his wealth and reputation while letting someone else navigate the regulatory storms. It was tempting. Hand off the operational burden, spend time on new projects, maybe start a venture fund or research lab.

But Shayne couldn't quite let go. Polymarket was his creation, his vision made real. Walking away while it faced existential threats felt like abandonment. More than that, he still believed in the mission. Prediction markets could make the world more rational, more informed, better at understanding uncertainty. Giving up on that vision because it was hard seemed like betraying something important.

"The road ahead is going to be brutal," he told his co-founders late one night in December 2024. "Longer legal battles, tougher competition, more criticism. We might lose. We might get shut down or regulated into irrelevance. But we're close to something real, a way to aggregate information that actually works. I can't walk away from that yet."

They nodded, exhausted but committed. They'd come too far to quit now.

The road ahead was uncertain, dangerous, and longer than anyone had expected. But it was still there, still passable, still leading somewhere worth going. Whether that destination was the triumphant future Shayne had imagined or something completely different remained to be seen.

But one thing was certain: the journey was far from over. If anything, the hardest part was just beginning.

Chapter 27

The Future of Prediction Markets

Dr. Philip Tetlock had spent four decades studying forecasting, from his early research on expert political judgment to his groundbreaking work on "superforecasters", ordinary people who consistently outperformed intelligence analysts at predicting geopolitical events. In December 2024, sitting in his University of Pennsylvania office, he reflected on what Polymarket's sudden prominence meant for the field he'd helped create.

"We're at an inflection point," he said. "For years, prediction markets were an academic curiosity, a neat idea that worked in controlled settings but couldn't scale. Polymarket has proven that it's wrong, millions of people will participate, billions of dollars will flow through these markets, and the forecasts can be remarkably accurate. The question now isn't whether prediction markets work. It's how we integrate them into society without causing more harm than good."

That question, how prediction markets would evolve from crypto novelty to societal infrastructure would shape the 2020s and beyond. The answer would determine not just Polymarket's fate but the future of forecasting, decision-making, and collective intelligence in an increasingly uncertain world.

The Institutional Adoption Wave

The most immediate future for prediction markets lay in institutional adoption. Polymarket had proven the concept to a skeptical world. Now, organizations ranging from corporations to governments were beginning to explore how they could harness prediction markets for their own purposes.

Major corporations had already begun experimenting. Google had run internal prediction markets for years, asking employees to forecast project completion dates, product success, and business metrics. The results had been impressive, employee markets often outperformed management estimates and formal planning processes.

By 2025, dozens of Fortune 500 companies were testing similar systems. Pharmaceutical companies used prediction markets to forecast drug trial outcomes, helping them allocate R&D resources more efficiently. Technology companies created markets on product launch dates and feature adoption. Manufacturing firms forecasted supply chain disruptions and demand fluctuations.

The corporate use case was compelling: companies already spent enormous resources on forecasting, planning, and risk management. If prediction markets could improve those forecasts even marginally, the value could be enormous. A 1% improvement in demand forecasting for a major retailer could be worth tens of millions of dollars.

But corporate prediction markets faced challenges. Employees had complex incentives, would an engineer bet against their own project? Would middle managers manipulate markets to influence resource allocation decisions? Companies needed to design market structures that aligned individual incentives with organizational interests, a delicate balancing act.

The solution, many organizations discovered, involved anonymous markets, play-money currencies that couldn't be gamed for personal profit, and careful integration with existing decision processes. Prediction markets weren't replacements for management judgment, they were additional data sources that could surface information otherwise hidden in organizational silos.

Beyond individual companies, entire industries were exploring prediction market applications. Insurance companies saw potential for catastrophe forecasting. Agricultural businesses wanted crop yield predictions. Energy companies needed demand forecasts that accounted for weather, policy changes, and consumer behavior.

The institutional adoption wave would unfold over decades, not years. Organizations moved slowly, especially when implementing new decision-making tools. But the direction was clear: prediction markets were transitioning from speculative trading venues to serious business intelligence infrastructure.

Government and Policy Applications

Perhaps the most transformative potential lay in government adoption of prediction markets. The idea seemed radical, having bureaucrats and citizens bet on policy outcomes but the logic was compelling.

Governments made decisions under profound uncertainty. Would an infrastructure bill reduce unemployment? Would a military intervention achieve its objectives? Would a public health policy contain an epidemic? Traditional methods of answering these questions, expert committees, modeling, and political negotiation had mixed track records.

Prediction markets offered an alternative: aggregate the dispersed knowledge of experts, practitioners, and affected citizens into probability estimates that could inform policy decisions. Done right, this could reduce costly mistakes and improve governance.

Several small-scale experiments had already occurred. In 2023, the U.S. Department of Defense had quietly tested prediction markets for forecasting geopolitical events, building on earlier DARPA research. The results were classified, but participants reported that markets had identified several emerging crises before traditional intelligence assessments.

Local governments proved more willing to experiment openly. Several cities created prediction markets for residents to forecast municipal outcomes, would a new transit line meet ridership projections? Would a zoning change increase housing construction? The markets provided useful reality checks on optimistic official projections.

The real breakthrough would come if federal governments embraced prediction markets systematically. Imagine a system where every major policy proposal had associated prediction markets estimating its likely effects. Legislators could see probability distributions for outcomes before voting. Agencies could use market prices to trigger contingency plans. The public could observe whether government forecasts aligned with market consensus.

Robin Hanson, the economist who had championed prediction markets for decades, proposed an even more radical vision: "futarchy," where prediction markets directly determined policy. Instead of voting on policies, citizens would vote on goals, and markets would select the policies most likely to achieve those goals.

"If we say our goal is to maximize GDP growth while maintaining environmental standards, we create markets estimating which policies achieve that," Hanson explained. "The policies with the highest probability of success get implemented. It's governance by market consensus rather than political compromise."

Most observers considered futarchy too radical for near-term adoption. Democratic governance involved more than optimizing for measurable outcomes, it required balancing competing values, protecting minority rights, and expressing collective identity. Markets couldn't capture all of that.

But milder versions were plausible. Governments could use prediction markets as advisory tools, one input among many in policy decisions. They could create markets to hold agencies accountable, if an agency claimed a program would succeed, a market showing low probability of success would trigger scrutiny.

The political obstacles were substantial. Politicians had little incentive to embrace tools that might expose their optimistic forecasts as unrealistic. Bureaucracies resisted external accountability mechanisms. And the optics of government officials betting on policy outcomes troubled many voters.

Yet the potential benefits, better resource allocation, fewer policy disasters, improved public trust through transparent forecasting were significant enough that experimentation would continue. By the 2030s, prediction markets might be as routine in government as cost-benefit analysis, another tool in the policymaker's toolkit.

Integration with Artificial Intelligence

The convergence of prediction markets and artificial intelligence represented perhaps the most fascinating frontier. Both technologies aimed to forecast the future, but they worked differently. Markets aggregated human judgment; AI analyzed patterns in data. The question was how they might complement each other.

In one direction, AI could enhance prediction markets. Machine learning algorithms could detect manipulation, identify informed traders, and optimize market-making. Natural language processing could create markets automatically by scanning news and generating relevant questions. Computer vision could resolve markets by analyzing images and video.

Polymarket and its competitors had already begun integrating AI tools. Automated trading bots used machine learning to identify profitable opportunities. AI systems monitored for suspicious trading patterns that might indicate manipulation or insider information. Machine learning models helped with market resolution by analyzing multiple data sources.

But the more intriguing possibility was AI as a participant in prediction markets. What if sophisticated language models could trade alongside humans, buying and selling contracts based on their analysis of available information?

Early experiments in late 2024 showed promise. Researchers gave GPT-4 access to news feeds and prediction market prices, then allowed it to trade. The AI performed surprisingly well, often matching or exceeding average human traders. It processed vast amounts of information quickly, identified relevant factors humans might miss, and updated its beliefs as new data emerged.

If AI traders became sophisticated enough, they could provide liquidity and keep markets efficient. When markets diverged from the probability estimates that AI calculated from available information, the bots could profit by correcting the mispricing. This would make markets more accurate while generating returns for the bot operators.

But AI participation also raised concerns. If bots dominated trading, were markets still aggregating human wisdom or just reflecting algorithmic pattern matching? If an AI made a large bet that moved market prices, and news organizations reported those prices as meaningful signals, had the AI manipulated public perception?

The deeper question was whether markets and AI were competitors or complements. Robin Hanson argued they were complements: "AI is good at processing public information systematically. Markets are good at aggregating private information, what individuals know from experience that isn't written down anywhere. The future is AI models providing baseline forecasts, and markets allowing humans to bet on whether they know something the AI missed."

This hybrid approach made sense for many applications. An AI could analyze all public polling, economic data, and news to generate election forecasts. Then prediction markets would allow traders with private information, local political knowledge, unreleased polling, or ground-level campaign insights to improve those forecasts.

By 2030, the most accurate forecasts would likely come from AI-human hybrid systems: machine learning models providing the base layer, prediction markets capturing additional information, and human analysts interpreting the combined signals. The organizations that mastered this integration would have enormous advantages in planning and decision-making.

The Decentralized Information Revolution

Zoom out further, and prediction markets fit into a broader transformation: the decentralization of information authority. For centuries, society had relied on centralized institutions, newspapers, universities, government agencies, expert panels to tell us what was true and what would happen.

That system was breaking down. Trust in traditional institutions had declined sharply. Media fragmentation meant different groups consumed entirely different information. The internet allowed anyone to claim expertise, making it harder to distinguish signal from noise.

Prediction markets offered a potential solution: instead of trusting authorities to tell us what's true, we could observe what people with money on the line believed. Markets forced accountability in ways that expert pronouncements didn't. A pundit could be wrong repeatedly without consequence; a trader who was consistently wrong would lose money and influence.

"This is part of a larger shift toward decentralized verification," argued technology theorist Balaji Srinivasan. "Blockchain verifies transactions without banks. Wikipedia verifies information without encyclopedia editors. Prediction markets verify forecasts without expert committees. We're building systems where truth emerges from process rather than being declared by authority."

The vision was appealing but also troubling. Markets could reveal consensus beliefs, but consensus could be wrong. The wisdom of crowds worked best when participants had diverse information and perspectives. If everyone was reading the same sources and making similar assumptions, markets might just amplify conventional wisdom rather than discovering truth.

Moreover, decentralized systems raised questions about accountability. If a traditional forecasting institution made a catastrophically wrong prediction, there were people to blame, reforms to implement, institutions to rebuild. If a prediction market was wrong, who was accountable? The faceless crowd? The platform that hosted the market?

The tension between decentralized information discovery and the need for institutional accountability would shape prediction markets' evolution. The most likely outcome wasn't pure decentralization but hybrid systems: traditional institutions using prediction markets as tools, market prices informing but not replacing expert judgment, and new forms of decentralized organization emerging to govern prediction market platforms.

Challenges to Overcome

For prediction markets to achieve their transformative potential, several major challenges needed solutions:

The manipulation problem: As markets became more influential, the incentive to manipulate them would grow. Foreign governments, political operatives, corporate competitors, and ideological activists all had reasons to spend money moving market prices in desired directions. Technical solutions such as better anomaly detection, reputation systems and collateral requirements could help but not eliminate the risk.

The influence paradox: Markets worked best when they predicted events they couldn't influence. But many of the most valuable forecasting questions involved events where public perception mattered, elections, consumer behavior and social trends. As prediction markets became widely cited, they would increasingly influence the outcomes they predicted. Resolving this paradox might require new market designs or acceptance that some topics weren't suitable for prediction markets.

The sample problem: Prediction markets only aggregated the views of people who chose to participate. If participants were systematically unrepresentative, wealthier, more risk-tolerant, more ideologically extreme than the general population, market prices might be biased. Expanding participation required making markets more accessible and creating incentives for diverse groups to trade.

The long-horizon challenge: Markets struggled with questions whose resolution was years or decades away. Few traders wanted to lock up capital for years, and the information environment could change dramatically over time. Yet many of the most important forecasting questions, climate change impacts, technological breakthroughs and demographic trends operated on these timescales.

The ethical boundaries: Society still needed to determine what should and shouldn't be subject to prediction markets. Most people felt uncomfortable with markets on individual deaths or criminal acts. But where exactly was the line? Natural disasters? Wars? Celebrity divorces? Each platform drew boundaries differently, and there was no clear principle guiding these decisions.

The regulatory framework: For prediction markets to integrate into mainstream institutions, governments needed to develop appropriate regulatory frameworks. The current situation, some platforms licensed, others operating offshore, users circumventing restrictions with VPNs was unstable. Clear rules distinguishing prediction markets from gambling and from regulated financial products were essential.

The Ten-Year Horizon

Looking ahead to 2035, several scenarios seemed plausible:

Scenario 1: Mainstream Integration Prediction markets become ubiquitous infrastructure. Major news organizations run their own markets alongside traditional polling. Corporations routinely use internal markets for forecasting and planning. Governments create public markets on policy outcomes. Regulatory frameworks are clear and well-established. Multiple platforms compete, offering services for different niches. Prediction market data is as common and accepted as stock prices or weather forecasts.

Scenario 2: Niche Persistence Prediction markets remain useful but niche tools. Professional traders and financial institutions use them for specific applications. Some governments and corporations experiment but adoption is limited. Regulatory uncertainty persists, keeping markets in gray zones. The technology works but never achieves mainstream legitimacy. Prediction markets occupy a space similar to hedge funds, specialized tools for sophisticated users, not mass-market products.

Scenario 3: Regulatory Suppression Governments crack down on prediction markets, classifying them as gambling or unregistered securities. Major platforms are shut down or forced to de-list most markets. Innovation moves to offshore jurisdictions with minimal regulatory oversight. Markets continue to operate but become increasingly marginalized and associated with crypto gray markets. The promise of prediction markets is recognized but not realized due to political and regulatory opposition.

Scenario 4: AI Displacement Artificial intelligence becomes so good at forecasting that prediction markets become unnecessary for most applications. AI models can analyze all public information more thoroughly than human traders, making market prices less informative. Humans still participate in narrow domains where private knowledge matters, but most forecasting shifts to AI systems. Prediction markets become historical curiosities, like telegraph operators after the telephone.

Scenario 5: Evolution and Transformation Prediction markets evolve into something quite different from their 2024 form. Perhaps they merge with social media, becoming integrated into how people discuss and debate future events. Perhaps they become embedded in AI systems, serving as training data or verification mechanisms. Perhaps they transform into decentralized autonomous organizations that govern themselves through market mechanisms. The core insight, that markets aggregate information persists, but the implementation changes dramatically.

Which scenario unfolds will depend on technological development, regulatory decisions, competitive dynamics, and whether prediction markets can solve their fundamental challenges while delivering sufficient value to justify their costs and risks.

The Philosophical Stakes

Underlying these practical questions were deeper philosophical issues about knowledge, democracy, and truth.

Prediction markets embodied a particular epistemology: truth emerges from the aggregation of individual beliefs, weighted by willingness to bear risk. This was fundamentally liberal and decentralized, it trusted markets over authorities, process over pronouncement.

But critics argued this approach had blind spots. Markets revealed what traders believed, not what was true. They worked when information was dispersed and participants were sophisticated, but they could amplify errors when everyone was wrong in the same direction. They measured probability but couldn't capture non-quantifiable values or moral considerations.

The deeper concern was that prediction markets might change how society thought about the future. If everything became subject to betting markets, did we reduce all questions to mere probabilities? Did we lose something important, moral reasoning, collective deliberation, shared meaning when we financialized every aspect of life?

"There's a difference between saying 'I predict X will happen' and 'I'm betting money that X will happen,'" argued philosopher Michael Sandel. "The latter introduces economic calculation into domains where it might not belong. Not everything should be a market. Some forms of knowledge and some types of social interaction are corrupted by commodification."

The counterargument was that prediction markets revealed existing beliefs rather than creating them. People already formed opinions about future events; markets simply made those beliefs explicit and testable. Better to have transparent probability estimates that forced accountability than opaque expert judgments that couldn't be evaluated.

This philosophical debate wouldn't be resolved quickly. It would play out over decades as prediction markets either integrated into societal decision-making or remained on the margins. The outcome would reveal something fundamental about what kind of society we wanted to build—one that trusted markets to discover truth, or one that preserved space for forms of knowledge that markets couldn't capture.

The Unwritten Future

Standing at the beginning of 2025, prediction markets' future remained genuinely uncertain. Polymarket had demonstrated that the technology could scale and attract mainstream attention. But sustainability, legitimacy, and social value were still unproven.

The optimistic case was compelling: prediction markets could make organizations smarter, governments more accountable, and citizens better informed about uncertainty. They could reduce cognitive biases, surface hidden information, and improve collective decision-making. As society faced increasingly complex challenges, climate change, technological disruption, geopolitical instability, tools for better forecasting were desperately needed.

The pessimistic case was equally plausible: prediction markets might remain forever controversial, trapped between gambling regulation and financial oversight. They might be manipulated by bad actors or dominated by algorithms. They might financialize aspects of life that shouldn't be markets, corroding social bonds and shared meaning. They might simply fail to deliver enough value to justify their costs and risks.

Most likely, the future would be somewhere in between, prediction markets would find their niche, solving certain problems well while failing to transform society as dramatically as either advocates hoped or critics feared. They would become one tool among many for forecasting and decision-making, valuable but not revolutionary, accepted but not universal.

What seemed certain was that the question Polymarket had forced onto the agenda, how should society aggregate information and forecast the future wasn't going away. Whether prediction markets provided the answer or just revealed the question's difficulty, Shayne Coplan had ensured that the conversation would continue for years to come.

The future of prediction markets was itself uncertain, probabilistic and contested which seemed somehow appropriate. After all, if we could predict the future with certainty, we wouldn't need prediction markets at all.

Chapter 28

Legacy in the Making

History doesn't wait for stories to finish before passing judgment. By early 2025, Shayne Coplan's legacy was already being written in real-time, debated in congressional hearings, analyzed in academic papers, celebrated in crypto forums, and condemned in op-eds. The narrative was still being contested, the ending still uncertain, but the impact was undeniable.

At 26, Shayne had built something that would outlast him, for better or worse. Whether Polymarket survived its regulatory challenges or collapsed under legal pressure, whether prediction markets became infrastructure or remained controversial, the seeds had been planted. The question wasn't whether Shayne Coplan mattered, but how and what lessons his improbable journey held for others.

What Has Already Been Accomplished

Strip away the controversy and legal uncertainty, and Shayne's achievements were remarkable. In four years, he had taken prediction markets from academic curiosity to mainstream phenomenon. Billions of dollars had flowed through Polymarket. Millions of people had discovered probabilistic thinking. The platform had influenced election coverage, political strategy, and public discourse in ways that would have seemed impossible in 2020.

Most significantly, Polymarket had proven the concept. Skeptics had long argued that prediction markets couldn't scale, couldn't achieve accuracy, couldn't attract serious participants. The 2024 election had demolished those arguments. When Polymarket's prices proved more accurate than nearly every poll and pundit, it forced a reckoning with the wisdom of crowds.

"Shayne made prediction markets real," said Robin Hanson, who had spent decades advocating for the technology. "Before Polymarket, they were an interesting idea with small-scale implementations. Now they're part of how society processes information about the future. That's a genuine paradigm shift, even if it's still early and fragile."

The technical accomplishments were equally substantial. Polymarket had solved difficult problems in market design, blockchain integration, and user experience. The platform had demonstrated that crypto could serve practical purposes beyond speculation. It had shown that automated market makers could provide liquidity efficiently. It had proven that smart contracts could settle complex markets fairly.

Beyond technology, Polymarket had built a community. Thousands of sophisticated traders had made the platform their primary venue for forecasting and analysis. Data scientists had developed tools and models based on Polymarket prices. Journalists had learned to interpret prediction market signals. An entire ecosystem had emerged around the platform.

The cultural impact was harder to quantify but perhaps more important. Polymarket had popularized probabilistic thinking, the idea that events had likelihoods rather than certainties. It has made forecasting transparent and accountable. It had demonstrated alternatives to traditional polling and expert opinion. These shifts in how people thought about the future would persist regardless of Polymarket's fate.

"Even if Polymarket disappeared tomorrow," observed Nate Silver, the statistician who had pioneered probabilistic election forecasting, "the conversation has changed permanently. People now understand that elections have probabilities, that confidence intervals matter, that good forecasting requires skin in the game. That's Shayne's legacy."

A Generation Defining Itself

Shayne's story resonated particularly with his generation of millennials and Gen Z who had come of age during crypto's rise and traditional institutions' decline. He embodied a particular archetype: the young founder who moved fast and broke things, who prioritized innovation over permission, who believed technology could route around regulatory obstacles.

This approach has produced remarkable successes: Uber transforming transportation, Airbnb revolutionizing lodging, Stripe modernizing payments. But it had also produced catastrophic failures: Theranos's fraud, WeWork's delusion, FTX's collapse. Shayne existed somewhere in the ambiguous middle, neither obvious success nor clear failure, but a contested figure whose ultimate judgment remained pending.

The generational aspect mattered because Shayne's approach reflected broader beliefs about how change happened. Older generations had generally worked within systems, seeking permission, building consensus, respecting established processes. Shayne's generation often rejected that path as too slow, too captured by entrenched interests, too unlikely to produce meaningful innovation.

"We grew up watching institutions fail," Shayne had said in a 2023 interview. "The financial crisis, Iraq, the pandemic response, we saw experts and authorities get huge things catastrophically wrong while insisting they knew best. So yeah, we're skeptical of the whole 'ask permission first' approach. Sometimes you have to build the thing, prove it works, and let regulators catch up."

This philosophy had its champions. Venture capitalists celebrated "permissionless innovation" and "regulatory arbitrage." Crypto advocates saw it as returning power to individuals. Technology optimists viewed it as the only way to overcome institutional sclerosis.

But critics saw it differently: as privilege dressed up as principle, as disruption that externalized costs onto society, as recklessness disguised as boldness. They noted that successful rule-breaking was often only successful because the rule-breakers were wealthy, well-connected, and could afford expensive lawyers. Those without such advantages who broke rules usually just went to prison.

"Shayne Coplan represents a very specific kind of privilege," argued technology critic Jathan Sadowski. "He can build an unlicensed financial platform, attract millions in venture capital, operate in legal gray zones, and face an FBI raid while still being featured sympathetically in major media. Try that as a working-class person of color and see how it goes. The 'move fast and break things' approach only works if you're in a position where breaking things doesn't break you."

The critique had force. Shayne had attended elite schools, had access to venture capital networks, and had the safety net that allowed him to take enormous risks. His story couldn't be easily replicated by someone without those advantages, even if they had equivalent vision and talent.

Yet defenders argued that all innovation involved risk and that regulatory frameworks often protected incumbents rather than serving public interest. The question wasn't whether Shayne had advantages, obviously he did but whether the world was better off with prediction markets existing than without them.

This debate about privilege, innovation, regulation, and social good would define not just Shayne's legacy but his generation's broader impact on technology and society.

Lessons for Other Founders

Whatever his ultimate fate, Shayne's journey offered lessons for other entrepreneurs navigating the space between innovation and regulation:

Lesson 1: Technical excellence isn't enough Polymarket's technology was sophisticated and effective, but that didn't shield the company from regulatory pressure. Founders in regulated industries needed to engage with legal frameworks early, even if those frameworks seemed outdated or inappropriate. Ignoring regulation didn't make it disappear; it just meant confronting it later from a position of weakness.

Lesson 2: Growth creates enemies When Polymarket was small, regulators largely ignored it. Success brought scrutiny. Every startup in a controversial space faced a similar dynamic: stay small and marginal, or grow large and face powerful opposition. Managing that transition required political sophistication that many technical founders lacked.

Lesson 3: Community is defensible Polymarket's strongest asset wasn't its technology, competitors could copy that. It was the community of traders, developers, and supporters who had invested in the platform's success. Building genuine community rather than just user bases created resilience that regulatory pressure couldn't easily destroy.

Lesson 4: Narratives matter How people understood Polymarket, as gambling, as forecasting, as financial markets, as civic infrastructure shaped its legitimacy. Shayne had sometimes been sloppy about narrative framing, allowing critics to define the platform. Founders needed to actively shape how their products were understood, not just focus on functionality.

Lesson 5: Offshore doesn't mean safe Operating offshore provided flexibility but not immunity. If you served American users or had American operations, U.S. law could reach you. The belief that blockchain's borderless nature provided protection from regulation had proven naive. Geography still mattered, even in the crypto era.

Lesson 6: Success has a cost The pressure of running a high-stakes startup while under federal investigation had visibly aged Shayne. Founders often underestimated the personal toll of building controversial companies. The wealth and recognition came with sleepless nights, strained relationships, and constant anxiety. Glorifying the founder's struggle ignored the very real psychological damage it could cause.

The Risks Still Ahead

Shayne's legacy remained unfinished because significant risks still loomed. The FBI investigation could result in criminal charges that would destroy both his company and his freedom. Regulatory crackdowns could make Polymarket's business model untenable. Competitors could fragment the market and erode his platform's dominance. Technical failures or security breaches could shatter user trust.

More subtly, Polymarket could succeed as a business but fail in its broader mission. If the platform became primarily a vehicle for gambling rather than forecasting, if it enabled manipulation rather than revealing truth, if it exacerbated social problems rather than solving them then Shayne's legacy would be mixed at best.

The most dangerous risk was complacency. Polymarket's 2024 success had generated enormous confidence and media celebration. That could breed the arrogance that preceded many spectacular failures in tech history. Founders who believed their own hype often made catastrophic mistakes, assuming that past success guaranteed future triumph.

"The hard part isn't getting here," one of Shayne's advisors warned him. "It's staying here while everyone's trying to knock you down. Success makes you a target. The question is whether you can be disciplined enough, paranoid enough, and humble enough to survive it."

Shayne's youth was both an advantage and liability. At 26, he had the energy, adaptability, and risk tolerance that older founders might lack. But he also lacked the experience, judgment, and caution that came with age. He hadn't yet faced the kind of existential setback that taught hard lessons about hubris and limits.

Whether he could learn those lessons without experiencing the disasters that usually taught them would determine his ultimate success or failure.

The Broader Impact on Crypto

Shayne's story intersected with crypto's larger narrative arc. By 2025, cryptocurrency had survived numerous boom-bust cycles, regulatory crackdowns, and spectacular frauds. The industry was maturing, moving from pure speculation toward practical applications. Polymarket represented one of the strongest use cases, a real product solving real problems rather than just token speculation.

If Polymarket succeeded, it would validate the crypto thesis: that blockchain technology enabled new forms of organization and value exchange that improved on traditional systems. It would show that crypto was more than a bubble, that decentralization had genuine utility, that the technology's promise could be realized.

But if Polymarket failed, especially if it failed due to fraud, manipulation, or regulatory non-compliance it would reinforce crypto's worst reputation. It would be added to the list alongside FTX, Terra/Luna, and countless other projects that had promised innovation but delivered disaster.

"Shayne bears an unfair burden," observed Vitalik Buterin, Ethereum's creator. "He's being judged not just on whether Polymarket works, but on whether all of crypto can build legitimate businesses. That's not reasonable, one company shouldn't represent an entire technological paradigm. But that's the reality he faces."

The burden manifested in how Polymarket was covered and regulated. Every misstep was magnified as evidence of crypto's fundamental problems. Every success was minimized as an exception that proved the rule. Shayne had to be not just good but perfect, not just successful but unimpeachable, because he was representing a technology that much of the establishment wanted to fail.

This dynamic created immense pressure. It also created opportunity, if Polymarket could succeed despite skepticism and opposition, it would demonstrate resilience and legitimacy that pure hype could never achieve.

How History Might Remember This Moment

Step back far enough, and individual companies became footnotes in larger technological transitions. The question wasn't whether Polymarket specifically survived but whether prediction markets became established infrastructure and what role Shayne played in that transition.

Several historical analogies suggested themselves:

The Netscape analogy: Marc Andreessen's company had pioneered web browsers and popularized the internet. Netscape itself had failed, losing to Microsoft and eventually being absorbed into AOL. But Andreessen was remembered as a visionary who had made the internet accessible. Perhaps Shayne would be remembered similarly, the person who made prediction markets real, even if his specific company didn't dominate.

The Napster analogy: Shawn Fanning's file-sharing service had been shut down by legal action, but it had transformed how people thought about music distribution. Spotify and other legal services had later realized Napster's vision through compliant means. Perhaps Polymarket would be crushed by regulators, but Kalshi or another platform would later build the mainstream prediction market industry.

The PayPal analogy: Peter Thiel's company had operated in regulatory gray zones, faced government pressure, but ultimately achieved legitimacy and transformed payments. Perhaps Polymarket would similarly navigate regulatory challenges and emerge as an established player.

The Silk Road analogy: Ross Ulbricht's darknet marketplace had been shut down and its founder imprisoned, becoming a cautionary tale about the limits of crypto anarchism. Perhaps Shayne would face similar fate, his platform remembered as a failed experiment in regulatory arbitrage.

Which analogy proved closest would depend on decisions Shayne and others made in the coming years, on regulatory choices by governments, and on whether prediction markets delivered sufficient value to justify their costs and risks.

Historians in 2050 might describe this period as the moment when prediction markets either became mainstream or were rejected by society. They might view Shayne as a pioneer who opened new possibilities or as an example of tech hubris. They might barely mention him at all, focusing instead on systemic forces and broader trends.

What seemed certain was that the 2020s would be remembered as an inflection point for how society aggregated information and made forecasts. The polling industry's failures, the pandemic's unpredictability, political polarization's effects on shared reality, all had created demand for new approaches to understanding the future. Polymarket had emerged at the right moment with a compelling answer.

Whether that answer was correct, whether it could be implemented responsibly, whether it improved society or caused new problems, those questions remained open. But they were being asked, debated, and tested in ways that wouldn't have happened without Shayne Coplan's vision and audacity.

The Unfinished Story

Legacy typically required completion, knowing how the story ended before judging its protagonist. But Shayne's story remained radically incomplete.

He might be heading toward vindication or imprisonment, toward lasting success or imminent failure. The uncertainty was profound.

Yet perhaps that incompleteness was itself part of the legacy. Shayne had forced society to confront questions about markets, information, regulation, and truth before those questions had clear answers. He had built something real and consequential while the rules governing it were still being written. He had demonstrated both the promise and the peril of moving fast in regulated spaces.

"What I hope people remember," Shayne said in a rare reflective moment, "is that we tried to build something that made the world more rational. We tried to create tools for understanding uncertainty. We didn't get everything right, probably got a lot wrong but we were genuinely trying to solve a real problem. Prediction markets can help people make better decisions if we design them right. That's what I care about. The rest is just noise."

It was a generous self-assessment, one that elided the complications and controversies. But it captured something real about Shayne's motivations. Whatever his flaws and missteps, he genuinely believed in prediction markets' potential. That belief had driven him to take enormous risks and had produced something remarkable, even if that something remained unstable and contested.

As 2025 unfolded, with investigations pending and competition intensifying, Shayne Coplan's legacy remained very much in the making. The first chapters had been written, but the ending triumphant or tragic, transformative or cautionary remained to be determined.

History would judge. But for now, all anyone could do was watch, wait, and wonder what probability the prediction markets themselves would assign to Shayne's ultimate success.

www.ingramcontent.com/pod-product-compliance
Lightning Source LLC
LaVergne TN
LVHW052025200926
848481LV00005B/1585
* 9 7 9 8 2 3 2 3 1 6 1 3 6 *